VEGETARIAN
EUROPE

300 places to eat
in Europe's
top travel destinations

edited by **Alex Bourke**

published by **Vegetarian Guides, London**

Vegetarian Europe edited by Alex Bourke
published by Vegetarian Guides Ltd
PO Box 2284, London W1A 5UH, England.
www.vegetarianguides.co.uk, info@vegetarianguides.co.uk

ISBN 1-902259 02 5. First published October 2000.
Cover designed by Mark Halunga, lj13@telia.com
City maps by Ronny Worsey, Paris map by Marc Vyvyan-Jones
Country maps by Mickael Charbonnel
Printed by Cox and Wyman, Reading, England

UK and worldwide distributor: Portfolio Books
Unit 5, Perivale Industrial Park, Horsenden Lane South, Greenford,
Middlesex UB6 7RL, England.
Tel: (+44) 020-8997 9000, Fax: (+44) 020-8997 9097
sales@portfoliobooks.com
USA distributor: Seven Hills Book Distributors
1531 Tremont Street, Cincinatti, OH 45214.
Sales call toll-free 1-800-545 2005.
Fax toll-free 1-888-777 7799. www.sevenhillsbooks.com

Also published by Vegetarian Guides:
Vegetarian Britain, over 500 places to eat and sleep, 256 pages
Vegetarian France, 150 places to eat and sleep, 128 pages
Vegetarian London, 400 places to eat and shop, 224 pages

An extensive range of vegetarian travel guides including
America, Australia, Israel and Worldwide is available from the
publishers. See order form at the end of this guide or browse
and buy online at www.vegetarianguides.co.uk

The small print:
Restaurants are constantly changing their opening hours and owners. Whilst every effort
has been made to ensure the accuracy of information contained in this book, we accept
no liability for any errors. Before making a special journey, you are advised to call a
place to confirm its details. Acceptance of advertisements does not imply endorsement of
either the advertisers or their products or services.

RESEARCHERS Paul Appleby (Oxford), **Marina Berati** (Florence, Milan, Rome, Venice), **Gabor Borsodi** (Budapest), **Alex Bourke** (Brussels, London, Paris, Prague, Zurich), **Andrew Butler** (Lake Garda), **Vanessa Clarke** (Malaga), **Pat Collins** (Berlin, Frankfurt, Munich, Salzburg, Vienna), **Akcelina Cvijetic** (Croatia and Serbia), **Simon England** (Munich), **Monica Engstrom** (Stockholm), **Paul Gaynor** (London), **Katrina Holland** (Barcelona, Cork, Dublin, Evora, Lisbon, Granada, Madrid, Seville), **Henk de Jong** (Amsterdam), **Kirsten Jungsberg** (Copenhagen, Malmo), **Johanna Jutila** (Helsinki), **Francisco Martin** (Malaga), **Dr Irena Medkova** (Moscow), **Claude Pasquini** (Luxembourg), **Tatyana Pavlova** (Moscow), **David Roman** (Alicante, Valencia), **Mieke Roscher** (Bremen, Hamburg, Oldenburg), **Henrik Scheutz** (Sweden), **Aris Skliros** (Athens), **Zofia Torun** (Poland, Krakow, Warsaw), **Ulla Troeng** (Stockholm), **Ania Truszkowska** (Gdansk, Warsaw), **Natalia Tsobkallo** (St Petersburg), **Jennifer Wharton** (Edinburgh), **Ronny Worsey** (Camden Town, Liverpool, Oxford), **Roar Waagen** (Bergen, Oslo)

ADVERTISING Alex Bourke, Kate Gallagher

COVER DESIGN Mark Halunga   VIGNETTES Marion Gillet

EDITING AND PROOFING Alex Bourke, Katrina Holland, Zofia Torun, Jennifer Wharton, Ronny Worsey

MAPS Mickael Charbonnel (countries), **Marc Vyvyan-Jones** (Paris), **Ronny Worsey** (cities).

MARKETING AND PR
Carol Farley (Portfolio Books), **Samantha Calvert**

POEMS: Bernie Laprade of www.ThePoemShop.co.uk

WEBSITE & ONLINE STORE www.vegetarianguides.co.uk
Original design **Andy and Libby Purves** of veganvillage.co.uk, additional graphics **Mark Halunga**, webmaster **Graham Brown**

WORDLISTS Mickael Charbonnel (French), **Brigitte Kehrwisch** (German), **David Roman** (Spanish), **Zofia Torun** (Polish), **Stefania Vinci** (Italian)

WITH THANKS TO Ann Casey, Mike Bourke, Hugh Brune, Vanessa Clarke, Liz Cook, Dave Cope, Dr Michael Grill, Thomas Hamre, Sheila Hyslop, Hartley Jackson, Brian Longstaff, Gina Madison, Sherry Nicholls, Bill Norris, Chris Olivant, Rob Olver, Bettina Rehberg, Andrew Richards, Colin Russell, Ewa Suskiewicz, Steve Trayler, Toni Vernelli, Jacqueline Walsh, Tony Weston, Hugh Wilson ... and all who contributed ... **THANK YOU!**

CONTENTS

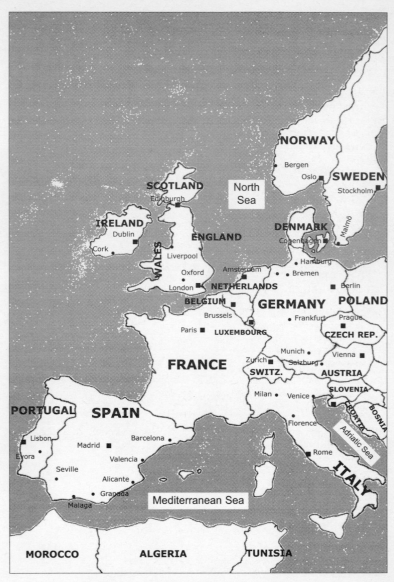

Now I take life in my veggie stride

EUROPE

by Mickael Charbonnel

as I travel with my veggie guide

VEGETARIAN TRAVELLERS CHECKS

Every week we help hundreds of our members with their travel plans, offering them advice on where to stay and where to eat both at home and abroad.

Our members are also entitled to discounts at over 800 establishments worldwide and their exclusive hotline provides useful translations and phrases and lists of guest houses, restaurants and health food stores.

By giving us your support you will enable us to campaign throughout the UK to make the benefits of vegetarianism more widely known. Our activities range from major promotions such as National Vegetarian Week to hard hitting issue–based campaigns against the exotic meat trade, battery farming and intensive fishing.

We are an independent voice when it comes to issues such as BSE and vegetarian nutrition. To let that voice be heard we need your support.

For a free starter pack and membership details call today on **0161 925 2000**.

Parkdale Dunham Road Altrincham
Cheshire WA14 4QG
Tel: 0161 925 2000 www.vegsoc.org
REGISTERED CHARITY NO. 259358

real men fake it!

"I know leather isn't a material, it's somebody's skin. So I chose synthetic." —*Jerome Flynn*

Fashion with a conscience.

leather:massmarketmassslaughter

 PO Box 3169, London SW18 4WJ
contact us on 020 8870 3966
or on our website www.peta-online.org

Where to Go First

Vegetarian Guides founder Alex Bourke gives his selection of
the top five European cities of veggie culture.

Tumbling airfares mean it's now often cheaper to cross the
channel than to visit your in-laws. They have *la culture, l'ambience, tonnes* of *la romance*, plus art and architecture in abun-
dance. But what about the awful grub that tarnished your last
trip? *Mais non mes amis!* Europe is truly a gastronomic paradise when you know where to forage. Here's my pick of five
scrumptious cities and their hidden veggie eateries for a weekend or longer that I promise will leave you so stuffed and con-
tent you'll want to go back every month.

AMSTERDAM is the most fun city in Europe, and you won't
need a phrasebook since almost everyone speaks English better than we do.

PARIS is easy to get to, even from London, by plane, train or
coach and offers fabulous sightseeing and gourmet veggie
gorging.

Scenic **PRAGUE** is the hot, hip home of countless bars and dis-
cos, incredibly inexpensive, and it even has a central vegan
restaurant.

Stunningly beautiful **FLORENCE** has the greatest concentration of art treasures in the world.

Finally for those seasoned travellers who've scoffed and
quaffed in all of the above, let me propose **HELSINKI**, a delightful, friendly city surrounded by the most unspoilt, tranquil wilder-
ness in Europe.

You won't find many veggie lodgings in cities apart from
London. They tend to be in the country run by couples who've
left the rat race and the city behind. But who needs them?
European breakfasts are just coffee and rolls with jam anyway.
Let your travel agent, *Let's Go* or *Lonely Planet* find you a hotel
or backpacker hostel, then dine out in yummy restaurants or
picnic in the park.

There are dozens more great cities in this book, and with your help we'll be adding to them in future editions and forthcoming country guides.

And don't worry about the other continents. Apart from the other guides listed at the end of this one, we're already working on filling the gaps worldwide so that we won't be lonely veggies having a rough time any longer.

Bon voyage and happy scoffing!

Je suis un vegetarian

I am a veggie
Who had lost his way
But now I never
I never need to stray

Now I take life
In my veggie stride
As I travel
With my veggie guide

The towns and cities
Of the world are mine
Because I always
Know just where to dine

All my friends now
Follow me around
Je suis un veggie
Best books I ever found!

Bespoke and 'Ready-to-Wear' Poetry & Cards
*by **Bernie Laprade** at www.thepoemshop.co.uk*

14

Nutrition on the Road

*Should you take vitamins and which ones? How much to drink? How to beat blurred vision? With a degree in catering management and nutrition and 20 years experience, vegan nutritionist and author **Liz Cook** has the answers.*

WATER

Dehydration is the traveller's biggest enemy. Aim to drink two litres (four pints) of water a day, not from taps.

I'd also recommend that you don't drink more than two cups of coffee or three cups of tea per day because these can dehydrate you. Don't drink them immediately after a meal because the tannin in them binds with and inhibits iron absorption and overall stimulants deplete vitamin C.

Don't drink alcohol on the plane, it makes you feel terrible.

CARBOHYDRATE

Carry a good source of slow release carbohydrate for when meals are intermittent, starting with when they've lost your vegan meal on the plane! A packet of unsalted oatcakes from any healthfood store is terrific, whereas flapjacks give a sugar high and a subsequent low. Avoid sugar and salty snacks.

SNACKS

Dried fruit is nice, but watch out for sugary stuff in trail mix such as crystallized pineapple. Excellent fuels are cashew nuts and sundried bananas, which are compact because they're dehydrated and won't go off.

VITAMINS

The only vitamins to worry about on a short trip are the water soluble ones, particularly vitamin C. It's vital for fighting infection. Old oranges could have no vitamin C. If travelling for a long time take Zinc, a B vitamin and C.

If it's warm and you're in one place for two weeks, you can grow mung beans, which are a fantastic source of vitamin C and B vitamins, in a yogurt pot. Rinse morning and night.

GREENS

When eating out a lot always go for a green leafy vegetable at least once a day. Spinach, broccoli, kale, watercress or salad stuff can supply 9 out of your key 18 nutritional bases.

LONG TERM

If you're out there on a world tour, take some strips of ready to eat nori seaweed ready toasted for iodine.

Liz's latest book is **What Do You Eat?**, a gorgeous large format spiral bound book with wipe-clean pages that will last forever. It contains lots of easy vegan recipes and heaps of information about vegan nutrition and what to find where. In UK order for £12.95 inc. postage direct from E. Cook, 65 Lincoln Street, Brighton, East Sussex, BN2 2UG, England. Mention *Vegetarian Europe* and get a free laminated vegan nutrition chart to put on your kitchen wall worth £2.95, or send £2.95 for just the chart.

Overseas can order the book or chart and pay by credit card at www.stewartdistribution.com

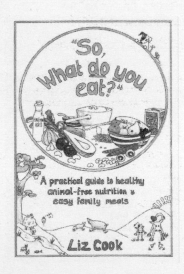

Liz's Trail Mix

Pumpkin seeds
Sesame seeds
Sunflower seeds
Chopped sun-dried
bananas
(for energy and vitamin B)
Dried apricots (for iron)
A handful of mixed nuts
like cashews and almonds

Campaigns   Education
Information   Youth Group
Advice   Exhibitions
Investigations Resources

Animal Aid
against all animal cruelty

Factory Farming
Animal Experiments
Hunting
Zoos and Circuses
Fur Trade
Vegetarianism
Livestock Markets
Humane Research
Living Without Cruelty

To find out more about the work we do and how you can become involved in helping to fight animal cruelty, please contact us at:

Animal Aid
The Old Chapel
Bradford Street
Tonbridge
Kent TN9 1AW
tel: (01732) 364546
fax: (01732)366533
email: info@animalaid.org.uk
web: www.animalaid.org.uk

Strictly
peaceful
campaigning

Be part of the solution

The actions of thoughtful and concerned people are the only thing that has ever changed the world. That's why here at Uncaged, one of our urgent priorities is to show people what they can do to help.

Join the Global boycott of P&G

Cruelty-free consuming

Perhaps the most basic and necessary step to take is to make sure that we are not supporting companies who carry out vivisection. If we buy products from animal-testing companies (eg. **Procter & Gamble, Unilever, Calvin Klein, L'Oreal, Johnson & Johnson, Wella** and many more) then we are effectively endorsing and funding these practices. On the other hand, by purchasing from cruelty-free companies, we are moving resources and thus power from cruel companies to humane and decent companies. It's this crucial fact that lead us to start the Global Boycott Procter & Gamble (P&G) Campaign.

Charitable giving

Unfortunately, some charities continue to spend some of their funds on animal experiments. Refuse to give to: **Imperial Cancer Research Fund** or **British Heart Foundation** amongst others.

Political pressure

Many of the decisions that affect animals are taken by politicians. Through our literature and quarterly magazine, Uncaged alerts the public to the stances of the political parties and informs them about urgent issues and debates they can participate in. **A well-informed and active public is a very powerful way of influencing decisions.**

The media

The influence of the media on public opinion cannot be overestimated. It is vital that we make sure that our message is heard in the media through letters pages, phone-ins, complaints and praise. **We must defend animals by challenging the promotion of vivisection wherever it rears its ugly head.**

The power of protest

Directly protesting against vivisection is one of the most potent and meaningful actions we can perform to challenge this terrible practice. Uncaged supports and publicises as many protests as possible - demonstrations send a clear message that **vivisection will no longer be tolerated by decent people!**

P&G experiment on monkeys and other animals

For details of a comprehensive 80 page CRUELTY-FREE shopping guide and more information about the work of Uncaged and how to join us, please contact:

Uncaged 14 Ridgeway Road Sheffield S12 2SS
Tel: (0114) 253 0020
email: uncaged.anti-viv@dial.pipex.com
website: www.uncaged.co.uk

Thank you

How to Learn a Language

English born Alex Bourke has lived in and travelled all over Europe. He is fluent in French, has an A-level in Russian, O-levels in Latin and classical Greek, and taught himself Italian from a BBC television course at 14. Here he covers how to get by in English, phrase books, fast track to fluency, and the lazy person's route to becoming multilingual.

Get by in English

English is all you'll ever need in Britain, Ireland, the Netherlands, Denmark, Sweden, Norway and Finland. Scandinavians and Dutch almost all speak English, perhaps because with small populations they import a lot of their tv and subtitle it rather than dubbing. In tourist centres throughout Europe anyone with a hotel, restaurant or souvenir shop will be fluent in the vocabulary needed to separate you from your money. By staying in hostels you can always find people from all over the world to trek around town with who are delighted to practise their English. But to do more than see Europe from the window of a tour bus, to catch trains into the mountains and explain what you do for a living to the locals, it's worth the effort to learn a few phrases.

Anyone can learn any language, it just takes repetition. Even if you're sticking to the beaten track, trying out a few phrases can be fun. For the independent traveller venturing into the countryside, some navigation, accommodation and shopping phrases will hugely enhance the pleasure of your holiday. Over the years I've learned to buy train tickets and ask the way to the supermarket in German, Greek, Japanese, Polish, Spanish and Turkish. It's easy when you know how and deeply satisfying. Here's how.

Phrase Books

A few months before a trip, I buy a Berlitz phrase book and cassette to listen to while walking around town, driving, on buses or lying in the park. There are other great courses too, but Berlitz is my favourite because of the ease of use and focus on the truly useful. They say you need about 34 repetitions to fix a word in your head, spread over a long period, so the sooner you start, the more fun you'll have later. Far from dismay at what you don't know, foreigners are flattered and pleased that you've made the effort to study their language and very willing to help you improve.

Which Language?

When choosing which language to learn, bear in mind where else you can use it. Spanish and Portuguese also work in south America. French, German, and Russian can help take you across Europe as they are widely taught in schools in the west, centre and east respectively, though in eastern Europe German and English are becoming much more popular. If you're British or Canadian, the obvious first choice is French. Americans would probably go for Spanish.

Fast Track to Fluency

If you've done the phrase book thing and want to go further, dump the telly one night a week and enroll in an evening class run by your local education authority, university or foreign residents' centre such as Alliance Française or London's Polish Centre in Hammersmith. Or invest in a thin teach yourself course and a pocket dictionary. Fat courses are scary and tend to get left on the shelf. Small ones seem more do-able. Plan a motivating holiday and seek out native speakers in your town to practise on such as students, au pairs and restaurant workers. You can find them by putting up a card seeking conversation exchange at your local English language school. You'd be amazed how many people come to learn English in your country then get stuck in a house full of foreigners, working in an ethnic restaurant run by immigrants and never a chance to practise English with us natives.

Multilingual Made Easy

If you fancy building a portfolio of languages for annual jaunts to Europe, south America, the Caribbean or Africa, it helps to know that the Indo-European language family includes three main groups in Europe: Germanic, Romance and Slavonic. Once you know one member of a group, it's easy to learn another. However if beginning two languages at the same time, it's a good idea to avoid a pair that are very similar.

The Germanic, or Teutonic, languages include English, Dutch, German, Luxemburgish and Yiddish in one subgroup and Danish, Norwegian, Swedish, Icelandic and Faroese in another. For an English speaker it's easy to learn basic German as many of the everyday, short words are similar such as *hand, buch und apfel*. In Scandinavia and the Netherlands you'll encounter few folk who don't speak English. So once you've learnt German, which is only really useful in Germany, there's nowhere to go.

The Romance languages are descended from Latin and include Italian, French, Spanish, Portuguese, Romanian, Catalan and Romansch. Italian, Spanish and Portuguese are the easiest with highly regular pronunciation. I dropped Italian while learning Spanish because they're so similar that I kept mixing them up. French has trickier pronunciation but it's worth it since many French don't speak a word of English and the language sounds so, 'ow you say, downright sensual. You'll be able to explore rural France year after year (with your copy of *Vegetarian France*) and apply your new linguistic skills in Quebec, West Africa and Polynesia. Not to mention watching exquisite French films in arts cinemas and late night on channel 4. Learn French then follow up with Spanish or Italian. Or start with Spanish and add French later. The second language will take half as long.

The Slavonic languages cover most of eastern Europe. Russian and the very similar Bulgarian are, to put it bluntly, hard, with their own Cyrillic alphabet. Polish has more kinds of sh than a soft drinks factory and for a few weeks you think you'll never crack it, then suddenly everything falls into place. Czech and Slovak are 90% the same, though you'll get by in Prague with English or German. Serbian, with a Russian-like alphabet, and Croatian written in English letters, are also very similar and used to be lumped together as Serbo-Croat.

There are lesser known language groups within the Indo-European family. The Baltic languages Latvian and Lithuanian are different from but linked to their Slavonic neighbours. Albanian and Modern Greek are in groups by themselves. Greek has its own alphabet, but you can get by with the phonetic transcriptions in a phrase book. Just as the short words in English come from German, you'll find that many of our poly-syllabic utterances are combinations of Greek words, such as poly- which means many. The Celtic languages Welsh, Irish, Gaelic and Breton hang on surrounded by English and French.

Two more families of languages are completely unrelated to any of the above and their ancestry is shrouded in mystery. Estonian, Hungarian, Finnish and the Sami language of the Lapps all belong to the Uralic family. Basque, spoken around the Pyrenees, has no known relatives.

You may already live in a multicultural city. Learning languages opens up a lifetime of discovering the culture and cuisine of the homelands of our friends and neighbours. Investigate a beginner's course and tape at the local library or bookstore. Evening classes are fun and you'll make new friends. You can also eat out ethnically before and after your trip, buy a regional cook-book, shop at foreign grocery stores and get all Mediterranean or Polish in the kitchen. Have fun!

AUSTRIA

by Pat Collins

SALZBURG

Saltzburg is a beautiful city with great culture, famous for being the home of Mozart. With a backdrop second to none, veggies will be consoled with a limited selection. Fear not, this means less time wasted selecting and more time for that chamber concert. There are Mexican, Italian and Vietnamese places aplenty, but vegans beware because if the Austrians can slip cheese, cream or eggs into a dish, they will.

Look for health food stores called naturkostladen or reformhaus. Supermarket shopping is fairly straightforward. Anyone under 40 probably speaks English and labels on food are usually multilingual nowadays.

Spicy Spices
Wolf-Dietrich Str 1, right by the cliff
Salzburg, 5020
Tel: 664-213 82 45
Open: Mon-Sat 10-22.00, closed Sun
Bus to Mirabell
Vegetarian ayurvedic South Indian café with a small grocery section, a real backpacker haven and a good place to regroup and stock up on high energy fuel. Starters 20-40 AS like green salad, samosas, pakoras and bhajees. Main courses 60-70 AS such as basmati rice with vegetables and dhal. Desserts 17-25 AS include vegan halva and vegan cherry energyballs made with dried fruit and nuts. Fresh pressed juices 25-30 AS. They have soya milk and organic wine and cater for special diets. Also sells some wholefoods like tofu and Provamel stuff. English speaking staff. When we visited they were only open till 18.30 (Sat 13.30) but told us they were planning longer hours.

VIENNA

Leave the hustle and bustle behind in this elegant capital and find a more gentile pace to take in the atmosphere. Whether on crisp white linen or working class wooden tables, it's always a privilege to dine in Vienna and we veggies certainly have many choices.

Rupp's
Arbeitergasse 46
Vienna, 0 1050
Tel: 54 52 284
Open: Sun-Thu 18.00-02.00, Fri and Sat 19.00-04.00. (Sundays winter only Oct-May)
Do you wanna party? Check out this vegetarian pub with 262 whiskeys run by a vegetarian, in a working class neigh-bourhoold with a great pub atmosphere, sixties and seventies music. Choose from a selection of burgers 42 AA and dozens of small and large dishes 38-85 AS such as various pastas, 10 salads, 5 soups with croutons, goulash, chilli sin carne, soya schnitzel, many of them vegan. Gluten or wheat free no problem. English speaking staff. Midweek after 8pm it's probably full (there are 50 seats) so you'll probably have a small wait for a table.

Siddhartha
Fleischmarkt 16
Vienna, 1010
Tel: 015 13 11 97
Open: Mon-Sat 11.30-15.00 and 18-23.00
U-3 Stephansplatz
Vegetarian international restaurant catering for vegans. Starters 54-98 AS such as miso soup and spaghetti marinara. Salads 62-88 AS include artichoke vinaigrette, waldorf salad and roasted tofu salad. Main courses 124-164 AS like platter of curries with samosas and chapati, spinach ravioli, 3 or 4 vegan

options. 6 vegetarian desserts including fruit salad and chocolate mousse 46-72 AS, none vegan. House wine 26 AS glass,
beer 13-38 AS, coffee 32 AS.

Wrenkh

Bauernmarkt 10,
Vienna, 1010
Tel: 533 15 26
Open: Every day 11-24.00
Posh vegetarian restaurant which astonishingly has almost no
vegan choices on the menu, perhaps the last bastion in Europe
to defy the massive modern trend towards dairy free dining,
though they can adapt some dishes. One of our researchers
got rice with her meal instead of the polenta she'd ordered as
the cook had automatically added cheese. Anyway, enough of
our ranting, soups 42 AS, 8 mains (of which 3 or 4 could be
made vegan) 95-125 AS such as spinach gnocchi calabria with
veggies in sundried tomato sauce, courgette risotto with tofu,
vegies genovese with tofu and basil. Desserts from 60 AS. Beer
from 29 AS, house wine even less and bottles from 192 AS.
Herb tea 38 AS. Liqueurs and whiskies 35-45 AS. English menu
and most waiters speak English.

Aera

Gonzagagasse 11
Vienna, 1010
Open: evenings
Hip omnivorous late night café-bar in a renovated warehouse
with cement floor and big windows featuring live music some
nights or jungle, garage etc. This is hip for Vienna. Starters 45-
85 AS include salad, bread with beans and oyster mushrooms
(if vegan, ask for no 'speck') and spinach and mushrooms. Main
courses 72-92 AS include pizzas and spaghetti with tomato or
pesto. Little for vegans. Chips are available for 25 AS. Desserts
32-52 AS iinclude strudel but nothing vegan. Vegans will probably end up grazing on Beilage black bread, or chips for 25 AS.

House wine 19 AS per glass, beer 13-26 AS, coffee 31 AS. Cover charge 140-160 from 8pm on entertainment nights.

Café Teitelbaum

Dorotheergass 11, close to Grabstr.
Vienna,
Tel: 512 55 45
Open: Sun-Fri 10-20.00, closed Sat
U-3 Stephansplatz
Little modern kosher café-bar next to a gallery with lots of papers to read. Basically veggie and fish with loads of bagels, and the owner is a Konditormeister who makes his strudel. Lots of butter and eggs, something to do with quality apparently. Small meals 30-60 AS include bagels and tomato soup. Veg curry and rice with crusty bread and mango chutney is vegan. Desserts 29 AS include homemade cakes and strudels, sadly none vegan. House wine 23 AS, beer 13-30 AS, coffee 30 AS.

Rosa Elefant

Bauernmarkt 21 (corner 4 Fleischmarkt), West of Rotenturm,
Vienna, 1010
Tel: 01-533 75 30
U-3 Stephansplatz. U-Schwedenplatz
Old pub/Kneipe with a darkwood, rustic charm, country inn look. Our female researcher noted the cute young barmen and 70's soul train music. This omnivorous place has a couple of vegetarian options 50-94 AS to go with your booze, basically salads and chips. House wine 23 glass, 230 bottle, 4 kinds of pils on tap 13-34, coffee 31. English speaking staff.

Natur & Reform

Wahringers Str. 57
Vienna, 1090
Tel: 01-406 2630
Open: Mon-Fri 08.30-18.30, Sat 08.30-13.00
U-6 Volksoper
Vegetarian wholefood shop boasting 'all your needs under one roof'. Small takeaway selling veggieburgers and similar snacks for 27-34 AS, pastries 15-30 AS. Also soya milk, freshly squeezed juices, and those travellers weary of not being able to find a strudel fit for vegan consumption can tank up here on soya ice cream. Takes Visa, Mastercard, AmEx and Diners cards. English speaking staff.

Vegirant

Währingerstr. 57
Vienna, 1090
Tel: 407 82 87
Open: Mon-Fri 8.30-18.30, Sat 8.30-13.00
U-6 Volksoper
Vegetarian shop with a wholefood deli counter offering some tasty take-aways like spinach and sweetcorn veggieburger or pasties with leek and veg 27-34 AS. Various small pastries for dessert 15-30 AS. Freshly squeezed juices. All your favourite vegan brands under one roof for picnicking like Provamel, Tartex, Granovita and they have soya ice-cream. 50% off organic veggies on Saturday. Also beer and wine.

PLANNING YOUR TRIP ON THE WEB

Incredibly cheap flights:

www.**ryanair**.com
www.**easyjet**.com
www.**go-fly**.com

Coaches/buses to and around Europe:

www.**eurolines**.com
www.**gobycoach**.com

Rail travel to and around Europe:

www.**eurostar**.com
www.**raileurope**.com

The world's best **guides for budget travellers**, to help you decide where to go, where to stay, what to see and how much to spend:

www.**lonelyplanet**.com
www.**roughguides**.com
www.**letsgo**.com
and of course
www.**vegetarianguides**.com

If you've got a favourite travel site to recommend, please let us know at:
info@vegetarianguides.co.uk

Visit the links page at www.vegetarianguides.co.uk for more links and the best veggie sites worldwide.

BELGIUM

BRUSSELS

by Alex Bourke

Dolma
Elsense Steenweg 329
Brussels 1050
Tel: 02 649 89 81
Open: Mon-Sat 12-14.00 and 19-21.30, closed Sun
Vegetarian restaurant with Tibetan all-you-can eat buffet, near avenue Louise and Place Flagey (which has a Sunday market) in the centre. The buffet is 460 for lunch, 540 evenings, 230 or 270 respectively for children up to 10 years. There's also a "pot au feu tibétain" for two people for 1150 BF with seitan, tofu, veg, noodles, spices and fresh coriander but vegans will want it without the quorn and quail eggs. 10 starters 100-300 F include miso, Tibetan or soup of the day; vegetable tart with Greek salad; potatoes with Tibetan sauce. 8 main meals 290-550 F such as spaghetti bolognaise with seitan; marinated tofu with vegetables and seaweed; tofu or seitan schnitzel with grain and veg; Himalayan selection of samosas and momos. Extra wholegrains, vegetable or salad 100-200 BF. Desserts 140. Beers 70-100 from light to Trappist. Juices 100-130, apéritifs 120-300, mineral water from 60, lemonade or cola (with or without Guarana) 100. Wines from 100 glass, 290 half bottle, 560 bottle. All kinds of tea at 100 for a pot to drink with your meal, but beware the Tibetan tea contains butter. Warm wine 180, coffees 65, hot chocolate 100, even organic saké 180. Champagne 2000 or 300 for a glass.

Tsampa

109 rue de Livourne,
Brussels 1050
Tel: 02-647 03 67
Open: Mon-Sat 12-14.00 and 19-21.30, closed Sun.
International vegetarian restaurant and wholefood shop run by the same people as Dolma, near avenue Louise in the centre. Daily lunch menu includes soup 120-200 BF, salads 150-300 BF, vegetable flan 200 BF, main course Assiette Tsampa 300 (400 with salad or soup) or half portion for 280, bowl of grains and veg 220, or a daily mini menu of soup + 1/2 Tsampa + tea 400. A la carte offers 9 entrées 210-290 such as seaweed, Tibetain seitan ravioli, spring rolls. 8 main dishes 420-510 such as curry, Japanese pot-au-feu with tofu and wakame, seitan steak with grain and veg, tofu and spinach ravioli. Desserts 150 such as chestnut chocolate tart. An extensive drinks menu with organic wine from 95/glass, 285 half bottle, 525 bottle, apéritifs like Sherry 120 and saké 200, alcohol free juice cocktails 100, cider 320 for 3/4 litre, champagne 750-1400, beers with and without alcohol 80-100, juices 90, teas 50-100, coffee and coffee-free coffee 60. Shop and deli open from 10 a.m. Menu not in English, but usually one of the staff speak English.
Shop, open 10-21.30 Mon-Sat, has vegan goodies and take-away salads, tarts, Provamel products.

Les Feux de Bengale

Rue des Epéronniers 69
Brussels 1000
Tel: 02-513 51 63
Open: Every evening 18-24.00
500m from the Central Station
Central omnivorous Indian restaurant which we've included as it's open late on Sundays and they are Anglophone-friendly. A vegetarian thali costs 795 BF with rice, 4 kinds of vegetables and nan bread. They use vegetable ghee unless the customer asks for butter ghee. Usual Indian desserts, some vegan. All

kinds of wines and beers including Indian. Menu in English and they speak English.

Mister Big Beng

48 Grand Place, City Centre,
Brussels 1000
Tel: 02-513 18 03
Open: Weekdays 11-02.00. Fri and Sat until 05.00
200m from near the Grand Place

If you've just emerged fom a disco at 3am at the weekend with a severe case of midnight munchies, head for Mister Big Beng's omnivorous Indian take-away and grocery store which is open till dawn, next to Place St Jean. They offer a number of vege-tarian and vegan dishes like bhajias, samosas, pakoras, toma-to and lentil dhal, okra, basmati rice, nan bread and mixed veg-etables, to eat in or out. You can phone your order and it will be waiting for you. Great for a quick lunch too. Also sells heaps of groceries including nuts, soft drinks, exotic juices and wines. A full vegetarian meal of samosa, bhajia, rice, mixed veg and dhal for 250 BF. Menu in French, but you can see the food and they speak English. Student discount 20% on snacks and drinks.

La Saga (formerly Greenfields)

Av. de la Chevalerie 9
Brussels 1040
Tel: 02-734 40 98
Open: Mon-Fri 12-15.00, Fri-Sat 19-21.30
Shop open: Mon-Sat 08.00-20.00
Metro: Merode

Vegan organic restaurant in the back of a health food store with 36 seats, in the "European" quartier where the diplomats hang out. Very handy if you've just been lobbying for EC milk and meat subsidies to be transferred to helping farmers convert to growing organic vegetables. Have three courses for 550 BF or two for 430 BF, with vegan tarts and cakes for dessert, or get a take-away. Lots of civil servants and office workers at lunchtime. The shop sells organic food, vegetables, soya milk, soya yogurt, soya dessert, British Scheese soya cheese and even vegan ice-cream, heh heh heh. In warm weather you can dine in the garden. No smoking. Between them the staff speak a truly European Community of languges that include French, Dutch, Italian, Spanish and English.

CROATIA

by Akcelina Cvijetic

There is a strong macrobiotic movement in the countries that were once Yugoslavia. This means that if you're heading for the beautiful beaches and islands of Croatia, you'll be able to find what you're used to eating by looking out for the great macrobiotic shops and well supplied health food stores. Markets are excellent for fresh and organic food.

I am a vegetarian
Ja sam vegetarijanac (m), Ja sam vegetarijanka (f)
c is pronounced ts, j is like English y

I am vegan
Ja sam vegan *or* Ja sam viganac (m), Ja sam viganka (f)

We are vegans (strict vegetarians)
Mi smo vegani (strogi vegetarijanci)

We do not eat meat, chicken or fish.
Mi ne jedemo meso, kokos i ribu.

We do not eat eggs, milk, butter, cheese, honey
Mi ne jedemo jaja, mlijeko, maslo, sir, med

Where is a health food shop?
Gdje je prodavnica zdrave ishrane?

Where is a macrobiotic shop?
Gdje je prodavnica makrobiotike?

Is there a vegetarian restaurant near here?
Ima li blizu vegetarijanski restoran?

Please   Molim
Thank you   Hvala

This is Zorba, the Veggie Guides' travelling laughing Buddha. He's here in case you have one of those days, you know, when it's raining on holiday and you've had an argument and there's nothing to eat and nothing seems to be going right. "Buddha" means the one who knows. And Zorba knows that even if today isn't everything he'd expected, everything will turn out ok in the end. He's got his smile, he's got his flute, and he's got his tummy. Whenever you feel down, just pat Zorba's belly and everything will be ok.

CZECH REPUBLIC

PRAGUE

by Alex Bourke

Dominated by the hilltop castle, Prague offers delightful sight-seeing with quaint old squares, warm sunshine and the slinkiest local accents in Europe. With plenty of cheap hostels and bars, it's every inch a party town and magnet for backpackers and thousands of resident Yappies (Young Americans in Prague) enjoying a bargain gap year. Vegans beware, in the Czech Republic the four food groups are sausages, cheese, ice-cream and beer. Thus my soft voiced Slovak companion and I appreciated all the more Prague's well stocked veggie oases.

Country Life
Melantrichova 15
Prague, 0 11000
Tel: 42 02 24 21 3366
Open: Mon-Thu 9-15.00, 18-21.30. Fri 9-19.00, Sun 11-18.00.
Closed Sat.
Metro: Mustek
Centrally located, virtually vegan organic cafeteria style restaurant and wholefood shop just off the SW corner of the old town square Staromestske Nam. They sell a wide variety of tasty and fresh raw and cooked food to serve yourself with from a buffet, or stock up in the shop for a picnic. As well as tasty wholefood dishes and soups, they have vegan desserts, and it's all very inexpensive. Part of a worldwide chain run by Seventh Day Adventists. No alcohol or smoking. Shop open from 8am Mon-Fri. There is another branch of Country Life a few blocks south at Jungmannova 1.

FX Café in Radost Centre

Belehradska 120
Prague, 0 2
www.techno.cz/radostfx
Tel: 2425 4776
Open: 11.30 right through till 04.00 next morning.
Metro: I.P. Pavlova
Vegetarian café in the Radost complex, which has a gallery upstairs and a nightclub downstairs. Popular for its Sunday brunch, which is served until 3pm. Also serves pizzas, burritos, salads and similar snack meals. Some vegan options. Typical price 70-160 kr. No smoking area.

Lotos

Platnerska 13
Prague,
Tel: 232 2390
Open: Every day 12-22.00
Metro: Staromestska
Lovely vegetarian restaurant between the old town square and the river, where you might end up after walking back from "doing" the castle. Lots of vegan-friendly and macrobiotic tofu dishes and as with everything in Prague you'll marvel at the prices compared to eating in Western Europe, with dishes from 59 to 140 kr, average 80-90. This is the veggie restaurant in central Prague that also has beer, both with and without alcohol, and wine. Non smoking.

Govinda's

Soukenicka 27
Prague, 0
Tel: 02-2481 6631
Open: Mon-Sat 11-17.30 (maybe 18.00), closed Sun
Metro: Nam. Republiky
Busy Hare Krishna restaurant north of nam. (square) Republiky and close to Petrske nam. 60 kr for a medium menu with rice, dhal, savoury and two salads, or go for it wit hall-you-can-eat

for 75 kr. There's also a sweet shop with cakes and drinks. Some vegan food. Lots of tourists eat there and they speak English.
There's another smaller, simpler branch at Na hrazi 5, tel. 683 7226, open Mon-Fri 12-18.00, closed Sat-Sun. It's further east, two blocks north of Metro Palmovka on Line B, by a small supermarket. 60 kr for a main meal. They also speak English.

CZECH THE VEGGIES

I'm vegetarian
Jsem vegetarian (m), Jsem vegetarianka (f)

I'm vegan
Jsem vegán (m), Jsem vegánka (f)

I don't eat meat, chicken, fish
Nejim maso, kurata, ryby

I don't eat eggs, milk, butter, or cheese
Nejim vejce, mléko, máslo a syry

Do you have any vegetarian dishes?
Mate take nejaka vegetarianska jidla?

LET'S PARTY!

DENMARK

COPENHAGEN

by Kirsten Jungsberg

In Denmark in almost all supermarkets you can get soya milk, organic fresh vegetables and fruits and they usually also have a health food section where you can get canned and frozen vegetarian and vegan food, usually from Nutana, different dried fruit and beans from Urtekram. Tofutti vegan icecream and cheese will soon be available in healthfood shops in Denmark. Swedish Glace soya ice-cream can be bought at Brugsen supermarket, where they also have their own range of healthfoods.

In Copenhagen, mainly in the inner part of the city and the streets Vesterbrogade and Nørrebrogade, you can find many restaurants which offer a buffet with vegetarian and vegan dishes before 16.00 at very reasonable prices, e.g.. Ankara only 39 kr. There are also a lot of pizzerias, but be careful if you want falafel or chips because they very often use the same oil for chicken and fish. The best hotels can usually serve you an excellent but expensive vegetarian or vegan dinner with three courses.

Please note that København V and K and Frederiksberg C are the centre of Copenhagen and these streets each have their own numbers, whereas 2000 Frederiksberg and 2200 København N etc means a whole district.

Café Merkur

Willemoesgade 81
Copenhagen, 0 2100 Ø
Tel: 35 63 83 400
Open: Tue-Fri 11-21.00. Sat-Sun and holidays 11-19.00.
Nordhavn Station. Bus 3
95% organic café and take-away where you can enjoy a soya cappucino, herb tea or organic wine. It's a nice place with three rooms, two of them non-smoking. No muzak. Books and international papers to read and many cultural events take place here. In the summer it is possible to sit outside.

Den Grønne Kaelder (The Green Cellar)

Pilestræde 48,
Copenhagen, 1112 K
Tel: 33 93 01 40
Open: Mon-Sat 11-22.00 Sunday and holiday closed
Nørreport Station. Bus 1, 6, 5, 10, 19. 29. 31. 42, 43, 350S, 650S
S-train: Nørreport Station
Vegetarian world food restaurant in the middle of the old city with very good food. Many different salads and a wide variety of dishes you can combine, 7 hot ones, 3 of them vegan, and 7 salads of which 4 are vegan. The menu changes often. It's cheapest before 17.00, around 30 to 75kr, after 17.00 between 60 and 95 kr. Wine 25 kr glass, 135kr bottle, beer 25 kr, organic coffee 20kr. Organic wine, herb tea and organic coffee. High chairs for children and children's portions. Staff speak English.

Den Økologiske Cafe (The Organic Cafe)
Griffenfeldsgade 17
Copenhagen, 2200
Tel: 35 36 34 17
Open: Mon-Fri 10-20.00. Closed Sat, Sun and holidays.
Bus:3, 5, 16
Good value salad bar with hot vegetarian and vegan dishes and sandwiches from 20-50 kr, organic coffee 10kr and they have vegan icecream (sorbet). Also take-away food. The place is run by an organic society and started as a project for unemployed young people with an interest in the environment. They have a healthfood shop next door called Spidsroden. Takes Visa cards. High chairs for children and children's portions.

Govinda's
Nr. Farimagsgade 82
Copenhagen, 1314
Tel: 33 33 74 44
Open: Mon-Sat 12.00-20.30, Sunday and holiday closed
S-train Nørreport Station. Bus 5, 14, 16, 40, 42, 43.
Very popular vegetarian Indian Hare Krishna restaurant where a vegan can always get food. One meal daily which contains snacks, soup, salad, home-made bread, main course with rice and spring water, all you can eat for only 55kr. Eat there 10 times with their discount card and get 10% off. Monday and Thursday are vegan days. Samosas 15 kr, lasagne 35 kr, small or large salad 10-20 kr. Herb tea and barley cup. They always have soya milk. Desserts 10-20 kr. High chairs for children and children's portions. Staff speak English. No smoking or alcohol.

Morgenstedet
Bådsmandsstræde 43, Christiania,
Copenhagen, 0 1407 K
Open: Wed to Mon 14-20.00, Tuesday closed.
Bus 8 (for instance from Central Station) to the entrance.
Vegetarian meals inspired by the different cooks. Almost everything organic and fairly cheap. Morgenstedet's idea is to serve

healthy food which uplifts you, therefore smoking, alcohol and loud music are not allowed. Situated in the famous New Age community called Christiania, a former military camp and a very interesting place to visit but don't put on your best clothes! Caters for vegans and always has soya milk. High chairs for children and children's portions.

Ø-Sneglen

Istedgade 24
Copenhagen, 0 1650 V
Tel: 33 23 75 47
Open: Mon-Fri 06.30-18.00, Sat and Sun 06.30-15.00
Very close to the Central Station. Bus 16.
An old-fashioned organic dairy with sandwiches and vegan products.

Atlas Bar

LarsBjørnsstræde 18
Copenhagen, 0 1454 K
Tel: 33 15 03 52
Open: Mon-Sat 12.00-22.00, closed Sun.
Bar with take-away food situated very close to the pedestrian street Strøget. Many different salads, soups and meals also for vegans. The food is 50 % organic. Sit and enjoy the atmosphere in the Latin Quarter.

Cascabel Madhus

St. Kongensgade 80
Copenhagen, 1264
Tel: 33 93 77 97
Open: Mon-Sat 11-22.00, Sun.11-15.00, holidays closed.
Bus: 1, 6, 9, 19, 29, 650S
Omnivorous restaurant in the old city close the Queen's castle Amalienborg. Mostly vegetarian world foods with many different vegetarian and vegan dishes. Salad 25kr, soup 40kr and main course 85kr. Cascabel means chili in Spanish which they use a lot of in their food. Also take-away which is 10% cheaper.

House wine 27kr glass, 130kr bottle, beer 22kr, coffee 15kr, cappucino 17kr. They always have soya milk and soya ice cream. High chairs for children and children's portions. Staff speak English.

Cassiopeia

Gl. Kongevej 10
Copenhagen, 1610
Tel: 33 15 09 33
Open: Every day 11.30-21.30
S-train Vesterport Station. Buses 1, 14, 29
A very nice omnivorous restaurant in the Tycho Brahes Planetarium with a beautiful view over the Saint Jørgens Lake. 3 vegetarian dishes priced 78-89 kr. House wine 27 kr glass, 155kr bottle, beer 25kr, coffee 24kr. High chairs for children and children's portions. Menu in English, staff speak English, German, French and Italian.

Den Persiske Stue

Nørrebrogade 102,
Copenhagen, 2200
Tel: 35 35 35 72
Open: Every day 17-22.00
Bus 5, 16, 18, 350S
A rather new omnivorous Persian restaurant with small bright rooms, very popular with a good atmosphere, that can cater for vegans. Special offer menu 59kr for 3 dishes where you can choose from 4 salads, 4 main courses and 3 desserts, including vegan ice cream. House wine 25kr glass, 118kr bottle, beer 19kr, coffee 12kr. English menu. High chairs for children and children's portions.

India Palace

H.C. Andersens Boulevard 13
Copenhagen, 1553
Tel: 33 91 04 08
Open: Every day 11-24.00
Vesterport station.
Bus 2,6,8,11,14,16,28,29,30,34,67,68,69,150S,250S.
Large omnivorous Indian and Pakistani restaurant close to the Town Hall Square which caters for vegetarians and vegans. Big buffet from 11.00 till 3pm with vegetarian and vegan dishes for 59kr. They never use the same oil for vegetables and meat/fish. Starters 18-4kr of which onion bhaji and samosa are vegan. Main courses 20-25kr like dhal, tomato soup, bhindi bahaji (okra) and mushroom special which are all vegan. Wine 35kr glass, 120kr bottle, beer 20kr, coffee 12kr. Takes Visa, Mastercard, AmEx and Diners Club. High chairs for children and children's portions. English menu, staff speak English.

Indian Taj Restaurant

Jernbanegade 3 - 5
Copenhagen, 0 1608 V
Tel: 33 13 10 10
Open: Every day 12-24.00
Vesterport Station.
Bus 2,6,8,11,14,16,28,29,30,34,67,68,69,150S,250S
A very beautiful and elegant large omnivorous restaurant with genuine Indian atmosphere. Very close to the Town Hall Square. Uses only fresh ingredients with no tins or frozen vegetables. 3 different salads 28kr. 15 main dishes between 68 and 115kr. Desserts 32-38kr. Wine 45kr glass, 175kr bottle, beer 25kr, coffee 34kr. High chairs for children and children's portions. English menu, staff speak English

Leonora Christine

Nyhavn 9
Copenhagen, 1051 K
Tel: 33 13 50 40
Open: Every day 12-24.00
Bus 1, 6, 9, 10, 19, 29, 31, 42, 43, 350S, 650S
Omnivorous restaurant catering for vegetarians and vegans in the oldest building in Nyhavn dating from 1681, right by the water with a beautiful interior like a fairytale that you just have to see and a beautiful patio. Nyhavn is a restaurant street very close to the Royal Theatre and the King's New Square. This restaurant is one of the best, named after a daughter of Christian the 4th, who built a lot of famous tourist attractions such as The Round Tower, Nyboder, Børsen, Rosenborg Castle, Holmen's Church and many more. Starters from 85kr. Main course 185kr. Dessert 95kr including vegan ice-cream. House wine 35 kr glass, 175 k. bottle, beer 35 kr, coffee 28 kr. High chairs for children and children's portions. English menu, staff speak English. No non-smoking area. Takes Visa, Mastercard, Amex.

Picnic

Fælledvej 22B
Copenhagen, 0 2200 N
Tel: 35390953
Open: Mon-Fri 10-22.00, Sat 11-23.00, Sun 11-22.00
Bus 3, 5, 16, 350S
85% vegetarian, organic salad and sandwich bar with many hot dishes served in a cosy old-fashioned bar. Also herb teas and take-away service. Caters for vegans and macrobiotic diets. 1 salad 28 kr, 3 salads 54 kr, main dish 58 kr. They have soya milk. High chairs for children and children's portions. They take Visa. Staff speak English.

Riz Raz

Kompagnistræde 20
Copenhagen, 0 1208 K
Tel: 33150575
Open: Mon-Sat 11.30-23.00, Sun and holidays 11.30-24.00
Bus 2, 5, 6, 28, 29

Very large omnivorous Mediterranean and Middle East inspired restaurant with 200 seats, situated in a famous walking street where you can sit outside in summer. Very popular and famous for its wonderful vegetarian buffet with mostly vegan dishes for 49kr before 17.00 and 59 kr after. House wine 22 kr glass, 129 kr bottle, beer 20kr, coffee 12 kr. High chairs for children and children's portions. Staff speak English and German.

SIFA

Vesterbrogade 39
Copenhagen, 0 1620 V
Tel: 33 25 10 10
Open: Sun-Thu 11.00-24.00, Fri and Sat 11.00-02.00
Central Station. Bus: 6, 28, 550S

Very interesting large omnivorous Turkish restaurant, newly redecorated, with belly dancers on Friday and Saturday nights. Big buffet with many vegan and vegetarian dishes 49kr until 16.00, 59 kr after. A 3-course vegan or vegetarian dinner for 99 kr. House wine 24 kr glass, 109 kr bottle, beer 18 kr, coffee: 14kr. Takes Visa, Mastercard, AmEx. High chairs for children and children's portions.

City Helse

Vendersgade 6
Copenhagen, 0 1363 K
Tel: 331 408 92
Open: Mon-Thur 9.30-17.30, Fri 9.30-18.00, Sat 9.30 14.00
Nørreport Station. Bus 5, 14, 16.

Health food shop.

Det Esotiske Hjørne
Jagtvej 127, Copenhagen N,
Copenhagen, 0 2200 K
Tel: 35 83 05 80
Open: Mon-Fri 8-18.30, Sat 8-15.00
Bus 18
50-60% organic health food shop where you can also buy 9 vegetarian sandwiches of which 8 are vegan, 12 salads, soup and organic wine.

Det Rene Brød (The Pure Bread)
Rosenvængats Alle 17
Copenhagen, 0 2100 Ø
Tel: 35 43 18 14
Open: Every day
Bus 3, 6, 14, 650S
Organic bakery which sells very good vegan bread and vegan Danish pastries.

Drogisten
Finsensvej 92, Frederiksberg,
Copenhagen, 0 2000
Tel: 38 33 96 33
Open: Mon-Thu 10-17.30, Fri 10-18.30, Sat 10-13.00
Bus 13 and 39
Health food shop offering 10% discount to Vegetarian and Vegan Society members, so remember your membership card.

Helsehuset
Gl. Kongeveg 92, Frederiksberg,
Copenhagen, 1850 C
Tel: 33 21 44 21
Open: Mon-Fri 9.30-17.30, Sat 9-14.00
Bus 1 and 14
Health food shop.

Mælk og Honning

Valby Tingsted 6-8, Valby,
Copenhagen, 0 2500
Tel: 36 30 55 66
Open: Mon-Fri 10-17.30, Sat 10-13.30
Valby Station. Bus 6.
Health food shop near the organic market at Valby Tingsted,
which is open Tue 14-17.30 and Sat 9-14.00.

Mc Grail

Gl. Torv 6
Copenhagen, 1457 K
Tel: 33 13 20 43
Open: Mon-Thu 10-18.00, Fri 10-19.00, Sat 10-16.00
Health food shop near the City Hall Square and the pedestrian
street Strøget.

Solsikke

Blågårdsgade 33
Copenhagen, 0 2200 N
Tel: 35 39 53 11
Open: Mon-Thu 09-18.00, Fri 09-19.00, Sat 09-16.00
Bus 3, 5, 16
Health food shop

To be vegan, or not to be vegan
That is the question

I am vegetarian
Jeg er vegetar

I am vegan
Jeg er veganer

I don't eat meat, chicken, fish
Jeg spiser ikke kød, kylling, fisk

I don't eat eggs, milk, butter, cheese, honey
Jeg spiser ikke aeg, maelk, smør, ost, honning

ENGLAND

London 52

Liverpool 91

Oxford 95

VEGAN HEAVEN

Animal Free Shopper and Swedish Glace
Buying shoes in Brighton no more disgrace
Plamil chocolate and Country Life
Veggie Matchmakers found me a wife
Peta posters in underground stations
Vegan Society's public relations
Cruelty free guide, what more can you ask
Being a vegan was never an easier task
Is everyone living here really aware
That the rest of the world doesn't show as much care
So if you travel abroad please do not forget
To take part of vegan Britain with you in your pack
This is so much better than Christchurch or LA
"Vegan heaven" is what I call the UK!

Gina Madison

LONDON

by Alex Bourke & Paul Gaynor

SOHO

beatroot

92 Berwick Street, Soho W1V
Tel: 020 7437 8591
Tube: Oxford Circus, Tottenham Court Rd
Open: Mon-Sat 9-18.30
Vegan dessert heaven. Alex's favourite café in London, 80% vegan, at the south end of Berwick St by the fruit and veg market, with a couple of tables outside on the pavement. Choose any combination from 16 hot specials and salads, 8 are vegan, small £2.50, medium £3.50 or large £4.50. 5 cakes, mostly vegan, 90p-£1.30 including fabulous vegan chocolate dream cake with vegan custard and vegan tofu cheesecake. Truffles and flapjacks £1. Teas 90p, coffee £1. Gorgeous soya-fruit smoothies. They do take-away and sandwiches too. Couple of outside tables. Smoking allowed inside. No credit cards, cheques ok. We love this place.

Crazy Salads

128 Wardour Street
Soho W1
Tel: 020-7437 3286
Tube: Tottenham Court Rd,
Oxford Circus
Open: Mon-Fri lunch and
early afternoon
Great salad bar, serve yourself with a box of 3 from a selection of 40 for £1.99 or 4 for £2.25. See Goodge Street branch (Bloomsbury) for details.

CTJ Organic Vegan Restaurant

10 Greek Street, Soho W1V
Tel: 020-7287 3713
Tube: Tottenham Court Rd, Leicester Sq
Open: Mon-Sat 12.30-21.30, Sun 13-21.00

Organic vegan Chinese. London's newest veggie restaurant, run by a Buddhist temple, and already incredibly popular for its amazing value and delicious food. Mainly Chinese and Thai food, some Japanese. All you can eat buffet, as many trips as you like for £5, or £6 minimum charge evenings so have a drink, £3 for a take-away box. Rice, spring rolls, tofu, stir-fry veg, salad, soya meats, noodles, menu changes all the time. All vegetables are organic and the soya is GM free. Tea £1, all organic juices £2.50, soft drinks such as natural cola £1. Cash only. Non-smoking.

Govinda's Vegetarian Restaurant

9/10 Soho Street, Soho W1V
Tel: 020-7437 3662
Tube: Tottenham Court Road
Open: Mon-Sat 12-20.00, closed Sun

Popular Hare Krishna owned and staffed vegetarian, Indian restaurant and café, with some fast food, next door to temple just off Oxford Street near Tottenham Court Road. 2 vegan and 4 veggie starters such as pakoras or dahl with bread £1.50. Several vegan and 9 veggie choices to make your large £3.75 or regular £2 mixed salad. 10 main course dishes, but the best value of all is the 7 dish all-you-can-eat buffet £4.99. Vegans should check whether they are using butter ghee as it seems to vary from year to year. As well as Indian food there are lasagne, quiche, pizza, and baked potatoes for £1.50-3.00. Several desserts and cakes but usually only 1 vegan choice and proportionately more expensive at £2.50 than other courses. Soya milk, soya milkshakes available. Lots of juices and waters 75p-£1.20. (Decaf) tea or coffee or herb tea 80p. No eggs. Non smoking. Surplus grub is given to London's homeless after hours.

Mildreds

58 Greek Street
Soho W1V
Tel: 020-7494 1634
Tube: Tottenham Court Road
Open: Mon-Sat 12-23.00, Sun 12-17.00
Almost completely vegetarian café-restaurant and take-away in the heart of vibrant restaurant land with a menu that changes daily. Young and trendy place to eat with big lunchtime trade. Sometimes a queue and always crowded but always friendly and the food is worth the wait, especially if you wait in the pub opposite till the waitress comes to get you. Most of the food is vegan and clearly marked. Starters £2.30-3.50 like dahl with coconut cakes or artichoke soup. Main courses £4.50-5.80 are mostly vegan such as warm Catalan butter bean salad with carmelized fennel and leeks plus olive bread; lentil, courgette and pumpkin seed burger with aubergine, apricot relish and garlic mayonnaise served with salad and New York fries; stir fried veg in sesame oil with garlic and ginger on brown rice. Falafel with organic pitta bread £4.70 or take-away £2.80. Salads £2.20-5.00. At least one of the 8 more-ish desserts is vegan such as rich chocolate pudding £2.95, extra soya cream 60p. Organic wines from £8.20 bottle, £2.30 glass, organic lager £2.60, heck they even have organic Guy Pinard VSOP cognac £3. Teas 80p cup, £1 pot, coffee £1, soy cappuccino £1.25. Juices and soft drinks from £1.30. If you really can't wait, there's always CTJ opposite.

LEICESTER SQUARE

Cranks Leicester Square

17 Great Newport Street
by Leicester Square WC2
Tel: 020-7836 5226
Tube: Leicester Square
Open: Mon-Fri 08.00-21.00, Sat 10-21.00, Sun 11-19.00
Vegetarian health food café where you can fill up for a fiver or just have a coffee. Busy early evening with the post-work pre-cinema crowd, otherwise the perfect place to write a postcard while waiting for a friend. Just east of Leicester Square.

Cranks Charing Cross

8 Adelaide Street
Charing Cross WC2N
Tel: 020-7836 0660
Tube: Charing Cross
Open: Mon-Sat 08.00-20.00, closed Sun
Vegetarian fast health food café and take-away close to Charing Cross station. Sandwiches, stir-fry, pizza, quiche, hot dish of the day, soups, salads, juices and cakes. There's always something vegan. Small eating area.

International Vegetarian Union (IVU) presents

35th World Vegetarian Congress

'Food for all our futures'
Heriot Watt University, Edinburgh, Scotland
July 8-14, 2002

An enjoyable week's holiday with no worries about food! Mix with like-minded people from around the world and gain experience and information from top international speakers and workshop leaders. In addition, a post-congress holiday is being organised to take advantage of the unique scenic and historic heritage of Scotland. Hosted by The Vegetarian Society (UK).

Further information from Tina Fox, The Vegetarian Society (UK), Parkdale Dunham Road, Altrincham WA14 4QG, Cheshire, UK.
Tel: +44 (0)161 928 0793.   Fax: +44 (0)161 926 9182.
www.ivu.org/congress/2002/   email: congress@vegsoc.org

Country Life

3-4 Warwick Street
near Piccadilly W1
Tel: 020 71434 2922
Tube: Piccadilly Circus exit 1
Open: Sun-Thu 11.30-21.00 (last orders), Fri 11.30-15.00.
Closed Sat.

Herbivore heaven. London's central vegan restaurant reopened in 1998 in a new location at the south end of Warwick Street. Seventh Day Adventist managed but they won't try to conver you. More clinical and clean cut than their old premises with low key décor and paintwork. Mainly organic and wholefoods. Brilliant buffet all-you-can-eat lunch till 15.00 of mixed salads and hot dishes for which you pay 1p per gramme, roughly £5-6 a plate. In the evenings the chef has gone gourmet à la carte. Starters £1.50-2.50 could be grapefruit puree; gaucamole with tortilla chips; stuffed champignons au gratin; tofu spinach consomme; Indian lentil soup. Main courses around £10 with salad and wholegrain bread or rolls include basmati risotto, gratinated aubergines, seitan fillet Stroganoff, borlotti fricasse, potato souffle Picadilly, tofu-medallion "piccata", or a main course salad. Desserts £1.90-2.65 are all vegan with the exception of any containing honey (clearly labelled) and include Viennese apple strudel, Tofutti vanilla ice cream, blackberry terrine, tofu cheese cake. Alcohol free wine and other non alcoholic drinks. Smoke free. Booking advised in the evening. Family treats, business dinners or large special events catered for.

Superb wholefood shop with hundreds of delicious vegan foods, self-service nuts, dried fruits and grains, organic fruit and vegetables and books. Freshly home baked wholemeal breads and rolls, sandwiches, biscuits, cakes and snacks. Shop open Mon-Wed 9-18.00, Thu till 19.30, Fri till 15.00, Sun 11.30-16.00. Also cookery classes with true nutrition taught there by their resident vegan GP who is available for private consultations by appointment. Medical and dietary consultations available for good health and advice on particular conditions including heart

disease, cancer, osteoporosis, diabetes, food allergies, stress management and weight control.
Web site: www.countrylife-restaurant.co.uk

Woodlands Vegetarian Restaurant

37 Panton S, SW1t
(off Haymarket)
Tel: 020-7839 7258
Tube: Piccadilly Circus, Leicester Square
Open: Mon-Sat 12-14.30, 17.30-22.30. Sun 18-22.30
Vegetarian Indian restaurant off the south-west corner of Leicester Square. White tablecloths rather than flock wallpaper. Big menu with plenty of savouries for vegans. Starters like samosa and bhel poori £1.70-2.25. Lots of dosas £2.50-3.50, a South Indian crepe made from a batter of soaked and finely ground lentils and rice, fermented overnight and served with a lentil soup and coconut chutney. Uthappam is a lentil pizza for £2.75 plus 30p per extra topping. Veg korma curry with cashews and rice £3.95. Thalis £6.25 or £7.25. Steamed, lemon, coconut, bakala or pillau rice £1.50-2.75.

Gaby's

30 Charing Cross Road, WC2
by Leicester Square
Tel: 020-7836 4233
Tube: Leicester Square
Open: Mon-Sat 11-24.00, Sun 11-21.00
Uncomplicated omnivorous Mediterranean café 50 metres from Leicester Square tube station on the Covent Garden side of Charing Cross Rd. with stacks of veggie and vegan eat-ins and take-aways for a fiver or less. Real favourite because of its location and prices, though food can be a little on the oily side. Point to what you want in the deli style counter such as stuffed aubergine/pepper £5.50, pasta with herb and tomato sauce £4, excellent falafels £2.50. 20 salads £2-3. Chips £1.30. All kinds of alcohol, coffee, lemon and herb tea.

Eden Rock Café

22 Cranbourne Street, WC2
(by Leicester Square)
Tel: 020-7379 7737
Tube: Leicester Square
Open every day 08.00-04.00

Omnivorous Lebanese café open till 3 in the morning, close to the Hippodrome, Stringfellows, theatres and cinemas, and the Trafalgar Square night buses. Very handy after the disco when all the veggie places have been closed for hours with plenty even for vegans. Midnight munchies for revellers include falafel £3.75 (take-away £3.40), aubergine salad £2.95, mixed veg £2.95, tabouleh £2.40, veg soup £2.40. Large mixed vegetarian deli £5.95 with tabouleh, aubergine, rice, humous and salads. Chips £1 take-away. Lavazza coffee £1.50. Kaliber £1.50.

Holland & Barrett

65 Charing Cross Rd, WC2
by Leicester Square
Tel: 020-7287 3139
Tube: Leicester Square

Health food store just north of Leicester Square, great for flapjacks, dried fruit, nuts, vegan chocolate, drinks and snacks.

Prince Charles Cinema

Leicester Place, W1
north side of Leicester Square behind Haagen-Dazs
Tel: 020-494 4087
Tube: Leicester Square

Bargain alert!! Not a restaurant, not a café, but the cheapest cinema in London charging £3 in the daytime, or £3.50 evenings and weekends. Sometimes Monday is bargain day with films £1.99 all day. The films are almost new including blockbusters, with five different ones on every day, for a third of the price of other West End cinemas. There are even free postcards in the basement, plus a bar serving all drinks for £2. This will leave you with heaps more dough for the 30 veggie restaurants and cafés in the West End. If you're a student or skint person looking to spoil yourself we recommend preceding your cinema trip with the all-you-can-scoff buffet at Govinda's or CTJ. Or buy your ticket and grab a falafel for £2 at a café on the NW side of Leicester Square, about 100m from the cinema. Call above number for today's programme or 020-7437 8181 for the whole week. If going in the evening it's best to arrive half an hour early.

COVENT GARDEN

Food For Thought

31 Neal Street
Covent Garden WC2
Tel: 020 7836 9072/0239
Tube: Covent Garden
Open: Mon-Sat 9.30-20.30, Sun (and Bank Holidays) 12-17.00
Fabulous veggie take-away and café-restaurant in vaulted basement offering superb value and ultra-fresh food from around the world. Gets really crowded at peak times and its counter service and pine tables but that's part of its appeal. One of the oldest and most successful veggie restaurants in London. Menu changes daily so here are some examples: vegan oriental soup with babycorn and tofu £2.30; choice of 4 salads £2-£5 such as butterbean, cauliflower and toasted sesame seed with parsley dressing. 4 main courses £3.30-6.00, at least one of them vegan, such as mushroom, courgettes and red pepper goulasz; pasta arrabiata with aubergine and spinach; gado gado hot pot; Moroccan vegetable tagine; stir fry noodles and veg. Or really tuck in to a seasonal plate of main course plus salads £6. Several desserts £2.30-2.60 such as vegan apple and rhubarb crumble. Cakes from 90p, half of them vegan. Drinks 60p-£1 and they have soya milk. Bring your own booze, no corkage charge. No smoking. Alex feasts here at every opportunity and so will you.

Neal's Yard Bakery

6 Neal's Yard
Covent Garden WC2
Tel: 020-7836 5199
Tube: Covent Garden
Open: Mon-Sat 10.30-17.00, bread from 6am.
One of three vegetarian cafés in Neal's Yard This one has been established for 20 years and has a bakery specialising in bread and rolls made from organic wholewheat flour, such as three seeds, cheese and herb and sunflower and honey which are available from 6.30am in the morning.   Take-away service. Secluded, first-floor, non-smoking tearoom with free corkage. Menu caters well for vegans. Soup of the day £2.50. 4 salads daily such as mixed leaf, chickpea and French bean, organic pasta and roasted vegetables, curried mushroom £2.50-£2.80. Dish of the Day £3.15-£3.80 such as vegetarian lasagne, mushroom and cashew biryani, sweet potato korma or red dragon pie.   Savouries, such as baps, burgers and croissants for £2.10. Cakes, at least 3 vegan £1.

Neal's Yard Salad Bar

2 Neal's Yard
Covent Garden WC2
Tel: 020-7836 3233
Tube: Covent Garden
Open: Mon-Sat 11-18.00, but will stay open later on warm Summer days. Closed Sun.
Vegan owned vegetarian wholefood café with food prepared in the open kitchen before your very eyes, with a Brazilian, English, Italian, Lebanese and Oriental twist. Point to the food you want at the counter then chill out in the sun at an outside table. Different foods daily with three salads £2.00-3.90, dairy and wheat free vegetable soup £2, 4 main courses £3.10-5.50 such as Lebanes kibe with onion, fresh coriander and peppers; roasted aubergine stuffed with tomato, onion and coriander. Desserts £2-3 such as vegan Brazilian banana cinnamon cake,

sweet corn pudding, tropical fruit trifle. Tea £1.20, coffee £1.50, soya milkshakes too.

World Food Café

First Floor, 14 Neal's Yard
Covent Garden WC2
Tel: 020-7379 0298
Tube: Covent Garden
Open: Mon-Sat 12-17.00
Upstairs international wholefood vegetarian restaurant in the heart of veggieland, overlooking Neal's Yard. 90% vegan. There's an open plan kitchen in the centre so you can see all the food being prepared. Light meals from every continent (except penguinland) £4.95-5.25 such as Indian spicy veg masala with steamed brown rice; falafel with salad and hou-mous. Small mixed salad £4. Soup of the day £3.85. Big meals £7.45 could be thali with steamed brown rice; Turkish meze of aubergine and cabbage cooked with parsley, mint and tomatoes served with tabouleh salad, olives, mashed carrot, houmous and roasted pitta bread; West West African sweet potatoes and cabbage in creamy groundnut and cayenne sauce served with fresh banana, steamed brown rice and salad; Mexican refried beans, avocado guacamole, jalapeno salsa, olives, salad and corn chips; Large mixed plate of all the day's salads with guacamole, carrot, houmous, olives and pitta. Cakes, puddings, teas, coffes, juices. Tea time special after 3pm: carrot cake with tea or coffee £2.45. Minimum charge £4.85 at lunchtime and Saturdays. Close second in Time Out 1998 best vegetarian meal.

First Out Coffee Shop

52 St Giles High St
Covent Garden WC2
Tel: 020-7240 8042
Tube: Tottenham Court Road
Open: Mon-Sat 10.30-23.00, Sun 11-22.00

Smart, modern and very popular gay and lesbian vegetarian café with basement café/bar and international menu, close to Tottenham Court Road tube.   Music for all tastes and low enough not to be intrusive.   Can be lively or very laid back depending on time of day.   50 yards from Tottenham Court Road tube. Menu changes seasonally. Selection of salads for £3.25. Mains such as Tricolor Putanseca, Tamarind & coconut curry and rice and Black bean casserole £3.75, ratatouille and cous cous was the dish of the day for £3.75 when we called. Jacket potatoes and other savouries available. Generally good for vegans until you get to the cakes. Good selection of bottled beers around £2.30 and champagne £20. Smoking downstairs only. No credit cards.

London Vegetarian and Vegan Gay and Bisexual Men's group meets here on the last Sunday of every month, friends and women welcome, phone 0181-690 4792 for details.

Neal's Yard Wholefoods

21 Shorts Gardens
Covent Garden WC2H

Health food shop in Covent Garden now taken over by the Holland & Barratt chain though retaining more original features than some other outlets that went the same way. Open 7 days. They have some take-away food but for fresh organic fruit and veg you'll have to go to the nearby Tesco Metro.

BLOOMSBURY

Greenhouse

Drill Hall
16 Chenies Street
Bloomsbury WC1
Tel: 020-7637 8038
Tube: Goodge Street
Open: Mon-Sat 11-22.30, Sun 12-16.30
Busy vegetarian international wholefood basement café/restaurant below the Drill Hall Arts Centre. Very reasonable prices and just off Tottenham Court Road. Often has displays by local artists. Very popular at lunchtimes with office workers and shoppers. Menu changes daily and offers good sized home-made portions and always a vegan option. Vegan soup £2, main meal £4 such as gado gado and rice, roast potato and aubergine stew (both vegan), moussaka, lasagne, pizza, quiche, curries, bakes, burgers. Desserts £1.45 and cakes from 60p and there's always something vegan. Bring your own booze (free corkage) or get it from the theatre bar upstairs from 6pm. No bookings under 12 people.

Mandeer Restaurant

8 Bloomsbury Way,
Bloomsbury WC1
N.B. Will be temporarily closed for moving end 2000.
Tel: 020-7242 6202
Tube: Tottenham Court Rd, Holborn
Open: Mon-Sat 12-15.00, 17.30-22.00. Closed Sun.
London's oldest vegetarian restaurant, serving top quality Indian Ayurvedic gourmet cuisine since 1961, has moved to a new location where New Oxford Street forks into Bloomsbury Way. Big lunchtime buffet lunch £2.90-5.00 will get you a Veganosaurus Rex sized platter of bhajia, samosa, brown rice, veg, chickpeas and dhal. In the evening they go upmarket a la carte. Starters like dal vada, pani puri, dahi vada, kachori, dosa or samosa £2.25-4.95. Punjabi dishes £3.75-4.95 like Bombay

alu, tofu curry, tarka dal £3.75-5.50. Gujarati dishes include vegetable curry, beans of the day or vadi and onion. Basic vegan thali £8 ranging up to a Mandeer Deluxe £12.50 of pilau rice, bread, panir matar, Bomay alu, veg curry, beans, samosa, vada, papadom and chutney, dessert. Heaps of dairy based desserts plus 4 fruity ones for vegans, £2.50. Coffee or tea £1. Fully licensed for alcohol.

Alara Wholefoods

58 Marchmont Street
Bloomsbury WC1
Tel: 020-7837 1172
Tube: Russell Square
Open: Mon-Fri 9-18.00, Sat 10-18.00, closed Sun.
Huge take-away section in this big wholefood store and one of the best places to grab a lunch to go. Vegan and organic produce includes wine, beer, fruit & veg, cosmetics, food supplements and lots of bread. This is a fascinating street with lots of cafes, take-aways, cinema nearby and a real community feel.

OXFORD STREET

Cranks St Christopher's Place

23 Barrett Street, W1M
north of Bond Street underground
Tel: 020-7495 1340
Tube: Bond Street
Open: Mon-Fri 9.00-18.00, Sat 10.00-18.00, closed Sun
See Marshall Street branch for details. Vegetarian health food with cracking wholefood dishes for veggies and vegans. Average £5-6. Almost opposite Bond Street tube station, down an alleyway past Dillons bookshop that leads to a pedestrian area.

Nuthouse Vegetarian Restaurant

26 Kingly Street, W1R
Tel: 020-7437 9471
Tube: Oxford Circus
Open: Mon-Sat 10.30-19.00. Closed Sun.

Vegetarian café with first floor and basement seating. Round the back of Liberty and Hamleys mega toy store, close to Oxford Circus. Uses 70% organic ingredients. Great value munchies for West End shoppers to eat in (or take out) like baked potato £1.65 (£1.50), £3 (£2.50) with beans. Nut rissoles with tomato and onion sauce £1.75 (£1.55). Small salad £2.50 (2.25), large £3.50 (3.25). Two main courses daily £3.25 like mousakka, vegetable pancake, mixed beans casserole, stir fry. Cakes and beverages. What you see is what you pay: none of the usual cover or service or VAT "extras" and they won't take tips. Popular with non-veggies like Alex's folks.

Rasa W1

6 Dering Street, W1
off Oxford Street
Tel: 020-7629 1346
Tube: Oxford Circus
Open: Mon-Sat 12-15.00 & 18-23.00. Sun 18-23.00

Big sister to and up market version of the award winning Rasa in N16 on two floors. Indian food doesn't come much better than this. Vegetarian South Indian (Keralan) restaurant near Oxford Street. Gentle pastel colours, cool décor, tasteful objects and the smell of eastern spices perfectly invoke memories of southern India (but only if you've been there, otherwise its just a very nice feeling when you walk throught the door). Kerala is one of the riches places in the world for fruit and veg, they have over 250 kinds of banana alone, so no surprise that some of the best ingredients end up at Rasa. A cut above most Indian restaurants and loads for vegans, though you will be paying more than you might be used to. Pre meal snacks are on the menu for £4 and include nibbles made from root vegetables, rice, coconut milk, flour, lentils and seeds and all beautifully spiced. You can have them with home made chutneys £2.50 - but don't over do it yet. 10 starters come at £4.25 each and include Kappa cutlet which is Cassava root peeled and steamed in tumeric and flavoured with curry leaves and green chillies; Banana Boli is fried plantain dipped in rice and chick-pea batter with peanut and ginger sauce. The three soups are £4.50. The 8 mains are between £7.95-£8.25 and include dosas, semolina pancakes, vermicelli, and yeast cakes with a variety of exquisitely prepared sambars, chutneys, stews, curries and toppings. The 50 curry dishes, £5.75-£6.25, include a whole range of interesting ingredients such as sweet mangoes, green banana, breadfruit, tamarind, bottle gourd, coconut and many other Keralan delicacies. There are 6 side dishes at £5.25 such as shredded green papaya with fresh coconut and green chillies served with spiced dhal and mustard seeds. You then have a choice of 5 breads and 7 rice dishes. 12% option-al service charge is added to the bill and if you're going to pay it you might want to forsake the Dom Perignon 1990 at £95, for the Indian sparkling wine at £14.95. Beers are £2.75 and soft drinks £1.50. No smoking throughout.

Crazy Salads

47 Goodge Street, W1
Tel: 020-7323 3381
Tube: Goodge Street
Open: Mon-Fri 10-16.00

Brilliant snack bar and takeaway promoting the health benefits of salads. Located in an area with many restaurants, take-aways and cafes catering for the shoppers around Tottenham Court Road. Huge selection of green vegetable, bean, pasta, rice, fruit and non veg salads, nearly all of it vegan. A substan-tial selection of any three costs you £1.99, or four+ for £2.25. Limited seating at formica tables. Fresh fruit smoothies are a good deal at £1.75. Baked potatoes for £2.50. Baguettes, cia-batta or panini sandwiches are £2.50 with a filling. Good cold drinks, muffins, flapjacks (some vegan), juices and crisps also available. Other branches in Wardour Street, Soho, and at Holborn.

Holland & Barrett

Unit C12, West One Shopping Centre
corner of Davis St/Oxford St
by Bond Street underground
Tel: 020-7493 7988
Tube: Bond Street
Health food store in the Bond St underground station shopping complex with lots of take-away savouries including sandwiches and vegan pasties.

Holland & Barrett

123 Oxford St, W1R
Tel: 020-7287 3624
Open: Mon-Wed 8.30-18.45, Thur-Fri 8.30-19.45, Sat 10-18.45,
Sun 12-16.45
Half way between Oxford Circus and Tottenham Court Road, with less take-away food than at the bigger shop above, but plenty of vegan chocolate, flapjacks, dry fruit, nuts and other high energy food to keep you going.

Planet Organic

22 Torrington Place
London WC1A 7JE
Tel: 020-7436 1929
Tube: Goodge Street
Open: Mon-Fri 9.00-20.00, Sat 11-18.00, Sun 12-18.00
Picnickers' paradise. Brand new totally organic wholefood supermarket off Tottenham Court Road, in a sidestreet by Barclays Bank, with all you could possibly imagine for a splendid picnic in Regents Park. Every kind of pasta, pulse, grains from amarinth via quinoa to wheat, biscuits, huge macrobiotic range, gorgeous spread of organic fruit and veg, breads, salads, 15 kinds of tofu, pies, wraps, sandwiches. Also a breakfast bar with cereals, fruit, fruit salad, freshly squeezed juices, croissants, soyaccino, smoothies. Great wine selection, the majority labelled vegetarian or vegan. Wide range of women's things. Lots of baby foods, even biodegradable diapers and wipes. The

biggest health and body care section we've ever seen, all of it not tested on animals, run by a vegan with a chemistry degree to help you decipher what's what. Bulletin board where you can find drop-in yoga classes and other fun things to do in London.

THE CITY

Crazy Salads

54A Holborn Viaduct
Tel: 020-7298 5343
Tube: Farringdon, Barbican, St Paul's,
Chancery Lane, Blackfriars
Open: Mon-Fri lunch and early afternoon
Brilliant snack bar and takeaway in the city. Self-service buffet. See West End branch for details.

The Place Below

Crypt of St Mary-le-Bow Church
Tel: 020-7329 0789
Tube: St Paul's
Open: Mon-Fri 07.30-14.30. Hoping to extend hours soon. Phone to check.
Vegetarian restaurant and take-away with 80 seats in the Norman Crypt of a Wren church and 40 seats in the church-yard. The atmosphere is calm and serene under the arched ceilings after the road rage around Cheapside. Cuisine is Mediterranean/Middle-eastern and Asian influenced. Menu changes daily. Soup £1.90 take-away, £2.70 inside. Superb salads £4.70 take-away, £7 eat in. Main courses £4.50 take-away, £6-£7 eat in, could be potato, tomato and rosemary bake served with salad leaves; Boston village salad with wild rice, sun-dried tomatoes with rocket, broccoli and carrots and Puy lentils in balsamic vinaigrette. Desserts £2 out, £3 in, like apple and blackberry crumble or orange syrup cake. Brownies, muffins and scones. Bring your own booze £1.50 corkage. Unlimited cappucino, espresso, cofee, tea, herb tea £1.50

between 12 and 2 or £1 at all other times, 70p take-away. No smoking. Visa, MC. Available for private hire evenings.

Futures!! Café-Bar

2 Exchange Square
Off Primrose Street, EC2
Tel: 020-7638 6341
Tube: Liverpool Street
Open: Open: Mon-Fri 07.30-22.00 (Fri 23.00), bar only from 3pm. Closed at weekends

Big vegetarian café with interantional cuisine that becomes a bar in the evenings. On the edge of Liverpool Street station in lovely Exchange Square free from traffic and complete with waterfall and lawns. It has slick, modern décor, large conservatory and large sunny outside terraces. Haviing the feel of a wine bar means you can supp with a youngish selection of City slickers after work. Giant eat-in or take-away breakfast menu from 07.30-10.30am includes home made muesli £1.75 eat in (£1 take-away), full cooked brekkies £4.95, pastries, muffins, pot of tea £1.30 (65p) and 6 kinds of coffee. After a work or sightseeing break, pop back for for pastries with morning coffee or afternoon tea. The lunch menu changes monthly with daily specials Tue-Fri. Nibble savoury roasted almonds and cashews in soya sauce £1.75 before your soup of the day with roll £2.95, side salad £4.50, large salad £6.60, pasta of the day £6.25. Main courses £7 such as delicate dill pouch filled ith minced vegetable meat on a bed of sweetcorn and veloute mushroom sauce; palm hearts, asparagus and artichoke heart rissoto; Oriental vegetables in a piquant sauce on a bed of fresh spaghetti. Desserts £3.90 include exotic fruit platter or peach and almond tart. Vegan margarine used. Menu changes monthly. Fully licensed, house wine £9.75 bottle, £2.75 glass. No food in the evening, just a busy bar.

Futures! Vegetarian Takeaway

8 Botolph Alley
Eastcheap EC3
Tel: 0171-623 4529
Tube: Monument
Open: Mon-Fri breakfast 07.30-10.00, lunch 11.30-15.00.
Vegetarian take-away in a secluded pedestrianised alley in the
heart of the City with plenty for vegans including desserts. Main
course bake, hot pot or savouries £3.40 such as tagliatelle in
tomato sauce with spinach and mushrooms; or stir fried veg
with rice. Soup £1.75. Salads £1.15 or a combination £2.70.
Desserts £1.70 hot or cold such as vegan apple and apricot
crumble. Cake 90p. Drinks 45p-£1.20. Daily changing menu
faxed out nightly to 200 companies and city tycoons can check
it on Reuters City Screen LOLO L852/853 then order by phone.
See EC2 for brekkers menu. Parties and outside functions
catered. Credit cards accepted on orders over £15 delivered.

Fresh and Wild

196 Old Street, EC1
Tel: 020-7250 1708
Tube: Old Street
Open: Mon-Fri 9.30-19.30, Sat 10.30-16.30
Large wholefood store below the Community Health
Foundation New Age centre selling a huge range of organic fruit
& veg, take-away and pre-packed food and drinks, cosmetics,
toiletries, herbs, books and vitamins. Formerly called
'Freshlands'.

Spitalfields Organic Market

Commercial Street, E1
Tube: Liverpool Street
Open: Sunday 9am - 2pm
Who says London's dead on a Sunday morning? Only 5 minutes walk from Liverpool Street tube station, this indoor market
is a treasure with lots of craft stalls and good quality second-
hand goods. Excellent range of organic fresh fruit and veg as

well as dried, tinned and other processed organic foods, and on one side is an actual wholefood store. There is also an east Asian style food mart with a wide range of foods and even a falafel cafe.

KNIGHTSBRIDGE

The Lanesborough

Hyde Park Corner
Knightsbridge SW1X 7TA
Tel: 020-7259 5599
Tube: Hyde Park Corner
Open: For reservations in USA call toll free 1-800-999 1828, fax 1-800 937 8278
Luxury hotel popular with veggie rock and movie stars. Make sure you go better dressed than our photographer or be prepared to feel how unpleasant it is to have 'egg on your face'. Singles from £225, doubles from £325 up to the royal suite for £3500. Continental or fitness breakfast £14.50. Services include 24 hour butler, fitness studio, health club membership, video and CD in your room with a free library, all the sybaritic delights anyone could wish for. The in-house restaurant The Conservatory features gourmet vegetarian dinners, prepared by top chef Paul Gayler or one of his brigade of 40 chefs. Express lunch £15 which includes a main course, breads and glass of house wine or a bottle of water. 2 or 3 course lunch £21 or £26.50.

Veg of Knightsbridge

8 Egerton Garden Mews
Knightsbridge SW3
Tel: 020-7584 7007
Tube: Knightsbridge then a fair walk
Open: Mon-Sat 18.30-23.15, also lunch 12.30-14.30. Closed

Sundays.
Grand, intimate and spacious Chinese vegan restaurant in posh part of London close to Harrods. Veg uses staple Oriental ingredients to provide succulent dishes, with fake flesh food being a real speciality. The classical styles of cooking, by chefs trained in the best Chinese restaurants, along with the subtle spices, make the food here a real treat. Veg is not your typical veggie joint and is an ideal stepping stone for the carnivore in the party. 18 entrées £3-6.50, 2 salads £2.50-3.50, 40 main courses £4.50-8.50. Desserts £3. Set meal £12. With offerings such as Veg-Oysters and Sweet & Sour Veg-Chicken, imitation meats are the speciality here in many different forms. Genuine ingredients are used: real seaweed and naturally brewed soy sauce. The Vegetarian Dim Sum comes with a surprising and refreshing hot chili dip. Deep-fried Veg Oysters comprise aubergines and seaweed in batter. Tofu and Spinach Soup is a light classical Chinese variety. Seasonal vegetables are perfect: stir fried broccoli, pak soy and mange tout in a light sauce. Crispy Vegetarian Duck (deep-fried tofu skin) is rich, yet light as the wafer-thin pancakes it's wrapped in. Veg Beef in Black Bean Sauce is made from a traditional Chinese wheat gluten dish; a strong, meat-like taste. Desserts include toffee banana, toffee apple, frozen fragrant rice cream. Only drawback is that the alcohol is on the expensive side. No smoking. Credit cards being introduced as we go to print.

SLOANE ZONE

Holland & Barrett

Unit 15, Victoria Place Shopping Centre
Buckingham Palace Rd, SW1
Tel: 0171-828 5480
Tube: Victoria
Open: Mon-Fri 08.00-20.00, Sat 09.00-20.00, Sun 11-17.00.
Health food store at the back of Victoria rail station upstairs in the shopping centre where you can stock up on dried fruit and

nuts, small soya milk cartons, vegan chocolate and other supplies on the way to the National Express coach station for Britain and Europe. There is also a Body Shop nearby and a branch of Books Etc for your travel guides.

Revital Health Place

3a The Colonnades
123-151 Buckingham Palace Rd, SW1
Tel: 0171-976 6615
Tube: Victoria
Open: Mon-Fri 8.30-19.00, Sat 9-17.00
Health food shop between Victoria coach and train station with macrobiotic foods and a large range of sea vegetables. Also vegan desserts, pasties, pizza and cakes - all freshly made. Increasing organic range and Nelsons and BWC cosmetics. A great place to stock up before a coach journey. Superb range of books. Nutritionist based at shop.

Organic Café

The Auction Rooms
71 Lots Road, Chelsea SW10
Tel: 020-7351 7771
Tube: Fulham Broadway
Open: Fri-Sun 10-16.00, Mon 9-19.30
Vegetarian English and Thai dishes prepared by the vegan Thai proprietor Vip. Everything is organic, made freshly on site each day, and there's always something vegan. Main course for around £4, combination salad £3, main course and salad £4.95. Try Thai stir-fry rice noodles (padthai) every day, vegetarian shepherd's pie, hot pot, lasagne, moussaka, vegan spicy samosas and vegan sosage rolls. Five combination salad each week. Soup of the week £2.50 with seed loaf. Teas 70p, coffee and alternatives 90p, organic cakes like lemon, chocolate, banana (vegan) £1.35. The café is inside the auction rooms where antiques are being sold, and it cannot be seen from the street. If you want to watch, then viewing starts Thursday 5-8pm and continues through the weekend 10-16.00 and Monday

morning, with auctions on Monday 13-16.00 (modern) and 18-20.00 (antiques). If you're more into writing a long letter with a cuppa then Saturday is quite quiet, Sunday a bit busier, and Monday it's heaving all day with auction-goers.

EUSTON

Chutneys

beans

124 Drummond Street, NW1
Tel: 020-7388 0604
Tube: Euston, Euston Square
Open: Mon-Sun 12-22.45
Vegetarian South Indian restaurant. Thalis from £3.50, with a really good deluxe thali for £6.95 that's better than the £8-9 ones you'll find elsewhere. 9 starters £1.95-2.20 include dal soup, samosa, bhajias, vegetable kebabs. 9 South Indian dosas £2.60-4.30. Eat as much as you like buffet lunch daily and all day Sunday for £4.95. Licensed and quite swish with lots of people having quiet dinners and the odd party. Visa, MC.

Diwana Bhelpoori House

121-123 Drummond Street, NW1
Tel: 020-7387 5556
Tube: Euston, Euston Square
Open: Open: Every day 12.00-23.30
Vegetarian South Indian restaurant. Another of the original south Indian restauarants that has become an institution for London vegerarians. Great, cheap, snack food from southern India. Busy all you can eat buffet at lunchtime for £4.50 with a carafe of water on the table. Also a la carte all day. Bhel puri is the most popular starter with potatoes, onion, coriander, sweet and sour chutney, garlic and chilli chutney, puffed rice, crispy poori, sev crispy noodles, all mixed together in a bowl for £2.30. De luxe dosa crisply rice pancake with veg and coconut chutney and savoury sauce for £4.60, or thali £4-6.20. Specials every day for £4.80 such as pumpkin curry. Vegans can have lots of starters like bhajias, but the main courses like dosas often contain dairy products. Unfortunately no vegan desserts. Save money by bringing your own wine from the offie next door with no corkage charge.

Ravi Shankar

133-135 Drummond Street, NW1
Tel: 020-7388 6458
Tube: Euston, Euston Square
Open: Open 365 days a year 12-23.00 (last order 22.45)
Great value vegetarian South Indian restaurant in the street of veggie Indians close to Euston station that have become something of an institution in London. This is Indian snack food from Bombay at its best and cheapest. Some menu as the branch in Islington EC1. There's always plenty for vegans including cashew nut pilau, pancakes and loads of veg. Fully licensed. All you can eat lunchtime buffet. Visa, MC.

Health Food Centre

11 Warren Street, NW1
top of Tottenham Court Road
Tel: 020-7387 9289. Tube: Warren Street
Open: Mon-Fri 08.00-18.30
Vegetarian health food shop and take-away at the side of Warren Street tube station. Huge variety of hot and cold pastries, savouries, pies, snacks, salads, cakes and a range of sandwiches and rolls, many great for vegans. Choose two BSE-free sandwiches for only £2 in total from the big cabinet at the back of the store and top up with fruit from the nearby vendor next to the tube station. Handy for Euston or Regents Park.

WESTBOURNE GROVE

Planet Organic

42 Westbourne Grove
Westbourne Grove W2
Tel: 020-7221 7171
Tube: Bayswater
Open: Mon-Sat 9.30-20.00 & Sun 12-18.00
Picnic heaven. Load up here with every kind of veggie food and heaps you never even knew existed, then head for a lazy day in Hyde Park. 15 aisles makes this the largest retailer of orgasmic organic foods and alcoholic and non-alcoholic drinks, environmentally friendly household goods and exotic flowers in the UK. Not all vegetarain but the nasty stuff is right at the back of the store out of sight. No artificial additives in anything, no hydrogenated fat and no refined sugar. Juice and coffee bar.

CAMDEN

by Ronny Worsey

Fresh and Wild

41 Parkway
Camden Town NW1
Tube: Camden Town
Open: Every day 08.00-21.30
Load up here for a picnic in Regents Park. Large, well stocked organic supermarket with a wide range of vegetarian and vegan products, plus a few packaged corpses in one of the freezers at the back. Sells everything from tea to toothpaste and has a take-away food and juice bar with tasty muffins and cakes, some of them vegan. Good choice of organic fruit and vegetables. Formerly called 'Freshlands'.

HAMPSTEAD VILLAGE GUESTHOUSE

**2 Kemplay Road, Hampstead
London NW3 1SY**

Tel: +44 (0)20 7435 8679
Fax: +44 (0)20 7794 0254
Email: hvguesthouse@dial.pipex.com

Peaceful setting, close to Hampstead Heath, yet in the heart of lively Hampstead Village.

Close to underground and bus. Centre of London in 10 minutes.

Large rooms full of character, plus modern amenities: TV, fridge, kettle and direct-dial telephone.

Breakfast in the garden, weather permitting.

Accommodation from £48.
Two nights deposit required with booking.

No smoking.

"If you're looking for something a little different, make a beeline for Annemarie van der Meer's Hampstead home."

Chosen as one of the **"Hotels of the Year"**
THE WHICH? HOTEL GUIDE 2000

Organic Juice Bar
West Yard
Camden Lock Market
Tube: Camden Town
Open: Sat and Sun 10-17.00
Friendly, all-vegan drinks stall selling a range of freshly-squeezed organic fruit and vegetable juices and lovely foamy sesame and banana based 'mylk' shakes.
Prices from £2-4.00

The Veggie Stall
Row of food stalls, West Yard entrance
Camden Lock market NW1
Tube: Camden Town
Open: 10-17.00 Sat and Sun.
Stall selling falafels, drinks and large, homemade veggie burgers with a range of toppings such as avocado and pineapple. All are vegan except the cheeseburger. Prices £2-3.00.

HAMPSTEAD

Lively, historic Hampstead Village is a fun area with an art cinema, posh boutiques, lots of coffee shops and pubs, plus wonderful walks, views and even open air pond swimming on Hampstead Heath. A must see for visitors with the homes of famous folk from Dickens to Sting and Queen Boadicea is buried here. Freud's house and museum is at 20 Maresfield Gardens.

Hampstead Village Guesthouse

2 Kemplay Road
Hampstead NW3 1SY
Tel: 020-7435 8679, Fax: 020-7794 0254
Tube: Hampstead
Email: hvguesthouse@dial.pipex.com
5 rooms from £48-66 single, £72 upwards double, large studio flat.

Veggie friendly 1872 Victorian house in with a peaceful setting close to the heath and underground yet in the heart of Hampstead Village. The large, very comfortable rooms are full of character with sitting areas, writing desks, remote control TV, hairdryer, iron, fridge, kettle, telephone and books. Breakfast in the garden, weather permitting. En suite double £84, en suite single £66. Double £72, singles £48 and £54. Large studio with kitchen and shower £90 for 1, £120 for 2, £138 for 3, £150 for 4, £162 for 5. Optional breakfast £7 from 8.00, 9.00 at weekends until late, can be in the garden in summer and you can invite guests. Booking requires credit card, but pay on arrival in cash or sterling (travellers) cheques. Parking £10 per day. Non smoking.

Primrose Hill B&B

on Regents Park Road
Hampstead NW1 8XP
Tel: 020-7722 7139
Tube: Chalk Farm

Friendly, cosy, top floor apartment in Regency terrace in Primrose Hill village on the edge of the park. Prior booking essential for 2 double/twin rooms, one with own bathroom, one with shower, becomes self contained apartment with living room when both rooms taken. There's also a futon for an extra bed in one room. Double £50-60 per night, single £35-55 with inclusive self-service vegetarian organic breakfast, which can be vegan if you tell them in advance. Ideal central London location 2 min walk to underground, Primrose Hill and Regents Park nearby. Telephone booking essential, please do not just turn up.

Manna Vegetarian Restaurant

4 Erskine Road
Primrose Hill, NW3
Tel: 020-7722 8028
Tube: Chalk Farm
Open: Open every day 18.30-23.00, also Sat and Sun 12.30-15.00

Very classy international gourmet vegetarian restaurant with lots of vegan food, set in a picturesque street near Primrose Hill, still going strong after 30 years, with incredibly friendly and efficient service by staff from all over the world. The menu is constantly changing with the seasons and there are daily specials and 100% organic dishes in every section of the menu (soup, pasta, main, dessert), plus a fixed menu which changes quarterly. 9 starters and salads £3.95-5.75 include soup with organic bread or Thai aubergine kebabs with satay sauce. At least 7 mains such as Indonesian broccoli, tofu & coconut curry £9.50, Caribbean hotpot £9.25, Chef salad with crispy marinated tofu £8.95, organic pasta of the day £8.50. 7 "proper" desserts £2.95-4.50 like rich squidgy chocolate cake £4.50 and organic fruit crumble wth soya cream £4.25. A massive multipage drinks menu includes Kir £4.25, spirits £2.75, liqueurs, beers from £2.50, coconut fruit cooler £1.95, freshly squeezed juice £2.20, huge range of wines from £2.85 glass, £9.95 bottle, organic apple wine £9.75. Kosher wine and food no problem. Relaxed atmosphere, tranquil surroundings. They actually serve till 11pm which is unusual and it's advisable to book. Website www.manna-veg.com.

Hampstead Health Food Shop

57 Hampstead High Street
London NW3 1QH
Tel: 020-7435 6418
Tube: Hampstead
Open: M-F 10-6, sun 12-5

Health food store with all vegetarian and organic food including take-away cottage pies, veggie sausages, rice and curry, cakes and flapjacks.

NORTH LONDON

Dora Rothner Bed and Breakfast

23 The Ridgeway
Finchley N3 2PG
Tel: 020-8346 0246
Tube: Finchley Central

Private bed and breakfast where they're used to doing vegetarian or vegan breakfasts as the owner doesn't eat meat, and there's the excellent Rani Indian vegetarian restaurant very close by. 2 doubles and 1 single for £16 per person. TV in rooms. No smoking or pets. Handy for Finchley Central tube (Northern line), the North Circular and M1.

Rani Indian Vegetarian Restaurant

7 Long Lane
Finchley N3
Tel: 020-8349 4386/2636
Tube: Finchley Central
Open Mon-Sat 18-22.30, Sun 12.15-22.30

Excellent Gujarati and South Indian vegetarian restaurant at the top of Long Lane right by the tube station. More stylish than most and deservedly popular. Varied 6-7 dish set meal £22.90 for two people, comes with papadum, chutnies, pickles and mixed dal. Thali is £8.90. Choice of 3 spicy dhal soups for

£2.90. Cold starters for under £3 such as pooris, and delicious hot starters such as Bhakervelli, fried spiced vegetable mix in pastry roll with date chutney. Slow cooked bean and vegetable main courses £3.70-4.50, some with an East African influence, such as ripe bananas and fresh fenugreek leaves with a richly spiced tomato gravy; Undhia Kenyan aubergines, peas, guvar, valor, green beans, pigeon peas, and potato cooked with fried fenugreek balls. Good selection of breads - the essential accompaniment to Gujarati food. Don't miss the mithi roti which is sweetened lentil mix flavoured with cardamom and saffron, parcelled in unleavened dough, rolled flat, roasted in vegetable ghee and sprinkled with poppy seeds. 10 vegetarian desserts under £3, fresh fruit salad and sorbet are vegan. Menu indicates vegan dishes and ingredients likely to affect those with allergies. Braille menu available. Dairy and wheat free dishes are marked and they don't use egg, so it's good for vegans.

Indian Vegetarian Bhelpuri House

92-93 Chapel Market
Islington N1
Tel: 020-7837 4607
Tube: Angel
Open: Every day 12.00-15.00, 18.00-23.30
The original cut price vegetarian Indian All-You-Can-Eat-Buffet. Food does not come any cheaper in this area, especially since people found out that Tony Blair lives in Islington. You'll pay more for a sarnie in Pret a Manger just round the corner. They also promote the benefits of a vegetarian diet and were serving organic brown rice before most of us were eating hot dinners. Eat as much as you like for £2.75 in this big place with all your hungry mates. Great restaurant popular with London Vegans. They use vegetable oil not ghee. The only place we know of with vegan lassi yoghurt drink in three flavours and a wider range of vegan desserts than the average Indian restaurant, which usually have dairy everything. The only problem is that after the buffet you may not have room for one.

Oshobasho Cafe

Highgate Wood
Muswell Hill Road
Highgate N10
Tel: 020-8444 1505
Tube: Highgate
Open: every day except Mon, 8.30 till dusk, in summer till 21.00.

Completely vegetarian café, average £5 for a meal, in the middle of ancient Highgate Wood, between Muswell Hill and Highgate. Unique setting with a huge rose-filled garden and seating outside for 200. "Oshobasho means Heaven on Earth", and we think you'll find this is pretty close for veggies. Three evenings of music a week in summer with jazz on Wednesday, classical on Friday, and 2 DJ's on Saturday with old and new music. Wide variety of food such as Jamaican stew with yam and ciabatta bread £5.25. Puttanesca hot and spicy dish £5.25. Hummous and salad with a basket of bread £4.25. In winter try a warming butterbean stew or red kidney bean chilli, or a delicious soup of the day with basket of bread £3. Winter porridge with fresh fruit and raisins £2.50, or try a gigantic vegetarian grilled breakfast for £5 including sausages, grilled mushrooms and heaps more. Greek salad, pasta, grilled Italian bread sandwiches, daily soup. Desserts include vegan cheesecake, vegan apple pie, pastries, vegan cakes. All the usual teas, barley cup, coffee, soya milk, Whole Earth colas, lemonade, soda. Wine £1.90 glass, beer £2.

Rasa

55 Stoke Newington Church Street
Stoke Newington N16
Tel: 020-7249 0344
Tube: Angel then 73 bus
Open: dinner Sun-Thu 18-23.00, Fri-Sat 18-24.00.

Vegetarian South Indian restaurant that caters well for vegans as they don't use cheese or eggs at all, well worth a foray into north London. Three times Time Out Best Vegetarian

Restaurant winner and really popular despite all the competition in the street. Very relaxed, comfortable and friendly with classical Indian music in the background. Definitely a cut above most Indian restaurants with dishes that are always fresh and never oily. Masala dosa £4.25, a pancake made of rice and chickpea flour filled with spicy potato and giner served with chutney and a little vegetable curry. Pal curry £5 features steamed spongy rice cakes with a carrot and bean coconut stew. Finish off with vegan kesari £2.25, a semolina dessert with cashew nuts and sultanas. Very popular so book a couple of days ahead. No smoking throughout. Indian beer £3.50 for a big 650ml bottle (over a pint). House wine £2.25 glass, £7.95 bottle. 10% discount to Vegetarian Society members.

Bumblebee Wholefood Co-op

30, 32 and 33 Brecknock Road
London N7 6AA
Tel: 020-7607 1936
Open: Mon-Sat 9.30-18.30, Thu till 19.30
Tube: Kentish Town
Our favourite wholefood store is actually three shops containing a massive selection of healthy foods, organic produce, macrobiotic goodies and a bakery with yummy organic bread for your picnic. Lots of vegan and organic wines and beers. Take-way food and lunches 11.30-15.00 and always at least four vegan options.

WEST LONDON

Temple Lodge

51 Queen Caroline Street
Hammersmith W6 9QL
Tel: 020-8748 8388
Tube: Hammersmith
Large Georgian house with garden run by The Christian Community offering bed and breakfast accommodation. 2 sin-

gles £25, 3+ nights £22, £140 week. 4 twins £35, £190 week, which can be let as singles at the single rate. Washbasins in rooms. No TV. Continental vegetarian breakfast but vegans must request ahead. Classy vegetarian restaurant The Gate at same address. Close to the Thames and Olympia or Earls Court Exhibition Centres. Underground connection to the West End. No smoking in the house. An oasis of tranquility in a busy city.

The Gate Vegetarian Restaurant
51 Queen Caroline St
Hammersmith W6 9QL
Tel: 020-8748 6932
Tube: Hammersmith
Open: Mon-Fri 12-15.00,18-23.00, Sat 18-23.00, closed Sun
Top class international vegetarian restaurant set in an artist's studio and courtyard with with Mediterranean, Middle Eastern, Oriental, Indian and European cuisine. 7 starters (4 vegan) £3.50-4.90 such soupe du jour; wild asparagus salad with avo-cado, roasted onions, tomatoes with rocket and endive; Mexican tostada with refried beans, guacamole, fresh tomato salsa and tortillas. 4 main courses (one vegan) £8.50 such as vegan Green Thai curry with pan-fried broccoli, french beans, mange tout, asparagus and courgettes with coconut and lemongrass sauce served on basmati rice; Stonehenge veg-etables. Pasta of the day £6.80. Rocket salad with basamic vinegar dressing £3.50. 2 vegan and 4 veggie desserts such as glazed pear with a chilli anglaise. House wine £8.25 bottle, £1.90 glass. Tea or coffee £1.25, soya milk and milkshakes. Corkage charge £5.

Blah Blah Blah

78 Goldhawk Road
Shepherds Bush W12 8HA
Tel: 020 8746 1337
Tube: Shepherds Bush
Open: Mon-Sat 12.30-14.30, 19-23.00. Closed Sun.
Vegetarian restaurant near Shephards Bush Green with laid back feel, very low lighting, air conditioned basement and eclectic international menu that changes every month. Take-away service available. 6-7 starters which usually includes 2-3 salads £3.95-4.50, such as Plantain Friteroles, Halloumi Toasts, Saffron Tortino. At least 5 main courses £6.95-7.50, such as House Penne Pasta, Aubergine Schnitzel, Yam Enschilada and Noodle Laksa, which is flat noodles stir fried with courgettes, carrots, peppers, babycorn, with blackeye bean fritters with coconut sauce and fruit salsa. Usually 4 desserts, such as Strawberry Cheescake, Chocolate and Pear Tart, Knickerbocker Glory, Lemon and Meringue Pie with custard. Bring your own booze, corkage 95p. No credit cards. No cigars. Childrens portions on request. Separate party room. Not noted for their vegan sympathies which is a shame.

Bushwhacker Wholefoods

132 King Street
Hammersmith W6
Tel: 020-8748 2061
Open: Mon-Sat 10-18.00 (Tue from 11.00), closed Sun
Wholefood store with take-away vegan options. Organic fruit and vegetables too.

What's the difference between England, Britain, UK and the British Isles? Answer in a few pages.

SOUTH LONDON

Barrow House

45 Barrow Road
Streatham Common SW16 5PE
Tel: 020-8677 1925
Train: Streatham Common British Rail and close to the A23 to Gatwick

Vegetarian and vegan bed and breakfast. Luxurious accommodation is offered just 15 minutes by rail from Victoria Station in this Victorian family house situated in a quiet location. Two doubles and two singles. £50 double or £35 single. Breakfast features fruit salad, cereal and toast, and there are vegetarian restaurants in Streatham. Non smoking, no pets. There's a wholefood store called Natural Way at 252 Streatham High Rd and a couple of vegetarian restaurants nearby.

Cafe Pushkar

16c Market Row
Coldharbour Lane
Brixton SW9
Tel: 020-738 6161
Tube: Brixton
Open: Mon 10-17.00, Tue-Sat 9.30-17.00 (Wed till 14.00), closed Sun

Vegetarian café with International menu and take-away service on two floors. Top floor is no smoking. Right at the back of Brixton's covered market behind the underground station, you'll definitely need to ask for directions. Warm friendly atmosphere, very relaxed, simple décor and seating. All cakes cooked on the premises are vegan - yes! Soup, falafel, veg sausages and burgers £2.50. Variety of salads. Vegetarian or vegan main course with rice or potatoes and salad, such as tofu red wine casserole, potato and pepper layered bake for under £5. Various crumbles, cakes (not to be missed) and fruit salads for under £2, soya milkshakes, soya cappucino. Lots of papers to read. Free corkage. Children's portions. Highchairs. Nearby is the excellent Brixton Wholefoods shop at 59 Atlantic Road.

Heather's Vegetarian Restaurant

74 McMillan Street
Deptford SE8
Tel: 020-8691 6665
Train: Deptford British Rail (from Charing Cross or Greenwich)
Open: Tue-Fri 12-14.30,19-23.30. Sat 19-23.30. Sun 12.30-15.30,18.30-21.30.

A favourite virtually vegan restaurant and well worth the trek to sarf-east London for a friends' night out. This is the best use you can make of a converted pub. Well designed with central service area, spacious main eating area, outside seating in the summer and plans for expansion onto the rood. They keep you in touch with a newspaper that is more professionally produced that most national daily papers and it includes details of their special events and theme nights. Loads of meat eaters go to this big restaurant in groups as the grub is so awesomely excellent and the atmosphere great fun. Superb eat as much as you like buffet £12 which you can go back to as many times as you like, including desserts, and the buffet is usually 100% vegan. Or select the components separately £3.50 soup, £7.50 plateful, £3.50 dessert. The components being West African chilled gaspacho, peanut soup, mushroom and red wine soup, wild rice and coriander salad, mushroom and horseradish salad, mushroom and chestnut pie, Ethiopian stew, brazilnut moussaka, Thai chick pea curry, mixed vegetable couscous and almond, braised Chinse leek and pumpkin, mushroom and chestnut pie, 8 salads. Not forgetting the delicous desserts like nutty chocolate pudding, red fruit trifle, apple and hazelnut shortbread, banana and toffee pie. Vegan ice-cream. For the less greedy it's possible to make a single visit to the buffet for £7.50 without soup or dessert, which does not entitle you to cheat by sneaking food from mates having the full buffet. Beer from £1.95, cider £1.75, house wine £6.50, glass £1.95, many other vegan and organic wines, champagne £19.75. You can bring your own alcohol and pay 90p corkage per person, but don't bring soft drinks. Teas from 60p, coffee 90p, soya milk, banana smoothie or soft drinks £1.10, juices 75p. Smoke free apart from the garden. +10% cover charge for groups of 7 or more. Closed Mondays. No credit cards. Booking advisable. Also catering from picnics to weddings, theme fortnights, monthly jazz, wine tastings.

For the benefit of confused foreign readers:

Mainland (Great) **Britain** = **England + Wales + Scotland**

The nation
United Kingdom (UK) = **Britain + Northern Ireland** (Ulster) plus the semi-independent tax havens of the Isle of Man (in the Irish Sea) and the Channel Islands (close to France) of Jersey, Guensey, Alderney and Sark.

The **Republic of Ireland** (Eire) is a separate nation.

Ireland and the UK together make up the British Isles.

LIVERPOOL

by Ronny

Liverpool attracts a lot of tourists due to the worldwide success of the band the Beatles who put it firmly on the map in the 1960's. Today's fans can visit a museum, a shop and can even see the houses where the 'fab four' grew up.

Liverpool boasts some splendid Victorian architecture including many unspoiled city centre pubs. Most of its docks are still in operation but Albert Dock has now been turned into a tourist attraction with lots of little shops and cafes and the impressive Tate modern art gallery. There are lots of museums to visit, including ones with certain historical themes, such as the Maritime Museum and the Museum of Liverpool Life.

Liverpool is a very compact city and it is easy to walk around the city centre. If you want all the usual high street shops, leave Central Station and walk straight ahead up Church street. The Beatles attractions and the Tourist Information Centre are also situated off this and the Docks are at the far end.

The most interesting area for vegetarians is Bold Street, which runs to the left of the station in the opposite direction. The small streets running parallel to and branching off Bold Street are full of pubs, clubs and cafés and are very lively in the evenings.

Liverpool is well served by railways and motorways and is a good base for exploring North Wales and the North West.

Green Fish Café

11 Upper Newington, Off Renshaw Street
Liverpool, L1
Tel: 0151 707 0764
Open: Mon-Sat 11-18.00
Transport: Liverpool Central

Cheap, modern-looking vegetarian café. Smaller and more up-market in appearance than The Egg. Starters £1.50 upwards include soup and salads which are mainly vegan. Main courses £2.75-£3.50 include lasagne, mouskka, buritos and pasta. At least 1 vegan choice, but not obvious. Desserts £1 upwards include cakes, pies and scones. Tea and coffee under £1. No soya milk.

Follow the directions for the Egg Café, but walk to the end of Newington, cross over the main road and Upper Newington is directly opposite.

The Egg Café

Top Floor, Newington Buildings,
Newington, Liverpool, L1 4ED
Tel: 0151 707 2755
Open: Mon-Sat 10-22.00, Sun 10-17.00
Transport: Liverpool Central

Vegetarian café. Friendly, cheap and popular with students and young workers. Starters £1.50-£3 such as soups, salads and garlic bread. Main courses £2-5.00 include pizzas, shepherds pie, curries and lasagne. Desserts are under £2 and include spicy apple crumble, chocolate crunch and several cakes. About half the food is vegan, including the desserts, and all the vegan options are clearly marked on the menu. Wide variety of teas and herb teas 80p, coffee 85p, also fruit juices and milk and soyamilk shakes. No alcohol. No non-smoking area. Children's portions and highchairs available. Lots of papers and flyers to read.

Walk up Bold Street and turn right at the Oxfam shop onto Newington (not signposted) and about half way along look out

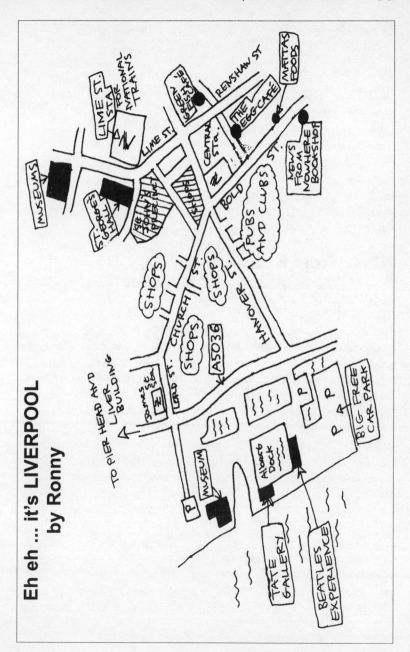

for a tall scruffy building on your right. Climb the stairs to the top
(2nd) floor and you're there.

Mattas International Foods

Bold Street, Liverpool
Open: Mon-Sat 9-18.00, Sun 10-16.00
Transport: Liverpool Central
Cheap international food shop, selling some meat but also very
well stocked with vegan products. Cheapest soya milk, tofu and
take away vegan pasties and samosas in town. Delivery of
vegan Turkish Delight every Thursday, ask at the counter!
Walk up Bold street and it's on the left, near the top.

News From Nowhere

Bold Street (almost right at the top), Liverpool
Open: Mon-Sat 9-5.30
Transport: Liverpool Central
Radical bookshop run by a women's workers' co-op. Stocks a
wide range of human and animal rights, gay and lesbian,
environmental and personal development books, postcards
and magazines. Good selection of vegetarian and vegan cookbooks. Very knowledgeable and helpful staff. Huge noticeboard
by the door packed with events and contacts in Liverpool.

OXFORD

by Paul Appleby, Alex Bourke and Ronny Worsey

Al-Salam

6 Park End Street, Oxford, OX1 2EB
Tel: 01865 245 710
Open: Every day 12-24.00
Lebanese restaurant catering well for vegetarians, in the premises formerly known as 'Entrees and Exits'. 42 starters, 90% of which are vegetarian and virtually all these are vegan, £1.80-3.50. 40 main courses, half of which are vegetarian and many vegan, £5.60-8.00. Licenced for alcohol.

Café MOMA

Museum of Modern Art, 30 Pembroke Street, Oxford, OX1 1BP
Tel: 01865 722 573
Open: Tue-Sat 9.30-17.30, also Thur 17.30-21.00. Sun 10.30-
17.30
Ground floor café in the Museum of Modern Art which has a largely vegetarian menu. There are veggie main meals, as well as salads, soup, baked potatoes and cakes. Some food is vegan. Relaxed atmosphere. No smoking.

Chutneys Indian Brasserie

36 St Michaels Street, Oxford, OX1 2EB
Tel: 01865-724 241
Open: Every day 12-23.00
Gloucester Green coach station
South Indian restaurant near the coach station with lots of vegetarian and vegan dishes. Licenced.

The Magic Café

110 Magdalen Road, Oxford
Open: Mon-Sat 10-18.00, also Fri 18-22.00
Spacious totally vegetarian café featuring cheerful décor and art exhibitions. Starters include hearty soups which are usually vegan such as spicy lentil and butterbean. Several salads, of which some are always vegan, for example exotic rice and mixed greens. Main courses include pies, which generally are not vegan, and a daily changing special. Desserts include a selection of cakes such as date and walnut and fruitcake, some of which are vegan. Fresh bread rolls baked on the premises. Non-smoking. Unlicensed but you can bring your own alcohol. Venue for the Oxford Vegetarians annual Christmas dinner and run by one of their members.

Uhuru Wholefoods

48 Cowley Road, Oxford, OX4 1HZ
Tel: 01865-248 249
Open: Mon-Fri 10-18.00, Sat 9.30-17.30.
Independent wholefood shop east of the city centre. Well stocked with a range of ethical products and very pro-vegan. Take-away counter with pasties etc., some of which are vegan.

FINLAND

HELSINKI

by Johanna Jutila

Helsinki is not just saunas and blue eyed blonds. It's now a multicultural city, an architectural paradise of neo-classical, Lutheran, Byzantine-Slavonic and modern, and a great place for veggie dining in restaurants where everyone speaks English. You can see it all on foot within a mile of the central station, and it's fairly flat. For ultimate tranquility, pack a picnic and head for the beach, islands or forest. From the last week of August, the two week Helsinki festival offers arts, dance, theatre and rock. If that's not enough, take a side trip to St Petersburg or the Baltic republics.

Café Zucchini

Fabianinkatu 4
00130 Helsinki
Tel: 09-622 2907
Open: Mon-Fri 11-16.00, closed Sat-Sun and in July
Vegetarian restaurant featuring a frequently changing menu. Wine 20mk glass, 90mk bottle. Coffee 8-13 mk. Staff speak English, Swedish and German. Takes Visa, Mastercard and Diners Club. Closed in July for staff holiday.

Iloinen Porkkana (Happy Carrot)

Malminrinne 2
00100 Helsinki
Tel: 09-693 2028
Open: Mon-Sat 10-21.00, Sun 11.30-20.00. Closed Juhannus (midsummer).
Metro Kamppi
Greek vegetarian restaurant, featuring a buffet where you can create your own meal. Small plate 30mk, big plate 39mk.

Choose from salads, pasta, couscous, lentils, steamed vegetables, olives, soya products, hummus, bread and various sauces. Different kind of soup every day. Coffee 5-7mk . Beer available. English and Swedish menu and staff speak English, Swedish and German. Visa, AmEx, Mastercard.

Orangerie

Hakaniemi's Hall (Market Hall), Hakaniemankatu 1,
00530 Helsinki
Open: Mon-Fri 9-18.00, Sat 9-16.00
Tram 1, 2, 3B/T, 6, 7A/B
Scandinavian take-away and juice bar with some vegan/veggie food for 18-26 mk. Wholefood ingredients used. Freshly made orange and organic carrot juices 7-15mk or drink a blended fruit nectar made from your choice of fruit, to drink standing there or take away. Staff speak English.

Organic Vegetables Shop

Hakaniemen Halli, Hakaniemen Tori (Market House, Hall 7),
00530 Helsinki
Open: Mon 10-17.00, Tue-Thu 9-17.00, Fri 8-18.00, Sat 8-16.00, closed Sun.
Metro Hakaniemi, Tram 1,2,3B/T, 6, 7A/B
Organic, vegan food shop selling vegetables, flowres, juices, organic and biodynamic products. In summertime they sell outside in Hakaniemi Market. Staff speak English and Swedish, maybe German.

Ravintola Kasvis

Korkeavuorenkatu 3
00140 Helsinki
Tel: 09-636 892
Open: Mon-Fri 11-18.00, Sat and Sun 12-20.00
Tram 10
Large vegetarian World food restaurant which caters well for vegans and special diets. Every day there are two soups for 25-

28 mk, one vegan, such as lentil or bean or potato and leek. Construct your own plate of salad for 43-49mk from their daily buffet of 10 different ones. Main course varies every day, 42-68mk, such as veggieburgers, Indian dishes and lasagne. Desserts 8-15mk at weekends such as cakes and buns. Organic wines and beers from 15mk, coffee 8mk. Some staff speak English and Swedish. Student discount.

Ruohonjuuri

Mannerhemintie 13A
00100 Helsinki
Tel: 09-445 465
Open: Mon-Fri 10-19.00, Sat 10-16.00, closed Sun
Central Station
The first organic food and ecological shop in Finland, with a wide range of products. Good selection of organic vegan foods for self-caterers such as bread, soya milk, tofu, soya burgers, tempeh, seitan, couscous, pasta, vegetable soups, soy puddings, vegan ice cream, biscuits, organic Fair Trade coffee, tea, chocolate and other sweets.   Also environmentally friendly washing up liquid, soaps and paper products. Staff speak English and Spanish. Visa, Mastercard.

Silvoplee

Toinen Linja 3
00530 Helsinki
Tel: 09-726 0900
Open: Tue-Thu 10-18.00, Fri and Sat 10-22.00.
Metro Hakeniemi, Tram 1, 2, 3B/T, 6, 7A/B
Large, almost vegetarian restaurant (apart from a few dodgy sandwiches) with Finnish and American wholefood style fare, 70% organic, including stacks of living/raw food which is all the rage now amongst Helsinki's healthy eaters. Living food breakfast of buckwheat, millet, oats and berry sauces 65mk/kg. For lunch or dinner go for the raw food buffet table, 95mk/kg, serve yourself and pay by weight. They have sprouts (such as mung, alfalfa, lentils), greens (sunflower, pea), regular salad (cucum-

ber, tomato, lettuce), special living food dishes, vegetables, fermented foods (such as sauerkraut, beans, carrot) and seaweed. A meal will cost about 39-59mk. There are also cooked soup and vegetarian dishes every day. Finish off your Finnish feast with vegan milkshakes or living food cake and sauce, 100mk/kg. House wine 24mk glass, 40mk bottle, beer 30 mk, coffee 7-13 mk. Wheatgrass juice. Staff speak English and Swedish. Takes Diners Club cards. No smoking. Monthly art exhibitions. Wheelchair access.

Vegetaari

Vanha Kauppahalli (Old Market Hall), Etelaranta 1,
00130 Helsinki
Open: Mon-Fri 8-18.00, Sat 8-15.00, closed Sun
Tram 3B/ 3T
Vegetarian and vegan health food shop with take-away food and juice bar, in a booth in a big market hall. Lots of vegan and organic products such as dried fruit and soya products, freshy made wheat grass juice and carrot juice. Living food "porridge" 48mk/kg, yoghurts and shakes 60mk/kg, Living food main dishes 85mk/kg such as fermented vegetables, sprouts, shoots and salads.. Menu in English. Staff speak English, Swedish, Spanish, German, French, maybe Italian. Takes Visa cards.

FINNS BUT NO FINS FOR ME

I am vegetarian
Olen kasvissyöjä

I am vegan
Olen vegaani

I don't eat meat, chicken, fish
En syö lihaa, kanaa, kalaa

I don't eat eggs, milk, butter, cheese, honey
En syö edes kanamunaa, maitoa, voita, juusto, hunajaa

FRANCE

PARIS

by Alex Bourke

"Ave you anything to declare?" asked the French customs offi-
cer in my dream. "Only my veganism." "Then Monsieur I advise
you to turn back." Now in Paris the nightmare is no more.
Having lived there for two years and visited at every opportunity, I can vouch that this favourite destination of lovers and bon
vivants offers not only a myriad of attractions, cafés and good
value hotels but also over a dozen delicious veggie eateries.
American veggies may find restaurant food a bit bland compared to what you're used to - the French haven't reached the
standards of the best U.S. and British places - but they've sure
come a long way and deserve to be encouraged. If you like
macrobiotic food then you'll be in heaven.

Get up early if you love the smell of freshly baked croissants
and real coffee in the morning. Start your walking tour at the
Louvre in the first arrondissement, then gawp at the extraordinary Pompidou Centre in the third with its plumbing on the outside and a fabulous view from the rooftop café. If it's not Friday
night or Saturday, wander on east for a light lunch at the Jewish
falafel bars in rue des Rosiers.

Crossing the river via Quasimodo's big island, you'll arrive at
the left bank or Latin quarter. This is the place to sup and write
those postcards in student thronged cafés and bars. After dinner, flop out at one of the many cinemas at Odéon or on the
Champs-Elysées showing films in V.O. (version originale) with
French subtitles. You can find what's on in the Time Out English
section of the weekly listings magazine Pariscope. If you're
weary of being a grown up, take the RER train from Les Halles
(1st) to Mickey Mouse land.

If you arrive late on the Eurostar at Gare du Nord, or you're about to leave, try the pedestrian street Passage Brady in the 10th arrondissement which is full of cheap Indian restaurants with plenty for us vegheads.

Restaurants here are listed by arrondissement, spiralling outward from the 1st. For the rest of France get a copy of our companion volume *Vegetarian France* from bookshops in Britain or our webshop at www.vegetarianguides.co.uk.

Entre Ciel et Terre

5 Rue Hérold, 1st Ar,
Paris, 75001
Tel: 1-45 08 49 84
Open: Mon-Fri 12-15.00 and 19-22.00.
Closed weekends and in August.
Metro Les Halles, Louvre Rivoli, Bourse
Vegetarian restaurant open weekdays north of the Louvre with plenty for vegans. Set meal from 74F or a la carte from 100F.

La Victoire Supreme du Coeur

41 Rue des Bourdonnais, 1st Ar,
Paris, 75001
Tel: 1-40 41 93 95
Open: Mon-Sat 12-22.00, closed Sunday
Metro Chatelet les Halles
Large vegetarian restaurant run by the followers of Sri Chinmoy, who teaches meditation at the United Nations. 45F-55F for a main course such as a vegetarian tart, also some vegan options such as salads, though vegans may miss out on desserts. Staff speak English.

Yes	Oui	three, four	trois, quatre
No	Non	five, six	cinq, six
Please	s'il vous plait	seven, eight	sept, huit
Thank you	Merci	nine, ten	neuf, dix
One, two	un, deux	A kilo ofUn kilo de	

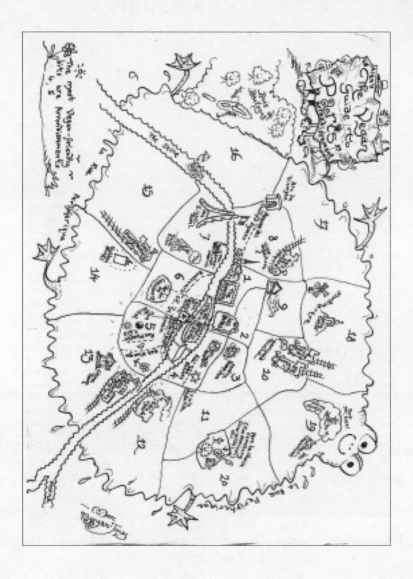

Parlez-vous Veggie?

FRUIT	LES FRUITS
apricot	un abricot
apple	une pomme
banana	une banane
blackcurrant	un cassis
cherry	une cerise
grape	un raisin
kiwi fruit	un kiwi
lemon	un citron
mango	une mangue
melon	un melon
orange	une orange
pear	une poire
peach	une pêche
plum	une prune
raspberry	une framboise
strawberry	une fraise

DRIED FRUIT	FRUITS SECS
date	une datte
figs	une figue
prune	un pruneau
raisin	un raisin sec
sultana	raisin (sec) de Smyrne

SALAD	LA SALADE
avocado	un avocat
beansprout	un germe de soja
celery	le céleri (en branches)
cucumber	un concombre
lettuce	une laitue
spinach	des épinards (m)
tomato	une tomate
watercress	le cresson (de fontaine)

HERBS	LES HERBES
basil	le basilic
bay leaves	la feuille de laurier
coriander	la coriandre
oregano	l'origan (m)
parsley	le persil
rosemary	le romarin

sage	la sauge

SPICES	LES ÉPICES (f)
chilli	le piment (rouge)
cumin	le cumin
ginger	le gingembre
nutmeg	la (noix) muscade

VEGETABLE	LÉGUMES (m)
aubergine	une aubergine
beetroot	la betterave
broccoli	brocoli
carrot	une carotte
cabbage	un chou
cauliflower	un chou-fleur
courgette (Brit) zucchini (US)	une courgette
french bean	le haricot vert
garlic	ail (m) ("eye")
leek	un poireau
mushroom	un champignon
onion	un oignon
parsnip	un panais
potatoe	la pomme de terre
peppers (yellow, green, red)	un poivron (jaune, vert, rouge)
runner bean	un haricot à rames
sweet potato	une patate douce
turnip	un navet

GRAINS	GRAINS (m)
barley	orge (f)
cereals	des céréales (f)
millet	le millet
noodles	nouilles (fpl)
oat flakes	flocons d'avoine
pasta	des pâtes
pitta bread	le pain grec/pitta
popcorn	popcorn
rice	le riz
long grain	long
short grain	rond
brown rice	le riz complet
rice cake	le gâteau de riz

wheat	le blé, le froment	tempeh	le tempeh
wholemeal bread	du pain complet	tofu	le tofu
		tomato ketchup	le ketchup
SEEDS	**GRAINES** (f)	vegan pesto	pesto végétalien
pumpkin seeds	de potiron		
sesame seeds	de sesame	**PULSES**	**LÉGUMINEUSES**
sunflower seeds	de tournesol	aduki beans	les azukis
		butterbean	le haricot blanc
NUTS	**LES NOIX** (f)	chick peas	pois chiches (f)
almond	une amande	green lentils	lentilles vertes
brazil	la noix du Brésil	haricot bean	le haricot blanc
cashew nut	la noix de cajou	mung bean	le haricot mung
hazelnut	une noisette	red lentils	lentilles rouges
peanut	une cacahuète		
peanut butter	le beurre de	**CUPBOARD**	**LE PLACARD**
	cacahuètes /	agar-agar	agar-agar
	arachides	baking powder	la levure
walnut	une noix	black pepper	le poivre (noir)
		burgamix	burgamix [cidre
TINNED FOOD	**ALIMENTS EN**	cider vinegar	le vinaigre de
	BOÎTES/CONSERVES	cocoa powder	cacao en poudre
coconut milk	le lait de coco	cornflour	farine de maïs
chick peas	les pois chiches	olive oil	de l'huile d'olive
sweetcorn	le maïs	extra virgin	extra vierge
kidney bean	le haricot rouge	olives	des olives
tomato purée	des tomates en	mustard	la moutarde
	purée	jam	la confiture
		marmalade	la marmelade
FROZEN	**SURGELÉS**	salt	le sel
pea	le petit pois	sea salt	du sel marin
soya ice-cream	la glace de soja	seaweed	les algues (f)
veggie sausages	saucisses	nori	le nori
	végétariennes	hiziki	le hiziki
veggie burgers	hamburgers	wakame	le wakame
	végétariens	soya cream	la crème de soja
		soya dessert	le dessert au soja
CHILLED	**ALIMENTS**	soya milk	le lait de soja
	FRAIS	sugar	le sucre
hummous	humus	sunflower oil	huile de tournesol
margarine	la margarine	soya sauce	la sauce de soja
miso	le miso	vanilla essence	l'essence de
orange juice	le jus d'orange		la vanille
soya cheese	le fromage de soja	yeast extract	extrait de levure
soya mayonnaise	mayonnaise de	yeast flakes	floccons de levure
	soja	nutritional yeast	la levure
soya yogurt	le yaourt de soja		nutritionelle
sundried tomato	la purée de	vegetable stock	bouillon de
paste	tomates sechées		légume

Piccolo Teatro

6 Rue des Ecouffes, 4th Ar,
Paris, 75004
Tel: 1-42 78 23 09
Open: Tue-Sun 12-15.00 and 19-23.30,
closed Mon. Metro: St Paul

Long established vegetarian restaurant with various set menus 52, 63, 85F for lunch, 90 or 120F for dinner. Popular with couples as they have candles on the tables, though it's quite a small place so you won't get any further than holding hands. Many of the dishes are gratin (containing cheese) but vegans can have miso soup or soupe du jour, various entrees and salads and tempeh dishes. Menu in English, staff speak English. Best to reserve for the evenings, unless arriving early, and weekends. Credit cards accepted.

Le Grand Appetit

9 rue de la Cerisaie, 4th Ar (near Bastille),
Paris, 75004
Tel: 1-40 27 04 95
Open: Restaurant Mon-Fri 12-15.00, Tearoom Mon-Thu 15-19.00, closed Sat-Sun, Easter.
Metro Bastille, exit bd Henri 4

Vegan restaurant, mainly macrobiotic, and take-away, the only vegan restaurant left in Paris that we know of now that La Truffe has closed and Country Life has closed for the moment. Soup, a meal and dessert for 90F or just a main couse for 60F. Lots of vegan dessert like cakes, apple or fruit tarts, with no eggs or dairy products. Juices, beer, teas and coffee available. Also a health food shop open Mon-Thu 9.30-19.30; Fri, Sun 9.30-16.00; Sat closed. They may close for a few days in August.

11, 12	onze, douze	19, 20	dix-neuf, vingt
13, 14	treize, quatorze	21	vingt et un(e)
15, 16	quinze, seize	22	vingt-deux
17, 18	dix-sept, dix-huit	30, 40	trente, quarante

Aquarius

54 Rue Sainte Croix de la Bretonnerie, 4th Ar,
Paris, 75004
Tel: 1-48 87 48 71
Open: Mon-Sat 12-22.30
Metro Hotel de Ville

Large vegetarian restaurant owned by a staff co-operative, which caters for vegans, with rustic interior. A set meal in the evening will set you back 95F or you can go a la carte, accompanied by wine, juice or cider. Run by the same people as the Aquarius restaurant in 14th Ar.

French Onions

I rode the Paris Metro
Then I took the RER
A luncheon so divine
I would have travelled twice as far

Then at the Gare de Lyon
All aboard SNCF
A lovely trip to Cassis
And the beach that I had left

In Paris I go shopping
And I dine in luxury
In the South I soak the sun
And skinny-dip the bright blue sea

I love this splendid country
And the passion it inspires
Now I'm off to ski the Alps
To quench untamed, inflamed, desires

Bespoke and 'Ready-to-Wear' Poetry & Cards
by Bernie Laprade at www.ThePoemShop.co.uk

Rami et Hanna

54 Rue des Rosiers, 4th Ar
Tel: 1-42 78 23 09
Open: Every day 12.00-02.00
Metro Saint Paul or Hotel de Ville

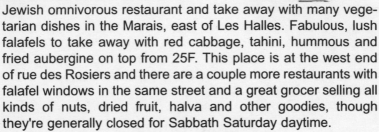

Jewish omnivorous restaurant and take away with many vegetarian dishes in the Marais, east of Les Halles. Fabulous, lush falafels to take away with red cabbage, tahini, hummous and fried aubergine on top from 25F. This place is at the west end of rue des Rosiers and there are a couple more restaurants with falafel windows in the same street and a great grocer selling all kinds of nuts, dried fruit, halva and other goodies, though they're generally closed for Sabbath Saturday daytime.

Le Grenier de Notre Dame

18 rue de la Bûcherie, 5th Ar (near Notre Dame)
Tel: 1-43 29 98 29
Open: Every day 12-14.30, 19-22.30 (23.00 Fri, Sat)
Metro Saint Michel

Vegetarian restaurant east of Place St Michel in a small side-street, featuring a huge menu and lots of macrobiotic options. The only non veggie dish is one fish soup. There is an economic menu for 79F which is great value as you can have several choices for each of the three courses, including vegan dessert. Organic wine. Also a small range of wholefoods on sale. Non-smoking area. Staff speak English and menus are in English. Best to reserve weekends as very busy. You can see all the menus in English on the web at www.legrenierde-notredame.com. To get there walk east from Place St Michel (the fountain is a good place to meet a friend) along rue de la Huchette past lots of smelly Greek restaurants and the odd falafel bar, which are just not in the same league as those in rue des Rosiers in the fourth, then continue east past the late night English language bookshop Shakespeare & Co. and a small park. R rue de la Bûcherie is set back one block from the river.

Les Quatre et Une Saveurs

72 rue du Cardinal-Lemoine, 5th Ar. Tel: 01-43 26 88 80
Open: Tue-Sun 12-14.30, 19-22.30. Closed Mon and August.
Metro: Cardinal Lemoine or Monge

Japanese style macrobiotic vegetarian (practically vegan) restaurant with the odd fish in bustling Place Contrescarpe, the heart of the 5th's bar and restaurant nightlife, where rue Cardinal-Lemoine meets picturesque rue Mouffetard. An "assiette" main couse with grains, vegetables and a vegan protein such as tempeh or seitan is 68F, or have the three course menu with soup and dessert for 130F. Same prices for lunch and dinner. No eggs or dairy, everything is vegan except one dessert. Nearby at 42 is Comptoir Mediterranee, a Lebanese fast food and take-away omnivorous place with falafels, hummous, tabouleh, stuffed vine leaves etc, open Mon-Sat 11-22.00

La Petite Legume

36 Rue des Boulangers, 5th
Tel: 1-40 46 06 85
Open: Mon-Sat 12-14.30 pm
and 19.30-10pm
Metro Cardinal Lemoine
or Jussieu

Quiet little vegetarian restaurant which caters for vegans. There is a take away service and a book and organic foo shop open 10-22 too. 3 set menus from 50, 64F and 75F. Afterwards you could try the Irish pub Finnegans Wake which is on the other side of the road just before Jussieu Metro. No smoking. They take credit cards and French cheques. Staff speak English.

Guenmaï

6 rue Cardinale, 6th Ar,
Paris, 75006
Tel: 1-43 26 03 24
Open: Mon-Sat 9.00-20.30, restaurant open 11.45-16.00.
Closed all of August.
Métro: Saint-Germain-des-Prés or Mabillon

Mainly vegan (no dairy, no eggs used in this place) and fish macrobiotic light and airy macrobiotic lunch restaurant, all day tea room and wholefood store, 90% organic, in the Latin Quarter. Dish of the day 64F. Also salads, soups, seitan and tofu dishes. Organic wine, organic beer with or without alcohol, fresh fruit juices and teas. Restaurant serves lunch from 11.45 till mid afternoon, or you can have tea and cake from 11.00-20.30, but they don't serve dinner. Lots of vegan organic wholefoods and snacks in the shop open from 9am till 20.30. Most cards accepted for 150F upwards and French cheques from 100F.

Veggie

38 Rue de Verneuil, 7th Ar,
Paris, 75007
Tel: 1-42 61 28 61
Open: Mon-Fri 12-14.30
Metro Rue de Bac

Nice little organic vegetarian shop, take away and snack bar open weekdays only where food is priced according to weight. Fairly basic but the only veggie oasis in this area where you can break your trek between the Eiffel Tower and St Michel with a complete meal for around 60F.

La Vie Claire

13 rue de Castellane, 8th Ar,
Paris, 75008
Tel: 1-42 65 16 80
Open: Mon-Fri 10-14.00, 15.30-19.00
Métro: Havre-Caumartin or Madeleine, RER: Auber.

Vegetarian organic fast-food shop and small restaurant with purified ionised air. 67F gets you the set meal with grains, veg, sesame bread, drink and dessert. The dish of the day is 42F, or get a take-away for 37F. A typical dish of the day is a platter of cereals and proteins like tofu steak with salad or vegetables. Also sandwiches, wine and fruit juice. Credit cards accepted. No smoking, wheelchair access. Booking advised for groups. Run by naturopaths who offer consultations and advice in French, lots of supplements on sale, wholefoods including soya milk and La Vie Claire soya desserts.

La Ville de Jagannath

101 Rue St Maur, 11th Ar,
Paris, 75011
Tel: 1-43 55 80 81
Open: Every day 19.30-23.30, Fri-Sat - 00.30.
Metro St Maur

If you've had enough of macrobiotic restaurants, check out this vegetarian Indian restaurant. They offer three kinds of thali, 90F if you have a small hunger, 130F medium, 160F if you're ravenous. The more you pay, the more bowls of veggies and dhal you get to go with your rice, Indian bread, chutney and dessert. Lots of Indian desserts in fact, but vegans will get a fruit salad of melon, grape, kiwi fruit and pineapple. Reservations advised. Credit cards ok. English spoken. They are considering opening for lunch Tue-Sat.

50, 60	cinquante, soixante	81	quatre-vingt-un(e)
70	soixante-dix	90	quatre-vingt-dix
71	soixante et onze	91	quatre-vingt-onze
72	soixante douze	100	cent
80	quatre-vingts	300	trois cents

Tenshin

8 rue Rochebrune, 11th Ar,
Paris, 75011
Tel: 1-47 00 62 44
Open: Mon-Sat 12-14.30 and 19-22.30, closed Sun and mid-
end August
Metro Voltaire
Vegetarian organic macrobiotic restaurant and take away serving some fish. Dishes include miso soup, vegetables, tofu steak and salads, so for example you'll pay 78F for soup followed by a main dish of cereals, 3 vegetables and seitan. No desserts. Organic wine is available, also organic apple and carrot juice. Staff speak English. Reservations advised for groups. No smoking.

Calypso

4 Boulevard Jules Ferry, 11th Ar,
Paris, 75011
Tel: 1-43 55 69 09
Open: Mon-Sat 12-16.00, closed Sun and bank holidays
Metro Republique or Parmentier
Vegetarian restaurant and takeaway, founded by its charming owner in 1988, near the Saint Martin canal featuring artworks, plants, flowers, light and love. Main meal with brown rice, veg, lentil, crudites, tarts, desserts 47F for a main dish, 20-25F desserts, compote de fruits maison 20F. House wine and juices available. Organic juice and wine: 18 juice, bottle of wine 50, 15 glass.

Aquarius

40 rue Gergovie, 14th Ar,
Paris, 75014
Tel: 1-45 41 36 88
Open: Mon-Sat 12- 14.15 and 19 to 22.30 (Fri-Sat 23.00),

PAIN

closed Sun and Xmas
Métro: Pernety or Plaisance
Vegetarian World food restaurant run by a workers' co-op, popular with vegans. Set menu at lunchtime for 65F Mon-Fri for a main course and dessert. Evenings and Saturday à la carte 90-120F for three courses, with individual dishes from 45F. Desserts include vegan carrot cake. Quarter litre of wine 20-30 F, carafe or bottle 40-90 F. Also beer, fresh carrot and other juices. CB, AmEx, Visa, Mastercard accepted. Two smoking and one non-smoking room. Fully accessible. 50% of clients are Anglophones so they have an English menu and English speaking staff. Best to reserve evenings Thu-Sat.

Dietetic Shop

11 Rue Delambre, 14th Ar,
Paris, 75014
Tel: 1 43 35 39 75
Open: Mon-Fri shop 11-22.30, restaurant 12-15.00, 19-22.30,
Sat 11- shop, resto 12-15.
Metro Vavain or Edgar Quinet
Vegetarian restaurant where meals are freshly prepared in front of the customers and dinner doesn't cost any more than lunch. 41 to 53F gets you a plate of brown rice, veggies, pulses, soya protein and salad. Desserts include fruit tarts or apple compote. Quaff wine, teas, herb teas or fruit juice cocktails. Also an organic wholefood shop with muesli, biscuits, bread, soya milk, soya yoghurt, organic wine and juice.

Joy in Food

2 Rue Truffaut, 17th Ar,
Paris, 75017
Tel: 1-43 87 96 79
Open: Mon-Sat 12-14.30. Also evenings by arrangement.
Metro Place Clichy
Vegetarian organic restaurant. International cuisine with American, African and Japanese dishes, 90% organic. 49F for a main meal, 63F two courses, 78F three courses. Lots of

desserts like cakes, tarts, and even sugar free vegan apple crumble. Organic beer, wine and cider. They'll open in the evenings if there are at least 10 of you. No Smoking.

Au Grain de Folie

24 Rue Lavieuville, 18th Ar,
Paris, 75018
Tel: 1-42 58 15 57
Open: Every day 12.30-15.00 and 19-22.30
Metro Abbesses
Long established vegetarian restaurant near the Sacré Coeur which caters well for vegans. Daytime set menu 55F, lots of other dishes 45-68F for a full meal. Apple crumble and chocolate cake with chocolate sauce, unfortunately not vegan, though they do have bananas glacées with chocolate sauce.

Rayons de Santé

8 Place Charles Dullin, 18th Ar,
Paris, 75018
Tel: 1-42 59 64 81
Open: Sun-Fri 12-15.00, Sun-Thu 18.30-21.30. Closed Fri night and all day Sat.
Metro Abbesses or Anvers
Vegetarian restaurant tucked away in a quiet corner with cheap prices for Paris. Good place for a swift lunch after "doing" the Sacré Coeur. The 45F fixed price menu gets you a starter and main course or a main course and dessert, or 59F for all three, excluding drinks. A la carte around 80F. They have alcohol free wine and beer and freshly made carrot juice. Non smoking, apart from the tables outside in the summer. Best to reserve for groups of four or more. Menu in English and German, but you'll need your dictionary for the dish of the day, unless your French matches the owner's "le minimum professionel d'anglais."

VIVE LA VEGOLUTION!

I am a vegetarian   Je suis végétarien (m), Je suis végétarienne (f)

I am vegan   Je suis végétalien (m), Je suis végétalienne (f)

I do not eat meat, chicken or fish
Je ne mange pas de viande, de poulet ou de poisson

I do not eat eggs, milk, butter, cheese or honey
Je ne mange pas d'œufs, lait, beurre, fromage ou miel

Where is ...?   Where is ...?
Avez-vous ...?   Do you have ...?

100g of ...   cent grammes de ...
200   deux cents
1,000 francs   1.000 F (mille francs)
a half, a third   un demi, un tiers
a quarter   un quart
ten per cent   dix pour cent

And here's the vocabulary you'll need if you're brave enough to explain veganism in French:

Véganisme (Végétalisme): l'attitude envers la vie, fondée sur des motivations diverses, par laquelle on s'efforce de vivre sans exploitation animale. On se nourrit d'aliments du royaume végétal. Tous les produits animaux tels que viande, poisson, volaille, oeuf, gélatine, lait d'animaux et produits laitiers comme le fromage, le beurre ou le yaourt etc; sont strictement rayés de l'alimentation. Alimentation typique: fruits, légumes, graines germées, céréales, oléagineux, légumineuses, plantes sauvages, algues.
L'horreur des pratiques cruelles liées aux industries du lait, du bétail et de la volaille est probablement la raison la plus connue pour adopter le véganisme.

Veganism: the attitude towards life based on a variety of motives where one tries as much as possible to live without any form of animal exploitation. One eats exclusively from the vegetable kingdom. All animal products such as meat, fish, poultry, eggs, honey, gelatin, animal milks and milk products such as cheese, butter or yogurt etc. are strictly excluded from the diet. Typical foods eaten: fruits, vegetables, sprouts, cereals, nuts, legumes, wild plants, seaweed.
The horrors of the cruel practices associated with the milk, livestock and poultry industries are perhaps the most well-known reasons for adopting veganism.

Vegan Shopping in France

ORGANIC FOOD
This is where being in France becomes a real joy. The French love organic food, which they call "biologique" or "bio". You can find organic produce everywhere, in the numerous street markets, supermarkets, and in health food (diététique) shops. Prices are cheaper than in Britain.

URBAN FORAGING
As you can't usually cook in hotels or hostels, you will have to forage for food that can be eaten raw. Indeed, your trip to Paris is a good opportunity to eat lots of healthy raw food, the natural diet for primates such as ourselves.

Your urban cooking kit contains only one essential item: a Swiss army knife or any cheap penknife with a bottle opener, tin opener, and a good sharp blade. You can stock up on a tin of peanut butter and some tinned kidney beans from a supermarket, wholemeal bread from the local baker, nuts and dried fruit from the Arab shops or markets, and lots of fruit from the markets. If you want to save money, buy a bottle of mineral water and keep refilling it from the tap. Parisian water is as safe as British.

Principal hunting grounds are:
1. Supermarkets   (le supermarché)
2. Street markets   (le marché)
3. Bakeries   (la boulangerie)
4. Health food shops   (le magasin diététique)
5. Chinese shops   (le magasin chinois)
6. Arab grocers   (l'épicier arabe)
7. The underground   (le métro)
   (subway)

1. SUPERMARKETS
These are some good supermarkets:
MONOPRIX: sells soya yoghurt, soya dessert, peanut butter.
ED L'ÉPICIER: very limited range of foods but incredibly cheap. The French equivalent of Britain's Kwiksave, with everything sold out of cartons.

2. STREET MARKETS

Everywhere in Paris. Just ask at your hotel or hostel where the nearest one is. Some good ones are at Place Maubert, rue Mouffetard (both in the 5th), and rue de Seine (6th).

3. BAKERIES

Your average froggie eats one baguette a day. This is a long white loaf that costs very little and goes rock hard within 24 hours. More expensive but tastier options from the extensive range of real bread are:

wholemeal bread	pain complet, pain au son
	pain cinq céreales
rye bread	pain de seigle

Beware of croissants which generally contain butter. Be very careful of cheap supermarket bread, which generally contains animal fat. Check for "graisse animale", or go for more expensive rye bread.

4. HEALTH FOOD SHOPS

These are the French version of Holland and Barrett, with everything in boxes and tins and high prices compared with the wholefood stores. You can pay 40F for a jar of peanut butter, but 15F for a tin in a supermarket. Only buy here what you can't get anywhere else, such as gorgeous smoked tofu or banana soya milk, or you're on a big bankroll.

5. CHINESE SHOPS

Very cheap source of nuts, tofu and beanshoots. These shops are mostly in the 13th arrondissement and run by Vietnamese boat people, but we've found some excellent ones in the 5th arrondissement near Notre Dame in Place Maubert.

6. ARAB GROCERS

These are the French equivalent of wholefood stores, with everything in sacks, such as nuts, dry fruit and olives. There are also stalls in the markets selling the same kind of stuff.

7. THE METRO

You will see lots of fruit for sale in the Metro at very low prices, according to what is in season. The standard price is 10F for some fruit, e.g. 4 avocados, 2kg of clementine oranges, 2 melons, 10 kiwi fruits, or a bunch of bananas.

April in Paris

by Alex Bourke

When I first moved to Paris I thought I'd arrived in Vegan Hell. Surely, I figured, les Misérables must be a play about British vegans in Paris starving to death. But after two years in the French capital I discovered to my delight that I could not have been more wrong. Paris, as well as being the most romantic and exciting city in Europe, is full of fantastic places for vegans to eat, mostly hidden away in the cobbled sidestreets. So let's venture beyond baguettes and berets into the treasures of vegan Paris.

Unlike London, where the attractions are mostly indoors, Paris is an outdoor city. Instead of pubs we had cafés, with tables spilling onto every pavement. Here you can linger sipping beer, wine, real coffee or herbal tea (*une infusion*) and watch the world walking by. The world being chic French businessmen and women, Swedish language students, dogs walking their retired owners, shoppers laden with designer clothes, designer-stubbled artists, and of course brightly costumed tourists and immigrants from every land.

Paris is divided neatly in two by the river Seine, with Notre Dame and a big flower market on the islands in the middle. On the Left (South) Bank are the student area of St Michel and the Eiffel Tower. A lovely walk on a Spring day starts at the fountain in Place St Michel, where you'll see young folk waiting for their friends. You can grab a falafel in the otherwise very meaty Greek area in rue de la Huchette. Head off west down quaint old rue St André des Arts, pausing now and then to browse in the many small shops. After an hour and a few hundred metres, turn left into rue de Seine, where there is a street market filled with fruit and the scent of flowers and a Monoprix supermarket.

Monoprix supermarkets, all over Paris, are by far the best for foraging vegans, and hence vegetarians. They sell many

flavours of delicious Sojasun soya yoghurts, and heaps of delicious and inexpensive plain chocolate that is even made with
soya lecithin. The hazelnut chocolate is absolutely incredible
and if you weren't a vegan you'd probably kill for some. You'll
want to take a few bars back home, perhaps a crate. Other bar-
gains in supermarkets are real coffee and of course wine. Your
duty-free allowance is now unlimited and they won't question
up to 60 litres of wine and 10 litres of spirits for personal consumption, plus all the food you can carry.

Continuing down rue de Seine across the café and cinema filled
boulevard St Germain, we stop at a café for a herb tea and to
relax and write a postcard. Pay on the way out and wend your
way to the big park called Jardin du Luxembourg to watch ten-
nis, chess and card players and put your feet up in the sun by
the boating pond.

My favourite secluded vegetarian restaurant on the Left Bank is
le Grenier de Notre Dame, which serves macrobiotic lunch and
dinner every day. From Place St Michel, walk east along the
river past the English language bookshop Shakespeare and
Co., then a small park, to 18 rue de la Bûcherie. The menu is
enormous and in English, with stacks of yummy vegan delicacies. Nearby you can pick up a big bags of nuts at the Chinese
shops in Place Maubert.

When I had weekend visitors, on Sunday morning we headed
for the organic market in boulevard Raspail, where they sell
some excellent organic vegan wines. After the obligatory stroll
around the Eiffel Tower and a look at the river, where you can
take a boat trip, continue north by Metro and get off at Charles
de Gaulle Étoile for the Arc de Triomphe. Whilst in the Metro
corridors you can pick up some vegan Easter avocados from
one of the many fruit sellers. The going rate is 10F for some
fruit, such as four avocados or 2kg of oranges. A penknife and
teaspoon are handy or use them later as butter in a baguette
with salad.   On every platform Metro there are also North
Africans selling snack-sized packets of nuts. Unlike the choco-

late machines in British stations, they're all totally vegan and you won't lose your 50p.

Having left the Arc de Triomphe by the subway, or been squashed flat running the gauntlet of several lanes of homicidal Renaults who didn't remove aggression before driving, there's the adventure of ambling along the Avenue des Champs-Elysées. We ogle the jewellery and glare at the spoiled bitches in the fur-filled fashion stores. This street has lean pickings for vegans so we settle in at a table on the pavement for some juice and coffee or a beer and write postcards.

After knocking back a beer and swigging from the half litre bottle of mineral water in your bag, you may be surprised at the toilet in some of the classy cafes. If squatting over a hole in the ground is just not you, it's time for the vegan game of dodging security guards in a burger bar. Wander in, gaze pointedly at the menu, glance at the long queue, then pop into the clean and comfy small room. This works best if a friend stands in line 'waiting' for you. When you emerge, check the menu once more and hit the exit.

If you're still on the Champs-Elysées in the evening, head for one of the many cinemas advertising films in the English version originale (V.O.). The weekly listings magazine *Pariscope* has an English *Time Out* section telling you what's on.

East of the Champs-Elysées, the area around Opéra is full of giant department stores such as Printemps, which covers three blocks. Unfortunately Country Life vegan restaurant in rue Daunou has closed for the moment so you'll need to keep going east for a good meal. From Opéra it's a short walk to the Louvre and the giant underground shopping complex at les Halles.

At les Halles you can catch the train for Euro Disney. I know this will destroy my street cred in certain quarters, but I've been twice and thoroughly enjoyed Star Tours and the Rocky Mountain Railroad, in front of which is a baked potato stand.

However if you'd rather give this a miss then there is still one extra special vegan treat for you in Paris.

Stroll east from les Halles, past the red light area of rue St Denis towards the Jewish quartier around rue des Rosiers. Here you'll find a mini-vegan paradise, with luscious special falafels like no falafel you've tasted before, piled high with salads, hummous and fried aubergine. Most of the bread and pastries are 'parve', containing no milk. Yes folks we are talking vegan chocolate croissants and more vegan cakes than Mr Kipling. And they are exceedingly moorish vegan cakes. Just ask if they're free of eggs (*C'est sans oeufs?*) and pig out.

We're very close to the most romantic vegetarian restaurant in Paris, Piccolo Teatro. It's tucked away in rue des Ecouffes, a bagel's throw from the Jewish section. Apart from lots of cheese dishes, there is some delicious vegan macrobiotic food. It's peaceful and warm, with candles and the most charming staff, and you'll see couples gazing lovingly into each other's veggie eyes. Possibly the most delightful, cosy, vegetarian restaurant in Europe, make sure you reserve for an evening date.

I almost forgot, high up over the north-east of Paris is the church of the Sacré-Coeur, from where the view is as good as from the Eiffel Tower but without the vertigo. Nestling nearby is the tiny vegetarian restaurant Au Grain de Folie at 24 rue de la Vieuville. It's open every day for lunch and dinner.

The most comfortable way to travel to Paris from London is on Eurostar through the Chunnel, which now takes two-thirds of the cross channel traffic. Returns start at £69 if you stay the right number of nights including a Saturday. Eurolines coaches from Victoria are ridiculously cheap but take eight hours though I love the ferry ride which gives a great view of the White Cliffs of Dover. Or get a cheap flight to Charles de Gaulle airport then take the RER A line to the centre of town. Paris is now a very affordable and attractive weekend for both lovers and gastronomic explorers, a treat that no vegan or veggie should miss.

GERMANY

BERLIN

by Pat Collins

Go ahead and bite off more than you can chew. Berlin can stretch even a veggie's energy limit and who needs to sleep with so many late night eateries? Do try matching up the daily itinerary with some great local eats, although some places will convince you to cross the entire city for a second sampling.

Abendmahl
Muskauerstr 9, Kreuzberg
Berlin 10997
Tel: 612 51 70
Metro: U-1 Gurlitzer Bhf
Open: 18.00-23.30 kitchen, closes 01.00
Gourmet vegetarian restaurant with some fish dishes. Mainly organic ingredients. Stylish interior featuring chandelier, red velvet and classic jazz singers for those looking for romance. Starters 9.50-16.50 DM including enchilada or soup. 4 salads, some vegan, 9.50-15.50 DM such as artichokes with thyme vinaigrette. One main course is vegan, such as mock chicken satay with peanut sauce and veggies in coconut sauce with basmati rice. Several desserts including crème caramel and vegan caipirinha sorbet. House wines from 5 DM per glass, 24 DM bottle, beer 3-4.80 DM, coffee 3.50 DM. Reserve for weekends. They also do catering.

ICH BIN EIN VEGANER

I am a vegetarian
Ich bin Vegetarier (m), Ich bin Vegetarierin (f)

I am a vegan
Ich bin Veganer (m), Veganerin (f)

I do not eat meat, chicken or fish
Ich esse kein Fleisch, auch kein Huhn und keinen Fisch

I do not eat eggs, milk, butter, cheese or honey
Ich esse keine Eier, Milch, Butter, Käse oder Honig

Good morning	Guten Morgen
Good afternoon	Guten Tag
Do you have..?	Haben Sie ...?
veggie dishes	vegetarische Gerichte
Please	Bitte
Thank you	Danke
Yes please	Ja, bitte
No thank you	Nein, danke
I'd like ...	Ich möchte ..
how much	Wieviel kostet es?
goodbye	Auf Wiedersehen

1, 2, 3, 4, 5	ein, zwei, drei, vier, fünf
6, 7, 8, 9, 10	sechs, sieben, acht, neun, zehn
11, 12, 13, 14	elf, zwölf, dreizehn, vierzehn
15, 16, 17, 18	fünfzehn, sechzehn, siebzehn, achtzehn
19, 20, 24	neunzehn, zwanzig, vierundzwanzig
30, 40, 42	dreissig, vierzig, zweiundvierzig
50, 60, 70, 80	fünfzig, sechzig, siebzig, achtzig
90, 100, 200	neunzig, hundert, zweihundert
300, 1000	dreihundert, tausend

Café V

Lausitzerplatz 12, Kreuzberg
Berlin
Tel: 612 45 05
Metro: U-2 Warschauer
Open: 10.00-02.00, kitchen 12-24.00, breakfast 10-15.00
Almost vegetarian restaurant (two fish dishes), featuring world music and a wide range of drinks. Several starters from 5 DM such as soup and the vegan option is sauteed mushrooms with onions and marinated beets. Salads 7.50-9.50 DM include hummous, mushroom and mixed. Main courses 10.50-13 DM such as pizza (can be vegan), stuffed dumpling (ravioli), chick pea polenta with curry sauce, seitan curry with basmati and wok veggies. Desserts 3.50-7 DM include cakes and fried banana with ice cream, which can be vegan. House wine 5 DM per glass, 21 litre, beer 3-3.50 DM, coffee or grain coffee 2.50 DM. Best to reserve after 20.00.

Hakuin

Martin Luther Str 1, Schönerberg
Berlin 10777
Tel: 030-218 20 27
Metro: Metro Wittenbergplatz
Open: Tue-Fri 16-23.30, Sat-Sun 12-23.30, closed Mon.
TOFUTTI ALERT. Vegetarian Zen Buddhist restaurant with vegan options clearly marked on the menu and all food freshly prepared. Starters 9.50 DM include Borsht broth and shitake and wakame herb tofu dumplings. Small house salad 9 DM, grilled courgettes and aubergine with herbs 15.50 DM, or avocado and vineleaf with tofu shitake quiche (can be vegan) 36 DM for two people. Main courses 26.50 DM such as cashew-shitake veg pockets or curry. Desserts from 12.50 DM including vegan Tofutti ice cream, hey hey. Organic wine from 8 DM, beer 4.70 DM, coffee 3.20 DM. English menu and English speaking staff. Outside seating in summer. Children's menu if you reserve. They also run a restaurant called Kokoro at Brunowstr 50, Tegel, 13507 Berlin. Tel. 030-434 90616. Open 12-22.00.

Sprechen Sie Veggie?

FRUIT	**OBST**	rosemary	Rosmarin
apricots	Aprikosen	sage	Salbei
apples	Äpfel		
bananas	Bananen	**SPICES**	**GEWÜRZE**
blackcurrants	schwarze	chilli	Chili
	Johannisbeeren	cumin	Kümmel
cherries	Kirschen	ginger	Ingwer
kiwi fruit	Kiwis	nutmeg	Muskatnuß
lemons	Zitronen		
mangoes	Mangos	**VEGETABLES**	**GEMÜSE**
melons	Melonen	aubergines	Auberginen
grapes	Weintrauben	beetroot	rote Beete
peaches	Pfirsiche	broccoli	Broccoli
plums	Pflaumen	carrots	Möhren,
raspberries	Himbeeren		Karotten
strawberries	Erdbeeren	cabbage	Kohl
oranges	Orangen,	cauliflower	Blumenkohl
	Apfelsinen	courgettes (Brit)	Zucchini
pears	Birnen	zuchinni (US)	
		garlic	Knoblauch
DRIED FRUIT	**TROCKENFRÜCHTE**	kale	Grünkohl
	(getrocknete)	leeks	Porree or Lauch
apricots	Aprikosen	mushrooms	Pilze
dates	Datteln	onions	Zwiebeln
figs	Feigen	potatoes	Kartoffeln
prunes	Pflaumen	spinach	Spinat
raisins	Rosinen	swede	Steckrüben
sultanas	Sultaninen		Kohlrüben
		peppers	Paprika
SALAD	**SALAT**	(yellow, green, red)	(gelb, grün, rot)
avocados	Avocados	sweet potatoes	Süßkartoffeln
beansprouts	Bohnenkeimlinge		
celery	Staudensellerie	**GRAINS**	**GETREIDE**
cucumber	Gurke	cereals	Frühstücksflocken
lettuce	Salat	barley	Gerste
spinach	Spinat	millet	Hirse
spring onions	Frühlingszwiebeln	noodles	Nudeln
tomatoes	Tomaten	rice noodles	Reisnudeln
watercress	Brunnenkresse	oats	Hafer
		pasta	Nudeln
HERBS	**KRÄUTER**	pitta bread	Pittabrot
basil	Basilikum	popcorn	Popcorn
bay leaves	Lorbeerblätter	rice	Reis
coriander	Koriander	long grain	Langkorn-
oregano	Oregano	brown rice	Naturreis
parsley	Petersilie	basmati	Basmati-

rice cakes	Puffreis	**PULSES**	**HÜLSEN**
wheatgerm	Weizenkeime		**FRÜCHTE**
wholemeal bread	Vollkornbrot	aduki beans	Azukibohnen
		chick peas	Kichererbsen
SEEDS	**SAMEN**	green lentils	Linsen
pumpkin seeds	Kürbiskerne	haricot beans	grüne Bohnen
sesame seeds	Sesamsamen	mung beans	Mungobohnen
sunflower seeds	Sonnen-	red lentils	rote Linsen
	blumenkerne		
		CUPBOARD	**VORRÄTE**
NUTS	**NÜSSE**	agar-agar	Agar-Agar
almonds	Mandeln	baking powder	Backpulver
brazils	Paranüsse	black pepper	schwarzer Pfeffer
cashew nuts	Cashewnüsse	burgamix	vegetarische
hazelnuts	Haselnüsse		Frikadellenmischung
peanuts	Erdnüsse	cider vinegar	Apfelessig
peanut butter	Erdnußbutter	cocoa posder	Kakaopulver
pine kernels	Pinienkerne	cornflour	Maismehl
walnuts	Walnüsse	custard powder	Puddingpulver
		olive oil	Olivenöl
TINNED FOOD	**KONSERVEN**	extra virgin	aus erster kalter
coconut milk	Kokosnußmilch		Pressung
chick peas	Kichererbsen	olives	Oliven
Sweetcorn	Mais	mustard	Senf
kidney beans	Kidneybohnen	jam	Marmelade
tinned tomatoes	Dosentomaten	Marmelade	Orangen-
tomato purée	Tomatenmark		marmelade
		(sea)salt	(Meer)Salz
FROZEN	**TIEFGEKÜHLT**	seaweed	Algen
peas	Erbsen	nori	Nori
soya ice-cream	Sojaeis	dulse	Dulse
soya mince	vegetarisches	hiziki	Hiziki
	Hack/gehacktes	kelp	Kelp
veggie sausages	vegetarische	wakame	Wakame
	Würstchen	soya cream	Sojasahne
veggie burgers	vegetarische	soya milk	Sojamilch
	Frikadellen	sunflower oil	Sonnenblumenöl
		soya sauce	Sojasoße
CHILLED	**GEKÜHLT**	tahini	Tahini [unknown!]
margarine	Margarine	yeast extract	Hefeextrakt
miso	Miso	yeast flakes	Hefeflocken
orange juice	Orangensaft	vegetable stock	pflanzliche
soya cheese	Sojakäse	cubes	Brühwürfel
soya mayonnaise	Sojamayonnaise	vegetable bouillon	pflanzliche
soya yogurt	Sojayogurt		Gemüsebrühe
tempeh	Tempeh		
tofu	Tofu		
tomato ketchup	Tomatenketchup		

Oren

Oranienburgerstr. 28
Berlin 10117
Tel: 030-282 8228
Metro: S Hackischermarkt, U6 Orenien Tor
Open: Sun-Thu 10.00-01.00, Fri and Sat 10.00-02.00
Traditional, mostly kosher vegetarian coffee house of days gone by serving vegetarian and some fish dishes and Israeli wines. Vegan food is available if you ask. Main meals from 18 DM such as "Orient Express" hummous falafel with aubergine in pitta and carrot salad combo. A hot veggie platter "Oren" with potatoes 19.50 DM can be vegan. Also blintzes. Desserts 5.50-8 DM such as baklava and strudel, which sadly aren't vegan, or fruit. House wine 7-11 DM, pils beer 4.50 DM, Israeli beer 6.50 DM, coffee 3.50 DM. English menu and English speaking staff.

Samadhi Vegetarisches Restaurant

Goethestr 6, Charlottenburg
Berlin 10623
Tel: 030-313 10 67
Metro: U-2 Ernst Reuter Platz
Open: Mon-Fri 12-15.00 and 18-23.00,
Sat 18-23.00, closed Sun.
Small Asian veggie corner restaurant that's great for vegans. Starters 6-6.50 DM include soups, corn fritters, crispy rice noodles and fried wonton tofu, all of which are vegan. Salads 8-12 DM include carrot, cabbage and papaya and tofu mushroom greens, again all vegan. 27 main courses, mostly vegan, such as stewed tofu with ginger in caramel sauce, aubergine in saté sauce and bittermelon curry. Special lunch menu 11.50-14.00. Five mostly vegan desserts including steamed banana and sticky rice in banana leaf with black bean and coconut cream. House wine 5.50 DM per glass, beer 3-5 DM, coffee 3.50 DM. Menu subtitled in amusing English. No smoking on Saturdays.

Satyam

Goethestr 5, Charlottenburg
Berlin 10623
Tel: 030-312 90 79
Email: jetontravels.sharma@t-online.de
Metro: U-2 Ernst Reuter Platz
Open: 11.00-01.00 every day
Indian vegetarian restaurant with a casual, deli feel. Starters
3.50-5.50 DM are all vegan and include samosas, onion bhajee
and soups. Various small and large salads 4.50-6.50 DM can
be made vegan if you ask. Main courses 6.50-12.50 DM include
biryani, which is vegan, dal, spicy soymince korma, veggie
kofta kebabs. A couple of desserts 2.50 DM include vegan barfi
and a gooey sticky milky non-vegany thingy. House wine 3.50
DM per glass. No music. English speaking staff.

Zenit Restaurant Café

Leibenwalderstr 2, Wedding
Berlin
Tel: 456 8272
Metro: U-9 Nauenauerplatz
Open: Mon-Fri 10-23.30, Sat-Sun 14-23.30
Omnivorous restaurant with a modern, warm feel, reminiscent
of a Biergarten with a courtyard, run as a training operation for
disadvantaged girls to train and qualify in business. Frequently
changing menu. Vegan food available, but must be asked for as
it is not always made obvious. A big main course with beautiful
colourful salads, bread basket and a free hors d'oeuvre with
drink and tip cost our researcher 18 DM - wow! Starters from
7.50 DM include Indian lentil soup and five vegetarian salads
which can be made vegan. 7 vegetarian main courses 12-14
DM such as fettucine in herb sauce, wheatberry fritters on wok
aubergine with garden salad. Desserts include cakes and icecreams but nuffink vegan. House wine 6 DM per glass, beer 3-
3.80 DM. English speaking staff. Close to Reineckerstr and S-
Bahn Markt.

FRANKFURT

by Pat Collins

Port of entry or business destination, Frankfurt makes a good veggie impression. Entertaining business colleagues at upmarket establishments or finding alternative apparel are two sides of the same coin. Frankfurt can provide for your needs and prepare you for the onward journey. Unfortunately as we go to press the veggie dining scene in Frankfurt has been decimated by the closure of Immergrün and Deux Lions, which lost their premises and couldn't get new ones such is the price of buildings in Frankfurt these days.

House of Youth Frankfurt
Deutschherrnufter 12
Frankfurt 60594
Tel: 069-61 00 15 0
Metro: Hauptbahnhof, then 46 bus (every 20 mins) to Frankensteiner Platz
Open: Daily from 12.00
Youth hostel and hotel with vegetarian food always available in the heart of Frankfurt on the banks fo the river Main, with a view of the skyscrapers and the old city. 500 beds. 26-33 DM per night according to age including sheets and breakfast, or 38.50 DM for hotel. Three course lunch (12.15-14.00) and dinner (18-19.30) 8.70 DM. Snacks and drinks in the cafeteria 15.00-22.30. Fully equipped for disabled. Close to major museums, the town hall, cathedral, Goethe's house, botanical garden. Website www.jugendherberge-frankfurt.de/english

Naturbar

Öderweg 26, Frankfurt 60318
Tel: 069-55 44 86
Metro: Eschenhemeir Turm, U-123
Open: Mon-Sat 11.30-15.30, 18-23.00, Sun closed.
Vegetarian wholefood restaurant with vegan dishes if you ask, though they have one fish dish.   80% organic ingredients. Around 15-24 DM for a meal. Tuck into home made bread, avocado, vegetables and rice, a bean dish or nine different salads. Wine from 6 DM glass, beer 4 DM, coffee 3.50 DM. Menu in German, but helpful staff speak English.

Bambusgarten

Eschersheimer Landstr. 156
Frankfurt 60322
Tel: 59 42 66
Metro: U 1,2,3
Open: Mon-Fri 11.30-15.00 and 17.30-23.30, Sat and Sun 11.30-23.30.
Chinese restaurant with typical cinnabar and dragon interior. Starters include spring roll and beansprout salad. 7 vegetarian and vegan main courses such as aubergine with chopped mushrooms and bamboo shoots, celery root, tofu and mushrooms, and greens with garlic. Lychees are available for dessert. House wine 5.50 DM per glass, 22-29 DM bottle, beer 3-3.50 DM, coffee 3 DM. Some of the menu is in English and most of the staff speak English. Accepts Visa, AmEx and Mastercard.

Vegan Shop & Versand

Höhenstrasse 50
Frankfurt 60385
Tel: 069-44 09 89
Metro: U-F / Bus 32
Open: Tue-Fri 13.00-18.00, Sat 10.00-13.00
Vegan wholefood, cosmetic and clothing shop stocking a wide range of organic and fairly traded products.

HAMBURG

by Mieke Roscher

Goldene Oase
Eppendorfer Baum 34
Hamburg 20249
Tel: 040-48 38 01
This restaurant is strictly organic and embraces a health orien-
tated ideology concerning food. Accordingly, smoking is not
allowed. There is also a bakery in the front room selling vegan
cake and bread.

Tassajara
Eppendorfer Landstraße 4
Hamburg 20249
Tel: 040-483890
This place is fairly expensive, but provides a decent and very
chic sourrounding.

Zorba the Buddha
Karolinenstraße 7
Hamburg 20357
Tel: 040-439 4762
Vegetarian restaurant and café. All dishes can be made vegan
using soy products instead of dairy if you ask.

Suryel
Thadenstraße 1
Hamburg 22767
Very cosy restaurant and café with extraordinary and yummy
salads.

Bioladen "Wilde Erdbeere"

Brigittenstraße 1
St.Pauli
Hamburg 20357
Hamburg has loads of health food and wholefood stores in the districts of Altona and Ottensen, and the three given here are examples.

Reformhaus Meyer

Große Bergstraße 199
Hamburg 22767
Health food store.

Yeo-Men Bioladen

Bahrenfelder Straße 169
Hamburg 22767
Health food store.

MUNICH

by Pat Collins

Munich is for living the good life. So, while ticking off the mandatory "sights seen" take time to savour the beer gardens and picnic spots. Think ahead and carry stocks from one of the many Reform/Naturkost Haus or the famous Viktualienmarkt. Weather not cooperating with al fresco plans? Munich's veggie venues won't let you down, even if you do begin to believe that Bavarian cities are built of Wurst und Schinken.

Alex's old flatmate Simon England now lives in Munich and adds the following tips. Prince Myshkin is a bit trendy, expensive but quite good. Das Gollier is by far and away the best place for vegans, like the inside of a pub. Speaking of pubs, O'Reilley's Irish Pub has great vegan food on request at

Maximilianstrasse 29, 80539 Munich, tel 089-29 33 11, open Mon-Thu 16.00-01.00, Sat 16.00-03.00, Sun 12.00-01.00. However if there is any soccer or rugby on they open earlier depending on kick-off time. All the restaurants will do vegan food and very friendly about it. Just take your Vegan Passport. One particularly good place is the Kartofellhaus which has an English menu. Most pasta here has egg, but all the real Italian restaurants make pizza base dough with water and flour only and will make you a vegan pizza without cheese.

Das Gollier

Gollier Street 83
Munich 80339
Tel: 089-271 0084, 501673
Metro: Heimeranplatz
Open: Mon-Fri 12-15.00 and 17-24.00, Sat 17-24.00,
Sun 10-24.00
Hearty vegetarian restaurant popular with campaigners. Starters 5-15 DM include soups and Greek salad platter. Vegans should ask for olive oil instead of butter. There are a range of 9 big salads costing 6.50-17 DM, 4 of which can be vegan. The many main courses include risotto, noodles, stir-fries, rosti (hash browns) and curries. 14 desserts 5-16 DM, sadly none are vegan, but fruit is available. Organic beers 4.40 and 5 DM. During happy hour (17-18.00 and 22.30-23.00) a complete meal costs 11DM. You should specify this when ordering to get the bill/check in the allotted hour. No credit cards apart from EC card. English-speaking staff.

Prinz Myshkin

Hackenstr. 2, just off Sendlingerstr.
Munich 80331
Tel: 089-265 596
Metro: Marienplatz or Sendlinger Tor
Open: 11.00 right through till 01.00
Fashionable vegetarian café/restaurant. 7 starters, 3 of them vegan, at 7-15.50 DM including miso soup, curry orange carrot

soup, chips and salsa, guacamole. Range of mainly vegan salads 7.50-17.50 DM from small mixed green to Mexican (avocado, pineapple, corn, celery, tomato, greens) or Forest & Field (sauteed oyster mushrooms on Rucola, endive, cherry tomatoes, olive oil and balsamic vinegar). Main courses 16.50-24.50 DM such as tofu veg stir-fry, Indian curry and Thai curry. Large range of fruit and cake desserts 5-13.50 DM, none vegan. Two pages of wines by region 6.50-9.50 DM glass, 26-60 DM bottle. Beer including organic 3-6.20 DM. Coffee 3.80-4.20 DM, teapot 6.70 DM. Wines are not vegetarian. Beers 3-6.20 DM. Half non-smoking though not well ventilated. Credit cards accepted.

Restaurant-Café Buxs

Frauenstr. 9
Munich 80469
Tel: 089-291 955-0
Metro: Marienplatz U & S Bahn
Open: Mon-Fri 11.00-20.30, Sat 11-15.30, Sun closed.
Closed 24 Dec-6 Jan.
Very busy vegetarian café-restaurant, mostly organic, with a huge international range of daily changing dishes which you pay for by weight.

Restaurant-Café Buxs

Amalienstr. 38
Munich 80799
Tel: 089-280 2994-0
Metro: Universität (University) U3 and U6
Open: Mon-Fri 11.00-15.00, Sat 11-15.00, Sun closed.
Closed 24 Dec-6 Jan.
As above.

BREMEN

by Mieke Roscher

Bremen is an interesting cultural centre and Oldenburg is a nearby small university city with a large population of young adults, which is a popular place to live and visit. Vegetarians and vegans can find food fairly easily in both places.

Bio Biss

Wulwestrasse 18, Bremen 28203
Tel: 0421-703 044
Open: 12-15.00 and 18-22.00
Organic wholefood restaurant. Fairly expensive. You can ask the chef to provide for extra dietary needs. Always say if you are vegan if you want to avoid finding dairy products in your meal although it might not be stated on the menu.

La Luna Pizzeria Vegetaria

Lübecker Strasse 37
Bremen 28203
Tel: 0421-700 750
Average prices, good food!

Sindbad

Ostertorsteinweg 83, Bremen
Open: 11 am 'til very late
Arabic foods. This cheap take away place has among other vegetarian/vegan specialities the best falafel in town.

Moto

Schlachte 22, Bremen
Open: Daily 12.00-21.00
Taiwanese cuisine. Fairly expensive, but wide range of vegan food. The mock duck is superb.

Kraut und Rüben
Wulwestrasse 5, Bremen
Organic and wholefood shop. This shop always has fresh organic veggies from the region. It is quite expensive though.

Reformhaus Lichte
Unser Lieber Frauen Kirchhof
Bremen
This shop has a separate shelf for vegan food, for those of you whose German is not sufficient enough to decipher the lists of ingredients.

AuTuMN
(Autonome Tier- und MenschenrechtlerInnen Norddeutschland)
c/o BBA-Infoladen
St.Pauli Strasse 10-12
28203 Bremen
Local animal rights group, which is happy to help out with contacts, assistance and support:

OLDENBURG

by Mieke Roscher

Safran
Mottenstrasse 19
Oldenburg
Cheap Persian take-away food, pizza, falafel, rollo. All available vegan by request

Tarisch
Dragonerstrasse 39
Oldenburg
Vegetarian fast food at average prices. A variety of vegan burgers and chillies is available.

RAINBOWS AND WELLIES

The Taigh na Mara Cookbook
by Jackie Redding and Tony Weston

Richly illustrated hardback. Vegan menus and recipes from the UK's Vegetarian Hotel of the Year in the Scottish Highlands, plus historical anecdotes and even the author doing the full monty on the cover. Wildly popular in some bookshops, banned in other hoity-toity ones, judge for yourselves whether Tony is more shocking than recipes for boiled animals. One thing's for sure this is gourmet vegan cuisine at its very finest.

**The perfect Christmas or birthday gift
for that special veggie in your life.**

"Distinctly Gourmet." - *Homes & Gardens*

"One read & you'll be on the first train North."
Here's Health

**£14.95 + postage
Order online at www.vegetarianguides.co.uk**
or using the order form at the end of this book
Vegetarian Guides Ltd, PO Box 2284, London W1A 5UH, UK

GREECE

In Athens head for the Plaka area, right by the Acropolis, where apart from Eden Vegetarian Restaurant there are heaps of ordinary places with veggie options like dolmades (rice stuffed in vine leaves), spinach, potatoes, eggplant dishes, Greek salad, and beans.

Elswhere in Greece stay away from seafront tourist traps full of chicken and burgers and head back a street or two to where the Greeks eat. All kinds of salads, bean dishes, rice (a staple on many islands), stuffed peppers, tomato or marrow and cheap wine are standard fare in tavernas. Meze, like in Lebanese restaurants, are a selection of starters with bread, such as aubergine or pepper dips. Once they know who you are, many places will make a special effort for the rest of your trip.

ATHENS

by Aris Skliros

Check opening times because they can vary with the season.

Amarando
Themistokleus 6 and Agia Paraskevis 20,
Halandri, Athens
Tel: 68 18 453
Open: 12.00-16.30
Vegetarian restaurant.

Diavlos
Draku 9, near Sigrou 70, FIX, Athens
Tel: 923 95 88, 923 26 22
Open: Evening till 02.00, closed Mon-Tue
Vegetarian restaurant.

IT'S ALL VEGAN TO ME!

I am a vegetarian. I do not eat meat or chicken.
Eemay hortofagos. Dthen troo krayas ee kotopoolo.

I don't eat fish either
Dthen troo psari

I'm vegan. I do not eat eggs, milk, butter cheese or feta.
Eemay veegkan. Dthen troo avga, gala, vootiro, teeree keh feta.

Igia Icologia

Panepistimiou 37
Athens
Tel: 32 10 966
Open: 11-23.00, Sun until 16.30
Vegetarian restaurant.

Ariston

Platonos 12 and Kipon
Nea Kifisia Square
Athens
Tel: 620 30 44
Open: Mon-Fri 18.00-02.00, Sat-Sun 12.00-02.00
Nearly vegetarian restaurant.

Eden

Lisiou 12 and Mnisikleus, Plaka
Athens
Tel: 32 48 858
Open: midday to midnight, closed Tuesday
We've heard that this is one of the best vegetarian restaurants
in Europe with lots of wholefood, brown rice, great salads, and

fabulous bread that they bake themselves. An air conditioned oasis in a meaty city at the foot of the Acropolis, some people eat there every day. Menu in English. They also sell organic food.

Icosistima

Leoforo Pendelis 106a, Halandri
Athens
Tel: 685 58 16/7/8
Open: 12.00-23.00
Nearly vegetarian restaurant.

Nectar ke Amvrosia

Filonos 49, Pireas
Athens
Tel: 412 56 16, 417 81 33
Open: Mon-Fri 11.00-16.00, Sat 11.00-14.00, closed Sunday.
Nearly vegetarian restaurant

Yogacharya **Aris Skliros**, B.S.Y.A., M.B.S.Y. (British School of Yoga Associate, full Member of the British School of Yoga), who compiled the information on Athens, started yoga in 1978. He travelled the world studying authentic yoga systems in their places of origin with the greatest teachers in India, USA, Austria, United Arab Emirates and England, where he lived for two and a half years. He continues to meet the world's best yoga teachers and is now practising advanced yoga techniques. He writes for magazines, is a people's guide for mountain walking, teaches Gentle Yoga, Asthanga, Iyengar, yoga for pregnancy, yoga introductory and Kriya seminars and is included in Yoga International's 2000 Teachers Guide.
Tel. Athens 22 81 964.

HUNGARY

by Gabor Borsodi

BUDAPEST

Elethaz

Boszormenyi ut 13-15
Budapest, 1126
Tel: 356 6533
Open: 12-21.00 Mon-Fri. Also Saturdays in Summer.
Red Line end sta. Deli pu, 2 stops with tram 59. Or bus 21 or 102 Southwest.
Vegetarian wholefood restaurant. Starters include soups 185-225 HUF which are often vegan. Main courses 579-795 HUF include pita with vegetables and are often vegan. Desserts 155 HUF like carob cake and halva are sometimes vegan. Wider choice in the summer. Children's portions. No alcohol or smoking.

Gandhi

Vigyazo Ferenc u.4
Budapest, 1051
Open: Mon-Sat 12-22.30
Deak Square (all lines)
Vegetarian restaurant which caters well for vegans. Starters 320 HUF include sweet potato soup and bean soup with cabbage. Salads priced according to weight, made with fresh vegetables, sprouts and seeds, mainly vegan. 2 main courses 860-1080 HUF, 1 vegan. Choose from 'Sun plate' or 'Moon plate' such as stuffed cabbage, mashed potato, courgette and dill sauce. Desserts 320 HUF such as apple and walnut slice are often vegan. Wine 290 HUF glass, 1160 HUF bottle. Beer 460 HUF. Coffee 200 HUF. English menu. Staff speak English and French.

Govinda

Belgrad rkp. 18
Budapest, 1056
Tel: 318 1144
Open: Tue-Sun 12-21.00

Blue line, Ferencziek Square station
South Indian Hare Krishna vegetarian restaurant which makes heavy use of cow extracts. Soups and salads available as starters. Main course 800-1100 HUF such as puri. 1 dessert. No alcohol. Children's portions. English menu, staff speak English. Cash only. Little for vegans.

Mirtusz

47 Zichy Jeno Street, 5th District,
Budapest,
Tel: 133 159 20
Open: Every day 12-22.00
Omnivorous. Caters for vegetarians. Soup, main courses, desserts and drinks are priced according to how much you eat, typically 1200-2500 HUF.

HUNGRY IN HUNGARY

I'm vegetarian
Vegetáriánus vagyok

I'm vegan
Végan vagyok

I don't eat meat, chicken, fish.
Nem eszek húst, baromfit, halat.

I don't eat egg, milk, cheese, dairy products, honey.
Nem eszek tojást, tejet, vajat, sajtot, tejterméket, mézet.

Do you have any vegetarian dishes?
Van vegetáriánus ételük?

IRELAND

by Katrina Holland

CORK

Café Paradiso

16 Lancaster Quay
Cork
Tel: 021 277939
Open: Tue-Sat 12.30-15.00, 18.30-22.30, Sun-Mon closed.
Vegetarian restaurant eight minutes walk from Cork centre. There is a peaceful ambience created by candles on the tables and friendly staff. Not a huge selection of food for vegans but they are happy to adapt most of their recipes to accommodate vegans or other special diets and they use a high percentage of organic ingredients. House Bread with organic olive oil costs £2.50, marinated olives £2.50, tossed salad £3. There are seven starters ranging from £4 to £6. Cannellini bean soup with roast pepper concasse and basil oil is £4; green bean salad with olives, broad beans, capers, oregano and a lemon garlic dressing is £6. Seven main courses range from £10 to £13. Two options are stir-fried mushrooms and greens in a sweet ginger and chilli sauce with noodles or rice at £11 and Thai cashew and tofu sandwich fritters, pan-fried in a crisp corn coating, pineapple chutney, coconut-stewed vegetables and fragrant basmati rice at £12. (We can highly recommend this dish!). There is a different menu at lunch time but the food is a similar style. Starters range from £4 to £6 and mains range from £5.80 to £7.80. The menu changes every few weeks. There are five desserts ranging form £2.80 to £3.20, unfortunately none are suitable for vegans. But vegan icecream with vegan chocolate sauce or fruit is available, and vegan chocolate. Licenced to sell wine only, the cheapest being £2.70 per glass and £10.50 per bottle. Cigarette smoking is allowed, though there is a non-smoking area, but big no to cigar and pipe smoking. Vegan margarine is always available, soya milk sometimes. Book a

table to avoid disappointment as they get busy. Visa and Mastercard welcome.

Quay Co-Op

24 Sullivan's Quay
Cork
Tel: 021 317026
Open: Mon-Sat 9.00-21.00 Bank holidays closed.
Vegetarian counter service café above a health food shop. They serve soups, salads, veggie burgers, hot pots, stews and desserts. Vegan, gluten-free and wheat-free diets are well catered for. Soup costs £1.55 on its own or with bread £1.85. A small salad is 80p and a large £1.20. Main dishes are served with two salads or two servings of hot vegetables. Two veggie burgers with two salads costs £4.50 and a stew or hot pot with two salads or two servings of hot vegetables is £5.25. French Country Stew was on the menu the day we went.
There are several desserts ranging from £1.50 to £1.80 and there is usually something for vegans. The fruit crumble at £1.60 was nice and was served with Provamel soya dessert on request. Vegan margarine and soya milk are available. Soya cappuccinos are £1.30. A mug of tea costs 70p, a pot for one is £1and a pot for two is £1.30. They are licenced to serve wine only. Upstairs is smoking and downstairs is non-smoking. Visa, Mastercard, and Amex accepted.

Crystal Inn

38 MacCurtain Street
Cork
Tel: 021-500271
Open: Sun-Thurs 17.00-00.30, Fri-Sat 17.00-1.00
Omnivorous Chinese restaurant with a decent selection of veg-etarian dishes, such as vegetables with black bean sauce and rice £5.70 eat in, or £4.40 take-away. They accept Visa and Access cards.

Indian Tandoori Take-Away

35 MacCurtain Street
Cork
Tel: 021 508382
Open: Sun-Thurs 17.00-3.00, Fri-Sat 17.00-4.00
Omnivorous Indian take-away with a few tables if you want to eat there. They have a reasonable selection of vegetarian food and it is the place to go if you happen to be out in the middle of the night and feeling a bit peckish. Vegetable samosas £1.50, and a veg kebab in fresh nan bread £3.50, or in pitta bread is £3. There is a selection of eight vegetarian main dishes ranging from £3.95 to £4.95 such as sag bhaji (mixed vegetables cooked with spinach) £3.95, dal tarka £3.95, Bombay aloo (potatoes cooked in spicy pickled sauce) £3.95, alu palik (potatoes and spinach) £3.95. Boiled rice £1.20, pilau rice £1.30.

Nature's Way

Paul Street
Cork
Tel: 021 270729
Open: Mon-Wed & Sat 9.00-18.00, Thu 9.00-19.00, Fri 9.00-20.00. Sun closed.
Health food store which stocks vegan icecreams, soya desserts, soya milk and vegan chocolate.

DUBLIN

Blazing Salads

25c Powerscourt Town Centre
Dublin 2
Tel: 01 6719552
Open: Mon-Sat 12.00-16.30, Sun closed.
Vegan heaven. Vegetarian counter service café on Level 2 of Powerscourt Shopping Centre with a daily changing menu. Lentil Soup and Carrot and Fresh Coriander Soup were on the

menu when we visited and cost £1.50. There is a selection of seven salads, five of which were vegan on the day we were there. It costs £2.20 for two salads, £3.30 for three and £4.40 for four. Mains included baked potato with two salads for £3.85 and kidney bean casserole with brown rice and two salads for £5.25. There was a wide choice of vegan desserts including apple pie with cashewnut topping at £1.85; date, oat and orange square £1.25; hot apple crumble £1.85; fruit and nut bar £1.20; and fresh fruit, tofu and almond slice £1.85. Vegan tofu nut cream is available with desserts at 30p extra. They have vegan margarine, soya milk, soya cappuccinos, and soya milk-shakes. They use organic ingredients as much as possible and cater for wheat free, yeast free and sugar free diets. Also do take-away food. Smoothies and juices can be taken away in cups for £1.65 or 1/2 litre bottles (juices £3 and smoothies £3.20). There is a discount for re-using bottles. The café seats about 50 people.

Unfortunately this branch of Blazing Salads is for sale, but should still be open at least through Winter 2000. We were told that when it is sold it will still be a vegetarian café, but the name and menu will be changing.

Blazing Salads

42 Drury Street
Dublin 2
Tel: 01 6719552
Open: Mon-Sat 9.00-17:30 (later in Summer), Sun Closed.
Vegetarian take-away using mainly organic ingredients, with a regularly changing menu. Soup of the day £1.50, miso soup £1.75.There is a self serve salad bar with a choice of twelve different salads. Cost is determined by weight, usually ranging from £3 to £6.50. Sandwiches are £2.25, such as homemade foccacia with hummous, spinach leaves, coriander, pesto, chilli oil and tomato. Organic wholemeal pitta filled with alfalfa, falafel, and a tahini and lemon dressing £2. Vegetable and lentil turnover £2, vegetable samosas £1.60 and vegetable and tofu spring rolls £1.60. There is range of slices and bars, all costing just over £1. Apricot slices and fruit and nut bars are

£1.10 and date, oat and orange squares £1.25. They cater for vegan, gluten-free and wheat-free diet and have soya milk, soya cappuccinos and soya milkshakes. Fresh juices and smoothies are £1.65 per cup and by the litre at £3 and £3.20 respectively. Visa, Mastercard and Amex accepted. Soymilk, rice milk and soya cream on sale by the carton.

Cornucopia

19 Wicklow Street
Dublin 2
Tel: 01 6777583
Open: Mon-Sat 9.00-20.00, except Thurs 9.00-21.00

Very busy vegetarian counter service café, with a great selection for vegans. Their menu changes daily and you will find a choice of soups, salads, mains, and cakes. There are always two different types of soup, of which one or both will be vegan such as tomato, cumin and red lentil soup or split pea and vegetable soup, small bowl £1.30, large £1.75. Ten salads, of which eight or nine vegan, such as garden salad, Chinese, Indian rice, pasta salad with roast vegetables, kidney bean and spinach in a garlic dressing. Small salad £1.20, large £1.95. Four or five main dishes, of which about three vegan, for example Moroccon lentil stew with rice and salad £5.20; spinach, mushroom and chickpea casserole with rice and salad £5.30. Selection of freshly baked bread by the slice. A thick slice of vegan soda bread costs 40p. Vegan margarine is available. Range of cakes and cookies of which about half are vegan. Examples include muesli bars, apple and almond slices and fruit and nut biscuits, all costing around £1.10. Tea, herbal tea, barley cup and coffee £1, cappuccino £1.30. Soy milk is available for tea or coffee and by the glass at 75p. They also have fresh juice.

A breakfast menu is served from 9.00-12.00, with a choice of a cooked breakfast, or a healthier alternative of fruit salad and muesli. Both come with bread, margarine and tea or coffee and will set you back £3.50. Unfortunately both breakfasts are more suited to veggies than vegans.

Cornucopia cater for vegan, yeast free, wheat free, gluten free and nut free diets, and all items are clearly marked which diets they are suitable for. Organic ingredients are used as much as possible. Take-away is available. Smoking allowed, non-smoking area.

Govinda's

4 Aungier Street
Dublin 2
Tel: 01 4750309
Open: Mon-Sat 12.00-21.00
Indian vegetarian restaurant maintaining the reputation of Hare Krishna places around the world for value, cheerfulness and very full plates. A plate of as much rice, dhal and salad as you can eat (vegans can omit one salad) will cost you £5, drinks extra. There's a different cake every day such as carob, so if you're vegan you'd better hope it's carrot cake day.

Juice

78-83 South Great Georges Street
Dublin 2
Tel: 01 4757856
Open: Sun-Wed 12.00-23.00, Thurs 12.00-24.00, Fri-Sat 12.00-1.00
Vegetarian restaurant with a friendly atmospere which would suit both a romantic dinner for two or a group of friends. It is also possible to sit at the front of the restaurant and just enjoy a fresh juice or a wine. Juice caters well for vegans and items are clearly marked whether they are vegan or if there is a vegan alternative. They use as many organic ingredients as possible. Starters include soup of the day which is always vegan, £3 and served with fresh bread. Vegan margarine is available on request. Miso broth is always on the menu for £3.50. Yam wedges served with a chilled tofu mayonnaise dip are another option to start your meal at £4.50. All the homemade dips are vegan and include tapenade (olivé pate), hummous, baba ganoush (aubergine and sesame seed paté), smoked pimento

pepper paté, and mushroom walnut rosemary paté. It costs £3.50 for one dip, £7.50 for three and £10 for five. Side dishes include wilted greens consisting of pak choi, Chinese leaves and spinach dressed in a shoyu marinade, topped with toasted sesame seeds. The side salad consists of mixed lettuce leaves and seasonal vegetables in a whole grain mustard dressing. Pesto mashed potatoes is baby new potatoes with garlic olive oil and fresh basil. These three dishes cost £3. Freshly-cut chunky potato chips cost £2.50. A selection of proteins are available as a side dish or starter. Tofu costs £3.50, tempeh £4.00 and seitan (wheat gluten) £4.50. All are sautéed and marinated in shoyu, garlic, ginger and chilli.

Main courses include Asian noodles in Ponzu sauce. This is vegan noodles and stir fried seasonal vegetables in a slightly sweet and spicy Asian-inspired sauce with tofu or tempeh and costs £11.50. Vegetable fried rice consists of assorted vegetable pieces diced and stir fried with garlic, ginger and brown basmati rice and mixed with tofu, tempeh or seitan and served with a side salad and costs £10. A Juiceburger & chips is a slightly cheaper option at £9.50. The burger is made of organic aduki beans and organic oats with a blend of fresh herbs and vegetables and served with homemade potato wedges, vegan mayonnaise and a side salad. Cashew and hazelnut roast at £11 is a toasted hazelnut and red pepper terrine with mango salsa served with a side salad.

Three types of organic vegan wine are offered, the cheapest being £2.95 per glass or £12.95 per bottle. Soya milk, soya cappucinno, and soya milkshakes are all available. There is a selection of homemade desserts and they have vVegan ice-cream! Service not included. Visa/Mastercard welcome, as well as debit cards and cheques with a cheque card. Seats about 60 people.

Shalimar

17 South Great Georges Street
Dublin 2
Tel: 01 6779922 / 6713770
Open: Every day 12.00-14.30 & 17.00-24.00
Omnivorous eat in or take-away Indian restaurant with a decent selection of fairly cheap vegetarian food. It's open late so a good place to go if you're coming back from the pub and have an attack of the munchies. Vegetable samosas and stuffed vegetarian parathas cost £2, and a vegetarian tandoori platter for two people is £6.95. There is a further selection of seven vegetarian dishes all priced at £4.50. They are happy to advise which dishes are suitable for vegans. Delivery to limited areas for a charge of £1. All major credit cards accepted. Licenced for alcohol.

Wagamama

South King Street
Dublin 2
Tel: 01 4782152
Open: Sun-Thurs 12.00-23.00, Fri-Sat 12.00-24.00
Omnivorous Japanese noodle bar with several branches also in London. Vegetarian dishes are clearly marked. Some are suitable for vegans. Reasonably priced. Non smoking. Licenced. They accept cheques backed by a guarantee card, Laser, Visa, Mastercard, Access, Amex and Diners Club.

Winding Stair Bookshop and Café

40 Lower Ormond Quay
(North side of Ha'penny Bridge)
Dublin 1
Tel: 01 8733292
Open: Mon-Sat 10.00-18.00, Sun 13.00-18.00.   Last orders 17.30
Omnivorous café and bookshop serving mainly vegetarian food. Most of the soups are vegetarian or vegan and are £1.80 per bowl. Options include red lentil and tomato, split pea, broc-

coli and almond, carrot and coriander, and courgette and
coriander. A salad sandwich costs £1.40 and a salad roll £1.65.
A special salad plate is £3.50. If you need anything on the
menu changed to suit your diet, they will be happy to accommodate. Fresh juices £1.80.

Nature's Way

Stephen's Green Shopping Centre
Grafton Street
Dublin 2
Tel: 01 478 0165
Open: Mon-Sat, (except Thu) 9.00-18.00, Thu 9.00-20.00
One of the six Nature's Way health food stores in Dublin.

Nature's Way

The Parnell Mall
The Ilac Centre
Dublin 1
Tel: 01 8728391
Open: Mon-Sat 9.00-18.00, except Thu 9.00-20.00
One of the six Nature's Way health food stores in Dublin.

Nature's Way

Unit 121
Blanchardstown Shopping Centre
Dublin 15
Tel: 01 822 2560
Metro: Bus 39
*Open: Mon-Tue & Sat 9.00-18.00, Wed-Fri 9.00-21.00, Sun
12.00-18.00*
One of the six Nature's Way health food stores in Dublin.

The General Health Food Store

93 Marlborough Street
Dublin 2
Tel: 01 8743290
Open: Mon-Sat 9.00-18.00.

Health Food Shop with a wide range of products, including pasties, flapjacks, date slices, flavoured soy milks etc.

ITALY

by Marina Berati

FLORENCE

Florence is so pretty that you'll want to steal some beauty and take it home with you. Bring a camera for the magical cobbled streets, orange roofs, palaces, piazzas, bridges, museums and churches such as Chiesa di Santa Croce where Galileo, Machiavelli and Michelangelo are buried.

You'll also see Leonardo and Raphael and I don't mean those cool talking turtle dudes. Italians live to love, sing, drink and eat. The trendy bottled Mediterranean fare that has come to dominate British restaurants is here fresher, lusher and brighter. They say that the river is purer the closer the source, so come be bewitched by the cuisine and culture of the jewel of Italy.

La Fonte - Ristorante Vegetariano

Via Lucignano 15
Monte Spertoli (FI)
Florence 50025
Tel: 0571-60914
Metro: Motorway/Superstrada Firenze-Livorno, exit/uscita 2 (Ginestre) for Monte Spertoli.
Open: Wed-Sat eve; Sun lunch & dinner, call to reserve.
Vegan organic macrobiotic restaurant with vegan proprietor, set in a lovely Tuscan setting in the Chianti hills, with a fireplace in winter and relaxing atmosphere. Menu changes regularly. 4 succulent starters at L 5000 such as 'crescione' (puff pastries stuffed with vegetables); almonds with chickpea cream; vegetables with walnut cream. 3 scrumptious first courses at L 8-9000 like pumpkin soup and croutons; basmati rice with carrots, ginger and sprouts; vegetable soup alla Garfagnine. 3 choices

of delicious second courses   at   L15000 such as seitan escalopes with white wine and sautéed turnip tops; baked and stuffed avocado with broccoli: tofu pie with mushroom, fennel and tahini. 5 tantalizing vegan desserts at L5000 such as pear/apple cake with tofu cream; chocolate cake; and ultimate vegan heaven - tiramisu, yumm.   House wine L2000 per glass and L8000 for a bottle, beer L5000, coffee L2500. The menu is in Italian but the friendly staff do speak English. Children's portions also available. Service charge L2000. No credit cards. The restaurant is closed for 15 days in July. Service charge L2,000.

Caffe d'Orzo
Via Reginaldo Giuliani 17R
Florence 50141
Tel: 055 411 905
Metro: Bus 8, 28, 14, 20
Open: Mon-Sat 7.30-19.30. Closed Sun and 15 days in August.
Only vegetarian and vegan snack bar in Florence. Salads L7,000. Main courses L6-7,000 such as pasta with olives and capers and rice with mushrooms and creamed tofu. Desserts L2,500-3,600 including chocolate cake and carrot and mandarin cake. House wine L2,000 glass, L10,000 bottle, beer L3,800, coffee L1,400. Soya cappuccinos and vegan cheese available. English speaking staff.

Il Vegetariano
Via delle Ruote 30R
Florence 50129
Tel: 055-47 50 30
Metro: Walking distance from railway station.
Open: Tue-Fri 12.30-2.30 and 19.30-22.30,
Sat-Sun 19.30-22.30.
Vegetarian and vegan Italian restaurant using 30% organic ingredients. Come for dinner, lunch, or a cake and herb tea. Menu varies each day. Starters L8-9,000 such as rice and green vegetables and pasta with turnip and tomato sauce.

Huge choice of salads, both raw and cooked, L6-8,000. Main courses L13,000 including diced seitan with broccoli, saffron and radish. Desserts L6,000 for example chocolate crumble tart. House wine L2,000 glass, L12,000 bottle, beer L4,000, coffee L2,000. Able to cater for gluten and wheat free diets.

Sedano Allegro

Borgo La Croce 20
Rosso
Florence 50121
Tel: 055-23 45 05
Metro: Walking distance from the Duomo.
Open: Tue-Sun 9-24.00, closed Mon. Closed in August.
Mediterranean and Italian vegetarian restaurant which has a fast lunch atmosphere during the day and a laid back, romantic feel in the evening with a candlelit patio. 9 vegetarian starters and salads L6-13,000 of which 5 are vegan including house salad, Palmito salad, and pearl barley salad. 11 vegetarian and 10 vegan first courses L8-15,000, such as risotto with radicchio, chick peas and spelt soup, ravioli with vegetable sauce or zuchini. Seven veggie and 5 vegan second courses L7-15,000 including seitan stew with beans, seitan alla Normanna (with mushrooms), vegetarian kebab and home made veggieburgers. Vegans must specify when ordering that they do not want parmesan cheese. House wine L4,000for 1/4 litre, beer L3,000, coffee L2,000. Menu in Italian but English speaking staff. Half the restaurant is no smoking in the evening. Takes Visa and Mastercard.

Amon

Via Palazzuolo 26/28 r
Florence 50123
Tel: 055 233 146
Open: Tue-Sun 12-15.00 and 18-23.00. Closed during August.
Good value Egyptian and Mediterranian omnivorous restaurant, popular with young vegans. Choose from 6 vegan options L4-6,000 including hummous with tomatoes, mousakka with

aubergines and tomatoes or broad beans, spices and tahini sauce in pitta bread. Baklavas are available for dessert, which are vegetarian but contain honey. Beer L3,000, coffee L1,000. Menus are available in English. Totally non-smoking.

Troponais Pasticceria Naturale

Via S. Gallo 92/R
Florence 50129
Tel: 055 483 017
Open: 9-19.00. Closed from Sat 13.00 till Mon 9am. Closed August.
Highly recommended vegetarian (almost vegan) bakery, the best in the whole of Tuscany, selling delicious vegan cakes, bread, eggless and dairy free quiches and pies and biscuits. Also sandwiches and other foods which are ideal for picnics, in fact only one dish is not vegan.

Naturasi

Viale Corsica 19/23
Florence
Tel: 055 366 024
Open: Mon 15.30-20.00, Tue-Thu 9-13.00 & 15.30-19.30, Fri 9-20.00, Sat 9-13.30.
Food shop selling fresh vegetables, fruit and take-away food for picnics like pizza, rolls, cakes, salads, desserts. Large proportion of organic food.

How much?	Quanto?	seventy	settanta
One, two	Uno, due	eighty	ottanta
three, four	tre, quattro	ninety	novanta
five, six	cinque, sei	one hundred	cento
seven, eight	sette, otto	two hundred	duecento
nine, ten	nove, dieci	one thousand	mille
twenty, thiry	venti, trenta	2,000 lire	duemila lire
forty	quaranta	five thousand	cinquemila
fifty	cinquanta	ten thousand	diecimila
sixty	sessanta	100,000	centomila

LAKE GARDA

Ohsawa

via Fratelli Bianchi 45
Maderno (BS)
Lake Garda
Tel: 0365-540860
Open: Tue-Sun 12-14.30, 18-24.00. Closed Monday.
Holiday in January.
Delicious and varied vegan dishes at this macrobiotic pure veg-
etarian restaurant on the shor of Lake Garda, just two hours
from Venice or half an hour by ferry from Torri de Benaco.
Really yummy yummy stuff, wholefoody but not righteous with
it, all organic. Set dinner for L20,000 or a la carte 35-40,000, all
of it vegan apart from some feta cheese, with vegan chocolate
and Italian biscuit pudding a highlight. Menu in English,
German, French. At the intersection of Via Fratelli Bianchi and
Via Carducci. (Review by Andrew Butler of PETA Europe)

VENI, VIDI, VEGI

I came, I saw, I ate vegetarian

I am vegetarian
Sono vegetariano (m), Sono vegetariana (f)

I am vegan
Sono vegano (m), Sono vegana (f)

I don't eat meat, chicken or fish
Non mangio carne, nè pollo o pesce

I don't eat eggs, milk, butter, cheese or honey
Non mangio uova, latte, burro, formaggio o miele

Do you have a vegetarian dish?
Avete un piatto vegetariano?

Si Parla Veggie?

FRUIT	FRUTTA
apricots	albicocche
apples	mele
banana	banana
blackcurrants	ribes nero
cherries	cileigie
grapes	uva
kiwi fruit	kiwi
lemons	limoni
mango	mango
melons	meloni
oranges	arance
pears	pere
peaches	pesche
plums	prugne/susine
raspberries	lamponi
strawberries	fragole

DRIED FRUIT	FRUTTA SECCA
apricots	alicocche
dates	datteri
(dried) figs	fichi (secchi)
prunes	prugne (secche)
raisins	uva passa
sultanas	uva passa

SALAD	INSALATA
avocado	avocado
beansprouts	germogli
celery	sedano
cucumber	cetriolo
lettuce	lattuga
spinach	spinaci
tomatoes	pomodori

HERBS	ERBE
basil	basilico
bay leaves	alloro
oregano	origano
parsley	prezzemolo
rosemary	rosmarino
sage	salvia

SPICES	SPEZIE
chilli	peperoncino
ginger	zenzero
nutmeg	noce moscata

VEGETABLES	VEGETALI
aubergines	melanzane
beetroot	barbabietola
broccoli	broccoli
carrots	carote
cabbage	cavolo
cauliflower	cavolfiore
courgettes	zucchine
garlic	aglio
kale	ravizzone
leeks	porri
mushrooms	funghi
onions	cipolle
parsnips	pastinaca
potatoes	patate
spinach	spinaci
peppers	peperoni
(yellow, green, red)	(gialli, verdi rossi)
sweet potatoes	patate dolci/americane

GRAINS	
barley	orzo
cereals	cereali
millet	niglio
oats	avena
pasta	pasta
popcorn	popcorn
rice	riso
wheatgerm	germe di grano
wholemeal bread	pane integrale

SEEDS   SEMI

pumpkin seeds semi di zucca
sesame seeds   semi di sesamo
sunflower s'ds semi di girasole

NUTS   NOCI (frutta secca)

almonds   mandorle
cashew nuts   anacardi
hazelnuts   nocciole
peanuts   arachidi
peanut butter burro di
               arachidi
pine kernels   pinoli
walnuts   noci

TINNED FOOD CIBO IN LATINA

coconut milk   latte di cocco
chick peas   ceci
sweetcorn   mais
tinned   pomodori pelati
  tomatoes
tomato purée   purè di pomodoro

FROZEN   SURGELATI

peas   piselli
soya ice-cream gelato alla soia
soya mince   salsicce vegetariani
veggie   salsicce
  sausages   vegetariani
veggie burgers hamurgher
               vegetariani

CHILLED   SURGELATI

margarine   margarina
orange juice   succo d'arancia
soya yogurt   yogurt alla soia
tofu   tofu
tomato ketchup ketchup

PULSES

chick peas   ceci
green lentils lenticchie verdi
red lentils   lenticchie rosse

CUPBOARD

agar-agar   agar-agar
baking powder lievito
black pepper   pepe nero
olive oil   olio d'oliva
extra virgin   extra vergine
olives   olive
mustard   mostarda
jam   marmellata
marmalade   marmellata
salt   sale
sea salt   sale marino
seaweed   alghe
soya dessert   dessert alla soia
soya milk   latte di soia
sunflower oil olio di girasole
tahini   tahini
vanilla essence essenza di vaniglia
yeast extract estratto di lievito
                 (di birra)
nutritional   lievito (di birra)
  yeast   alimentare
vegetable stock dadi di brodo
  cubes   vegetale
vegetable   brodo vegetale
  bouillon

In Italy there is not such an amazing brand of vegan foods as in Britain, but the good news is that there is a heavenly brand of soya products called Valsoia. Amazing desserts, lovely Italian style vegan ice-cream, snacks and of course soya milk. You can find them in almost every big supermarket like Coop, Sidis. To find other interesting foods you have to go to expensive health food shops.

Stefania Vinci

MILAN

Il Naviglio Macrobiotico

Via Casale 5
Milan 20144
Tel: 02-83 23 693
Open: Mon 12.30-14.30, Tues-Sat 12.30-14.30 and 20-22.30,
Sun 20-22.30.
Virtually vegan macrobiotic restaurant though fish is served once a week on Friday. Main course L25,000. Order a mixed dish of rice, pasta, vegetables, couscous salad, seitan and more, all of it vegan. Desserts L6,000, choose from fruit creams, pudding, cakes, strudel, pies and more, again all of it vegan. Bellissimo. They bake their own rice bread, 100% wheat and yeast free. House wine L2,000 glass, L20,000 bottle, beer L6,000, coffee L2,000. Totally non-smoking. Cover charge L2-3,000. They take Visa, Mastercard, AmEx and Diners cards. Staff speak English, French and Spanish. Closed Xmas, Easter, August. High chairs and children's portions.

Desiderata

Via Cagnola 6
Milan 20154
Tel: 02-33 60 30 03
Metro: tram 1, 28, 30
Open: Tue-Sat 12-15.00 and 18-21.00;
Sun eve only, Mon midday only.
Vegetarian restaurant serving tasty food which caters well for vegans. Starters L10-20,000 include lentil pate, hiziki salad and curry bulgar. Main courses L12-14,000 such as basmatti rice with vegetables, vegetable paella, pasta with veg, seitan steak. No desserts. House wine L3-6,000 glass, 16,000 bottle, beer up to L4-12,000, coffee L3,000. English speaking staff. No smoking in the evenings.

Joia

Via Panfilo Castaldi 18
Milan 20124
Tel: 02-20 49 244
Metro: Metro Line 1 Porta Venezia
Open: Mon-Fri 12.20-14.30, 19.30-22.30.
Closed Sat-Sun, Xmas and 10 days in August.
Almost vegetarian (some fish) avant garde gourmet restaurant, with vegan dishes marked on the menu. Starters L18-20,000 include 'variations on pumpkin' and 'the spiral of taste'. First courses L18-20,000 include cream of red lentils with chestnuts, black salsify, Madras curry and caramelised sweet verbena. Main courses L30-33,000 could be heart of cabbage and potato and portobello mushroom tart with vegetable mayonnaise, salad of herbs and sprouts with sesame oil. Four course set menus L65, 75 and 80,000. Menu changes with the season. House wine is L8,000 per glass, beer L10,000, coffee L5,000. Menu in English. Staff speak English, French and German.

Il Faraone

Via Masolino da Panicale 13
Milan 20100
Tel: 02-33 00 13 37
Open: Every day 12-15.00 and 19-23.00,
but closed on Wednesdays.
Egyptian omnivorous restaurant with plenty of veggie food which serves the best falafels in Milan. Starters L5-6,000 such as cous cous with bahhia, falafel and hummous. Salads L6-8,000. Main courses L8-12,000 include focaccia felfella which is pizza with falafel, tomatoes and tahini. There are special Egyptian desserts which are vegan, ask for more details. Can cater for special diets. They speak English and accept all cards.

Associazone Il Naviglio

Via Casale 5
Milan 20144
Tel: 02-83 23 593
Open: Mon-Sat 10-19.30. Closed during August.
Organic food shop selling vegetables, fruit and take-away food for picnis like ckaes, pizza and ready made pasta dishes. Also cruelty free clothes.

Progetto Gaia

Via Copernico 41
Milan 20125
Tel: 02-66 71 99 16
Open: Tue-Sat 10.30-19.30. Closed Christmas period
and August.
Shop selling organic food, take-away snacks and cruelty free clothes. Switch, Visa.

Noi Due

V. Col di Lana 1
Milan 20136
Tel: 02-58 101 593
Metro: MM2 Pta Genova, c/RAM 15-9-3-29-30
Open: Mon-Sat 12-15.00 and 20-22.30
Friendly omnivorous health food restaurant which caters for vegans. First course L7-10,000 such as rice with courgette and mint or tagliatelle with vegetables. Main courses include grain "hamburgers", aubergine cutlets, curry and tofu and seitan with tomato sauce. Dessert could be vegan yoghurt or ice cream. They have soya milk. No alcohol. Menu available in English. Staff speak English, German and French. They can do children's portions.

ROME

Arancia Blu

Via dei Latini 65
San Lorenzo
Rome
Open: 20-24.00 every day
Vegetarian restaurant. Starters L8,000 include hummous and tabouleh. There are 12 main courses L13-16,000, one of which is vegan, spicy vegetable terrine with chicory. 6 desserts L8-9,000, sadly none vegan. Beer L5,000, coffee L2,500. Staff speak English.

Margutta Vegetariano Ristorante

Via Margutta 118
Rome 00187
Tel: 0-32 65 05 77
Open: Tue-Sun 12.30-15.30 and 19.30-01.00, closed Mon
Vegetarian Italian restaurant. 7 starters 10-16,000, 6 salads 12-15,000, 23 mains 14-28,000 of which only Tuscan soup with beans is vegan. 9 desserts 12-15,000, niente vegano. Typical dishes are couscous or brown rice with mixed veg, pasta, pan cooked courgettes and mushrooms, roasted or steamed veg-etables, mixed salad. They asked us to point out they do not cater for vegans, only two dishes for them, and they can't (won't) alter the many veggie dishes. Well that may be true in the evening, but at lunchtime there's a self-service buffet for L16,000 with plenty of vegan stuff, apart from the desserts which all have milk and eggs. Organic beer L5,000, coffee L3,500. Discount for members of LAV, the Italian anti-vivisec-tion league.

Other branches with the same name at Piazza Rondanini 53, tel 06-68 13 45 44 near the Pantheon and via del Leoncino. Website www.marguttavegetariano.com.

Centro Macrobiotico Italiano
Via della Vite 14
Rome 00187
Tel: 06-67 92 25 09
Metro: Metro A
Open: Mon-Sat 10-24.00. Closed August and holidays.
Macrobiotic 100% organic restaurant that can get very busy
especially in the evenings. The menu changes fequently.
Starter 12,000 such as fantasia antipasti, salads such as chick
pea with ume vinegar L10,000. 9 vegan and 1 veggie main
course L14,000 include polenta with cream of tofu and herbs,
roast seitan steak, kamut with mushroom and pumpkin sauce.
Vegan desserts L6,000 such as rice pudding, or tiramisù with
soya milk which unfortunately for vegans contains egg - so near
yet so far! Staff speak English and French.

Indiano Himalaya Palace
Circonvallazione Gianicolense 277
Rome 00152
Tel: 06-58 26 001
Metro: Tram 30
Open: Daily 12-15.00, Tue-Sun 20-24.00,
closed Monday evening.
Omnivorous Indian Tandoori restaurant with about 20 vegetari-
an dishes L5-15,000 such as samosa, vegetable biryani, lentil
and red bean dalmakahani, chana masala. Beer L5,000, coffee
L2,500. English menu and English speaking staff. All major
credit cards accepted.

Un Punto Macrobiotico
Via Moricca 100
Rome
Tel: 06-39 75 10 39
Metro: Bus 495, 51, 490. Metro A + bus.
Open: Open Mon-Sat for lunch and dinner, closed Sun
Organic, macrobiotic restaurant which serves fish twice a week.
Daily set menu L12,000 excluding dessert, a bargain, and

there's discount for students and seniors. For this you could have vegetable and grain soup, followed by any of greens, grains and veg, millet croquettes, carrots and almonds, cream of lentils or mixed salad. Desserts L4,000 such as chestnut cake, fruit tarts or tiramisù, probably not vegan. They don't use soya. Reservations advised, and with these prices it's not surprising. They didn't want to be listed in this guide, we don't know why but perhaps it's because they already have enough business, so we probably ought to ask you not to go there or to hide the book or something, and it probably helps if you speak Italian. Also organic produce for sale.

Bottega E Natura

Centro Commerciale "I Granai"
via Mario Rigamonti 100
Rome
Tel: 06-50 31 484
Open: Mon 14-20.00, Tue-Fri 10-20.00, Sun closed
Organic fresh fruit and veg shop. Accepts Visa and debit cards.

Naturist Club

Via Della Vite 14
Rome
Tel: 06-67 92 509
Open: 10-24.00, closed Sunday, August and holidays
Oo-er Missus, it's not what you think but a totally organic food shop associated with the Centro Macrobiotico Ialiano, selling packaged and take-away picnic food. Takes Visa cards.

Yes	Sì
No	No
Please	Per favore
I'd like	Vorrei
Thank you	Grazie
Hello	Buongiorno
Goodbye	Arrivederci

UMBRIA

Country House Montali

Az. Agrituristica Montali
Via Montali, 23
Tavernelle di Panicale (PG) 06068 06068
Tel: 075-8350680
Metro: Website www.edisons.it/montali in English and Italian

Italy's only vegetarian hotel as far as we know. For a holiday in the fresh air, the Country House Montali is located in one of the most beautiful positions in Umbria and Tuscany. Situated on a plateau dominating the surrounding countryside with wonderful views in all directions of the Trasimeno Lake, Lower Tuscany and the valley of Perugia, including sunrise and sunset. The farm is surrounded by woods of ilex, arbutus and olive groves. You will arrive by a gravelled panoramic road. All around endless trails invite you for beautiful walks and excursions, right to the shores of the Trasimeno Lake.

In the centre of the property an old stone farm house, completely restored according to tradition (brick flooring, wooden beams, stone walls) welcomes guests in a wonderful and peaceful calm. Another stone building, hall for concerts, and two new houses built in the same style, offer ten comfortable rooms with private facilities (shower, wc), bar, garden, parking area. You can book half board with the possibility, on request, of having a light lunch, in case people want to spend all day on the farm enjoyng a dip in the swimming pool or a trek in the forest.

The owners take personal care of the cuisine which is exclusively vegetarian, with extensive use of organic farm and some dairy products. The menus, which are different every day, offer excellent dishes and delicious meals, according to recipes perfected from the owners' long experience in their own restaurant. They also organize vegetarian cooking courses. You can buy the farm's produce, unsurpassed olive oil, fruit jams, chutney and other seasonal goodies.

During your stay, besides the walks and trekking routes, you can make excursions to Assisi, Gubbio, Perugia, Todi, Orvieto, Spoleto, Montepulciano and many other beautiful cities of artistic importance, all more or less within 1 hour's drive. On special occasions the proprietors, themselves passionate musicians (this is Italy), organize live evening concerts of ethnic and world music.

Price per day per person, half board, is L 108 000 low season, and 118 000 high season which is 22 March to 3 April and 1 June to 30 September. Phone to book.

Website: www.edisons.it/montali in English and Italian

Email: montali@edisons.it

VENICE

Venice does not seem to have any truly vegetarian or vegan restaurants, but in each 'traditional' restaurant you can usually order at least one starter, a first course and vegetarian/vegan side dishes.

Please remember that in Venice there are a lot of 'tourist traps' where high prices will not guarantee high quality food. The same holds true for pizzerias, vegetarians usually have lots of choices, while vegans should order pizzas without thr mozzerella cheese. Again, beware of tourist traps when looking for a pizzeria.

Da Zorzi

Calle dei Fuseri 4359
S. Marco
Venice
Tel: 041-522 53 50
Open: Mon-Sat 11-15.00, closed Sun.
Omnivorous lunch restaurant serving many vegetarian and some vegan dishes. Takes Visa, AmEx and Switch cards. Licensed for alcohol.

Frary's Bar

Fondamenta Dei Frari 2559
(S. Polo)
Venice 30125
Tel: 041-720 050
Open: 9.30-24.00 every day. Closed for dinner on Tues.
Omnivorous restaurant and bar serving Greek, Italian, Lebanese, and Arabian cuisine. They provide a special 'fast' dinner for customers going to Vivaldi's music concerts in the nearby Scuola Grande di S. Giovanni Evangelista. The food is reasonably priced and of good quality. 6 vegan and 3 vegetarian starters L6-12,000, including dolmades (rice in vine leaves). Mixed salad L5-8,000 is vegan. 4 vegan and 4 veggie main

courses L13-16,000 including couscous, spaghetti with tomato and soup of the day. 6 vegetarian desserts, of which the melomaka (sweets with cinnamon and nuts) is vegan. House wine L7,000 per bottle, beer L 5,000, coffee L2,000. Cover charge L2,500. Menus available in English. Staff speak English. Takes Switch, Visa, Mastercard and AmEx.

Ganesh Ji
Rio Marin 2426
S. Polo
Venice 30125
Tel: 041-719804
Open: 12.30-15.00 and 18.30-24.00. Closed all day Wed and Thu lunchtime.
South Indian restaurant with good choice for some vegetarian and vegan dishes. Take away available. Starters, 5 of which are vegan L3-6,000 include samosas and paratha bread stuffed with vegetables. Main courses L16,000 include lentil daal and aloo palak (hot spinach and potatoes) which are vegan. English menu and English speaking staff. Takes Switch, Visa, Mastercard. Alcohol.

Pizzeria ae Oche
Calle Del Tintor 1552/B
S. Croce
Venice 30135
Tel: 041-5241 161
Open: Every day 12-15.00 and 19-24.00. Closed Sundays in Nov and Jan.
Pizza restaurant with wooden furnishing, very nice, and very good pizzas. Starters include grilled vegetables for L8,500 which are vegan. A variety of salads on offer L10-11,000, which can be made vegan with greens, tomatoes, carrots, olives, corn, mushrooms. First courses L9,000 like vegetable soup and spaghetti with tomato sauce. 10 veggie pizzas L7-14,000 to choose from, all of which can be made vegan if you ask for without (senza) mozzarella, for example mushroom or the vegetar-

ian pizza with spinach, courgettes (zucchini), aubergine (egg-plant) and asparagus. House wine L11,000 per bottle, pint of beer L7,000, coffee L2,000. Cover charge L2,000 + 12% service. Staff speak English and French.

Pizzeria da Sandro

Campello dei Meloni 1412
S. Polo
Venice 30125
Open: 11.30-00.30 every day except Friday.
Pizza restaurant. Starters from L8,000 include mixed vegetables. Main courses L 9-11,000 include tagliatelle alle verdure or spaghetti with garlic, oil and hot peppers. 7 different pizzas L9-13,000 which can be vegan if you ask them to make them without the mozzarella cheese. English menu and English speaking staff. Takes Switch, Visa and Mastercard. Alcohol.

Ecor

Mercato Ortofrutticolo Rialto
(vegetable market near Rialto Bridge)
Venice 30125
Tel: 0347-265 1374
Open: Mon-Sat 7-13.0, closed Sun and 2 weeks in August.
Organic fruit and veg stall selling some other food.

Erboristeria Cibele - Herbs and Food

Rio Tera S. Leonardo 1823
Canareggio
Venice
Tel: 041 52 42 113
Open: Mon Sat 9-12.45 and 15.30-19.45
Small herb and food shop, near railway station. Sells organic food. Takes Switch and Mastercard.

La Serenissima

Calle Fiubera 823
S. Marco
Venice 30124
Tel: 041-523 2346
Open: Mon-Sat 8-13 and 17-19.30
Small organic food shop with fruit and vegetables near San Marco.

Rialto Biocenter

Campo de le Becarie 366
S. Polo
Venice 30125
Tel: 041-523 9515
Open: Mon-Sat 8.30-13.00 & 16.30-20.00.
Small totally organic shop, with some fresh vegetables (for a wider selection go to Ecor, the open stall at the nearby Rialto market), fresh tofu, seitan, biscuits, sweets and cosmetics.

LUXEMBOURG

by Claude Pasquini

The Mesa Verde

11 Rue Du St Espirit
Luxembourg L-1475
Tel: +352-464 126
Open: Tues-Sat evenings.
Also lunchtimes on Wed and Thurs.
Predominantly vegetarian 'alternative' restaurant which can cater for vegans on request. Soups 190 F such as miso and vegetable are vegan. Main courses 650F include couscous with vegetables and seitan with mushrooms. Desserts 190-390F include sorbets and chocolate mousse. None appear to be vegan. Non-smoking area.

EarthSave

Imagine a world where the land is fertile, the water is clean, the air is fresh and all are fed. In this world nature is treated as a community, not a commodity, and our food is healthy for us as well as the planet. We all wish for this - but how do we get there from here?

One simple step is to move toward a plant-based diet, because our food choices profoundly affect the whole web of life on Earth. The good news is that the healthiest way to eat is also the most economical, the most compassionate and the least destructive. What's best for us personally is also best for the planet.

EarthSave is dedicated to helping create this world by showing the powerful impacts of our ordinary eating habits, and by promoting positive alternatives. We encourage sound nutrition, conservation of resources and sustainable agriculture. We show how an animal based diet and the factory farming that underlies it causes enormous depletion and pollution of the natural world, suffering for the animals, and danger to our own health.

EarthSave includes people of all kinds taking informed action to heal our lives and our planet. We encourage a responsible approach to restoring balance, kindness and health to our society. We welcome your participation!

The Unity of EarthSave

People everywhere are waking up and eager to make our world work. They want to do something. Since the beginning EarthSave has received letters asking "What can I do to help?" One of EarthSave's primary roles is to answer that question. We educate people and increase their awareness of the power of their choices. We show how they can make a difference. We supply them with tools and resources to succeed. And we connect with other caring individuals in their geographical areas so they can work together, pooling ideas, talents, and resources through the creation of Chapters.

It is undeniable that our world is facing severe health and environmental crises. Turning this around will take a concerted effort by millions of informed and caring people. That's why EarthSave is asking for your help. By becoming an EarthSave member, you amplify your voice for change. Your support will help us to educate people everywhere about the power of our food choices to create healthy people and a healthy planet. So we can all realise a more healthful future tomorrow.

As a member you will:

Receive a regular **newsletter** packed with interesting articles and practical tips for healthy living.

Have **opportunities to meet and socialise** with other members.

Be invited to attend informative and **educational meetings and events**.

Benefit from a **network of support**.

Be **investing in the future health of all life on earth**.

EarthSave UK, c/o Rozalind A Gruben, 1 Cassidy Place, New Town Road, Storrington, West Sussex RH20 4EY Tel/Fax: 01903-746572
Email: Rozgruben@aol.com
http://www.earthsave.org/

[ ] Student   [ ] Senior £15   [ ] Individual £25
[ ] Family £35   [ ] Patron £75   [ ] Sustaining £300
[ ] Benefactor £700   [ ] Founding £3000
Please make cheques payable to:EarthSave UK

Name:. . . . .

Address:. . . . .

Postcode:. . . . .

Tel:. . . . .   Email: . . . .

Interests/Hobbies:. . . . .

NETHERLANDS

AMSTERDAM

by Henk de Jong

There's much more to this town than tulips, clogs, dykes and space cake. Amsterdam is particularly popular with the young with its cheap, party atmosphere hostels, rock bottom bicycle hire (and no hills), no language barrier so it's easy to make friends, and an enlightened lack of formality or rules for rules' sake. Highlights are strolling through the canals, falafels, the hilarious Sex Museum or the Hemp Museum, Anne Frank house, Waterlooplein market, cafés and bars.

Maoz

1e van der Helsstraat 43
Amsterdam,
Open: Every day 11-2.00
Compact and original Israeli falafel take out bar in the centre, which offers an unlimited self-service salad bar of things to add to your falafel for free. The only non-vegan thing is the 'knoflook' (garlic) sauce. Eat yourself silly for just Dfl 6.

De Bolhoed

Prinsengracht 60-62
Amsterdam, 1015 DX
Tel: 020 626 1803
Open: Every day 12-22.00
Reasonably priced vegetarian restaurant (though not the cheapest) which has a vegan dish of the day for Dfl 26.50 such as tofu in roasted paprika dressing, brown rice, broccoli with mushroom, mixed veg in white wine, Dupuis lentils and salad too. As far as possible all ingredients are organic. Four 3-course menus Dfl 32.50-39.50 with a starter, main course and

choice of dessert. Dinner starters Dfl 7.50-19.75 such as soup, hummus with pitta, salads. Mains all around Dfl 25 such as enchilladas, burrito, casserole, platter of appetizers with salad, or pasta, but many of them cheesey though vegans can be accommodated with advance notice. Desserts from Dfl 8.50, some of which are vegan, and they have cookies and brownies.. Wide range of drinks from Dfl 3 including beer, wine, liqueurs, freshly squeezed juices, soymilk. Non-smoking area.

De Vliegende Schotel

Nieuwe Leliestraat 162
Amsterdam,
Tel: 625 20 41
Open: Every day 16.00 - 23:00

Their dish of the day, which comes in small and big portions, is usually vegan. So is this their goulash and a seitan dish. Mostly organic and very informal plus relaxed. You order at the counter. Wine but no beer (with alcohol in it). Popular with students. Separate smoking and non-smoking sections. Next to the Belly healthfood shop.

De Waaghals

Frans Halsstraat 29
Amsterdam,
Tel: 679 96 09
Open: Tues - Sun 17:00 - 21.30

Ovo-lacto with international menu, each month a different theme. If vegan, give them a call in advance and 'they can do anything'. 3 course menu Dfl 28. Organic vegan wines. Garden in the back where you can sit in summertime. Next to De Aanzet health food store.

Deshima

Weteringschans 65
Amsterdam,
Tel: 622 73 20
Open: Mon - Fri 12:00 - 14:00

Macrobiotic lunch room which is part of the Kushi Institute. The chef says fish (stock) is rarely used. There's soup and dessert and you can order a small or big meal. Lots of miso, noodles, rice, tofu and pickles. There's a very decent health food shop in the basement, called Freshop, which is open on Saturdays too. They provide great vegan snacks like home made pizza slices and tofu cream pies.

Golden Temple Restaurant

Utrechtsestraat 126
Amsterdam, 1017 UT
Tel: 020 626 8560
Open: Every day 17-21.30
Tram 4 from Central Station

Large, well established international vegetarian restaurant run by yoga practitioners since 1969. Extensive menu, with vegan options marked. Starters Dfl 7.5-9.5 include green salad, falafel, pakora, hummus, soup, guacamole. Main meal salads Dfl 19.50. Range of pizzas, two of which are vegan Dfl 13-19.50, and you can add as many toppings as you like for Dfl 1.50-4.00 each such as artichokes, baked tofu, olives and peppers. There is also a multiple choice thali where you select any four dishes from eight such as alu sabji, dhal, korma, kofta, braised tofu shishkebab, pakoras. Or go for the D-I-Y Middle Eastern platter with any from falafel, hummus, pumpkin or yam curry, baked tofu kebab, chickpea stew, dolmas. But no mixing between the platters, it confuses the cook. If you're still hungry there are a dozen side dishes for Dfl 2.75-6.00. Desserts Dfl 4-7 include home made soya ice-cream. Bring your own wine and pay Dfl 5 corkage per bottle. No smoking. Visa, Mastercard and AmEx accepted over Dfl 30. Service not included. Children's portions. English menu. 10% Countdown discount.

EATING DUTCH

I am a vegetarian
Ik ben een vegetarier

I am vegan
Ik ben veganist

I do not eat meat, chicken, fish
Ik eet geen vlees, kip, vis

I do not eat eggs, milk, butter, cheese, honey
Ik eet geen eieren, melk, boter, kaas, honing

Himalaya
Warmoesstraat 56
Amsterdam,
Tel: 626 08 99
Open: Mon 13-18.00, Tues-Sat 10-18.00, Thur till 21:00.
New age oasis in one of Amsterdam's most famous streets bordering on the red light district. It offers lunch fare: juices, herb tea, and snacks, a few of which are vegan like the samosa, tempeh bun and seitan burger.

De Groene Gewoonte
2e Helmessstraat 3
Amsterdam, 1054 CA
Tel: 020-68 98 952
Open: Every day except Tuesday 12-22.00
Tram 1 or 6 to Leidseplein then 3 minute walk
Organic 85% vegetarian café with an Internet connection. Salads and soup around Dfl 10, main meals Dfl 15.50-20 like lasagne, stew, tofu salad, stir-fried greens with burger, or a combination of two for Dfl 32.50. Finish with apple crunch for Dfl 7. Wide choice of teas, juices, coffees, hot chocolate, beers and

wine Dfl 3-5. Soya milkshakes and cappucinos available. Children's portions.

Orient

Van Baerlestraat 21
Amsterdam,
Tel: 673 49 58
Open: 17:00 - 22:00 daily

Good veggie choice in this Indonesian restaurant. A la carte and Rice tables: small one for Dfl 30, regular Dfl 38.50, consisting of 7 tofu and tempeh dishes, 6 veggie dishes and 5 side dishes. Let them point out to you what's vegan and not.

De Aanzet

Frans Halsstraat 27
Amsterdam,
Tel: 673 34 15
Open: Mon-Sat 8:30-18:00

The only store that can be truly called whole food with no pills and potions here. Practically everything they sell is organic. Loose grains and legumes, an excellent and low-priced organic produce section. Nuts, grains, dried fruits. Fresh organic and vegan breads. Best of all, unlike some Dutch wholefood stores, they don't sell any animal parts.

De Belly

Nieuwe Leliestraat 174 - 176
Amsterdam,
Tel: 624 52 81
Open: Mon-Sat 8.30-18.30

Excellent wholefood store. Next door to Vliegende Schotel restaurant.

De Weegschaal

Jodenbreestraat 20
Amsterdam,
Tel: 624 17 65
Open: Mon-Fri 9-18.00, Sat 9-17.00.
Small wholefood store near Waterlooplein flea market. Has its fruit and veggie section outside. Macrobiotic slant.

Gimsel

Huidenstraat 19
Amsterdam,
Tel: 624 80 87
Open: Mon-Fri 9:30-18:30, Sat 9-17.30
Centrally located health food store. They sell vegan cheese and Tofutti vegan ice cream.

De Natuurwinkel

Weteringschans 133 - 157
Amsterdam,
Tel: 638 40 83
Open: Mon-Sat 7-20.00, also Thurs till 21.00. Sun 11-18.00
Biggest health food store around. Sells absolutely everything, including alas organic meat.

NORWAY

by Roar Waagen

OSLO

Spisestedet

Hjelmsgt 3
Oslo, 0355
Tel: 22 69 01 30
Open: Mon-Fri 14-20.00
Totally vegetarian, mostly organic restaurant run by volunteers. Soup is available as a starter for 20 kr. There is one main course for 50 kr which varies each day. No alcohol. Staff speak English.

Vegeta Vertshus

Munkedamsveien 3B
Oslo, 0161
Tel: 22 83 40 20
Open: Every day 11-23.00
Nationaltheateret Stasion
Vegetarian buffet style restaurant and bar which caters for vegans. Established in 1938. Small plate 65 kr. Large plate 80 kr. Free coffee or tea when you buy dinner. English menu and English speaking staff. 10% discount for students.

Krishna Cusine

Kirkeveien 59B
Oslo, 0364
Tel: 22 60 62 50
Open: Mon-Fri 12-20.00
Hare Krishna restaurant. Cheap, but not much choice and very little for vegans. Small soup 15 kr. Main course is a daily changing special for 70 kr. No alcohol or smoking. English menu. English speaking staff.

Punjab Tandoori

Grønland 24
Oslo, 0188
Tel: 22 55 17 32
Open: Every day 12-23.00
Indian restaurant which sells some vegetarian and vegan food. There are 3 vegan meals, plus pakora, roti and nan bread. Pakoras start at 10 kr. Rice with dhal and roti 45 kr. Beer and wine on sale. English menu and English speaking staff.

Mucho Mas

Thorvald Mayersgt 36
Oslo, 0555
Open: Mon-Sat 11-0.30 Sun 13-0.30.
Small, friendly, Mexican omnivorous restaurant that caters for vegetarians and vegans. They are happy to prepare variations of all the items on their menu which contain no animal ingredients. Prices range from tacos 25 kr to burritos 60 kr. Non-smoking area. Sells beer, wine and spirits. English speaking staff.
In the same street nearby is the great Kjøkkenhagen restaurant with excellent salads.

Saigon's Lille Café

Bernt Ankersett
Oslo, 0183
Tel: 22 11 48 13
Open: Mon-Fri 11-23, Sat 11-01, Sun 11-01.
Vietnamese restaurant which is mostly meat, but features 5 good vegan main meals for 55-65 kr. Sells beer and wine. Non smoking area. English speaking staff.

BERGEN

Krishnas Kjøkken
Foggwinckelsgate 18
Bergen, 5007
Open: Mon-Fri
Vegetarian Hare Krishna restaurant which caters for vegans.
Soup is available every day which is vegan and costs 15-35
kr.There are a couple of salads which are 10-55 kr. Choose
between the vegetarian and the vegan main course, 60-80 kr.
There are 7 different dishes which change from day to day,
such as chutney, rice, vegetables and popadoms. Desserts 15-
20 kr, none vegan.

Millan
Vestne Strømhai 3A, Bergen
Tel: 55 31 45 00
Open: Every day 14-23.00
Indian restaurant offering 6 vegetarian and vegan starters 39 kr,
such as samosas and pakoras. Main courses 79-89 kr include
spiced mixed vegetables and chana masala. Licenced. Non
smoking. Visa cards taken. Menu available in English.

NO FISH FOR ME

I am a vegetarian
Jeg er vegetarianer

I am a vegan
Jeg er veganer

I do not eat meat, chicken or fish
Jeg spiser verken kjøtt, kylling eller fisk

I don't eat eggs, milk, butter, cheese, honey
Jeg spiser ikke egg, melk, smør, ost, honning

WHY I AM A VEGETARIAN

"The beef industry has contributed to more deaths than all the
wars in this century, all the natural disasters, and all
automobile accidents combined. If beef is your idea
of 'real food for real people', you'd better
live real close to a real good hospital."
Neal Barnard, M.D., www.pcrm.org

"I don't understand why asking people to eat a well-balanced
vegetarian diet is considered drastic, while it is medically
conservative to cut people open and put them on
powerful cholesterol-lowering drugs
for the rest of their lives."
Dean Ornish, M.D., Cardiologist

"If slaughterhouses had glass walls,
everyone would be a vegetarian."
Paul & Linda McCartney

"How good it is to be well-fed, healthy,
and kind all at the same time."
Henry Heimlich, M.D.

"If we live in peace and love, we will not kill our fellow creatures for
any reason, even to obtain food. There is no need to do so when
other foods are available to us that are both healthful and delicious."
Peter Max, artist

For information on going veggie follow the links at
www.vegetarianguides.co.uk/news

To get active, check out
www.CampaignAgainstCruelty.co.uk
or contact any of the organizations in this guide

"Never doubt that a small group of thoughtful committed citizens
can change the world. Indeed, it's the only thing that ever has."
Margaret Mead

POLAND

by Zofia Torun

Polish hospitality is fabled: "A guest in the house, God in the house." They are generous and gregarious people. All celebrations revolve around the table. Hours, even days, of preparation are then followed by several hours eating and all dishes must be sampled! For a visitor to leave their home hungry would be a great disgrace - instead guests are plied with food the moment they enter! Declining food is quite a struggle, and could cause offence.

Poles have dined at home, rather than out, a situation reinforced by the impoverishment and rationing during the Second World War and the Communist era. The catering industry is therefore fledgling, but growing explosively over the last five years.

Polish cuisine is traditionally stodgy and very animal-based. The quality of simple foods like bread and potatoes is paramount. The Poles have a fabulous selection of soups, both chilled and hearty ones for the heavy winters. Wild mushrooms, the picking of which is a national pastime, feature regularly on the menu - jadłospis.

Vegetarian food is more and more readily available along with health food shops. The recent proliferation of pizzerias and ethnic restaurants, although not always of good quality, are helping that transition.

One thing is for certain, eating out in Poland works out very cheaply for Westerners!

POLISH VOCABULARY

Jestem jaroszem / jaroszka	I'm a vegetarian (m/f)
Jestem weganinem / weganka	I'm a vegan
I do not eat meat chicken, fish	Nie jem miesa kury, ryby
I do not eat eggs, milk butter, cheese, honey	Nie jem jajek, mleka, masła, sera, miód
Smacznego!	Bon appetit!

Dania Jarskie
(traditional vegetarian dishes)

Savoury
Barszcz   beetroot soup

Pierogi   similar to ravioli
ruskie are filled with potato and cheese
and *z grzybami i kapusta* are with wild mushroom and cabbage, vegan and scrummy. If you're not in a veggie place, make sure they don't put any bacon bits as a garnish.
There are sweet versions too, try *z truskawkami* with strawberries.

placki ziemniaczane	potato pancakes
zestaw sałatek	pickled salads (sauerkraut, celeriac, carrot & beetroot)
kasza	roasted buckwheat
mizeria	cucumber and sour cream salad
bukiet jarzyn	a selection of cooked vegetables

SWEET

makowiec	poppy seed cake
sernik	amazing moist cheese cake
paczki	doughnuts with rose hip jam
nalesniki ("naleshniki")	fried stuffed pancakes

Drinks

vodka	vodka
piwo	beer
herbata z cytrynem	tea with lemon
	served without milk
kompot	stewed fruit drink of plums and pears which can also be a dessert

Beware!

smalec	lard
ryby	fish
mieso	meat
drób	poultry

Jadlodajnia

(types of eateries)

Bar Mleczny	Milk Bar
Stołówka	Canteen
Restauracja	Restaurant
Bar / Kawiarnia	Café

and, we can't escape them, fast-food establishments and pizzerias.

WARSAW

by Anna Truszkowska

Mata Hari
Nowy Swiat 52
Warsaw
Tel: 022-828 64 28
Metro: Ordynacka
Open: Mon-Sat 11-19.00
Tiny Indian vegetarian, 90% vegan, take-away and cafe with a few seats to eat in. Several kinds of salads - also hot ones - 3.2zl, or which 3 are always vegan. Soups with one vegan choice 3.2zl. Starters like samosas, pakora, kachori. Main meals 2.8-4.8zl like buckwheat or vegetable cutlets and stuffed peppers. Great variety of sweets 2-2.5zl. such as oat cookies with currants, sugar-free fruit and nut balls and fruit-filled buns. Herb or fruit tea 1.8-2zl.

Nowe Miasto
Rynek Nowego Miasta 13/15
Warsaw 00229
Tel: 022-831 43 79
Open: Mon-Sun 10-late
Mainly vegetarian restaurant, except that they serve also fish and seafood. You can eat there while listening to live music - guitar, violin, jazz - 5 times a week. A few vegan dishes. Starters including soups 9-21zl. Selection of salads 19-21zl. Main course like soya cutlets with shitake mashrooms, tofu cheese fried with shitake mushrooms or green lasagne with spinach, courgettes and broccoli 25-27zl. Wholegrain desserts 9-12zl such as soya pudding or sweet wheat dessert. French and German selected wines. Credit cards accepted.

Vega

ul. Jana Pawła II, 23B
Round the back of the Femina cinema
Warsaw 00141
Tel: 022-654 41 11
Bus or tram stop : Kino "Femina"
Open: Mon-Fri 11-17.00
A vegetarian cafe owned by "Pozywienie darem serca" (Food - a gift of the heart) foundation. Cheap and delicious, all veggie and 90% vegan, get your lunch here for about 5zl. Vegan choices also available. Soup (usually vegan) 1.5zl. Main dishes such as sabji (hot mixed vegetables), cutlets of peas or tofu cheese1.5-2zl. Daily changing menu. Some salads 3zl. Rice or cereals 1.5zl. Cakes 1.5-3zl but vegan choice not always available. Herb tea 1.5zl. They also do take-away.

Health Food Shops in Warsaw

New health food shops (sklepi ze zdrowa zywnosc) are spring-
ing up all the time and as we go to press we've just heard of a
new central shop in a street called Grojecka, with another
belonging to the same owner in Targowa.   Usually they are
small places, crammed full of miscellaneous wares - literature,
posture stools and now organic produce.   Service is usually
nice and polite, but perhaps not as profesional as you're used
to since owners are not necessarily vegetarians or trained nutri-
tionists. (Though if you've ever asked how to cook something
in Holland & Barrett....) Prices are high for Poles. Here we list
some central shops followed by a few in the suburbs.

A hot tip from a British vegan who regularly visits Warsaw:
McVities digestive biscuits in Poland are vegan, made there to
a different recipe and slightly smaller than in the UK.

Biosan
Ul. Poznanska 26, Central Warsaw
Tel: 621 27 61

Dormi
Al. Wyzwolenia 3/5, Central Warsaw
Tel: 621 81 00

Rosanna
Ul. Nowy Swiat 33, Central Warsaw
Tel: 826 44 03

Zdrowa Zywnosc
Ul. Zlota 11, Central Warsaw
Tel: 826 93 64

Zrodlo Zycia

Ul. Foksal 8, Central Warsaw
Tel: 827 76 11 w.11

Sante

Ul Sucha 29, Tartowek
Warsaw (East)
Tel: 679 59 77

Pestka

Ul. Woloska
Warsaw (south-west)
Tel: 844 06 61

Biosmak

Rondo Waszynglona
Praga, Warsaw (south-east)
Tel: 616 02 37

Feniks

Ul. Topograficzna 11/28
Rembertow, Warsaw (south-east)
Tel 612 91 44

Gaja

Al. "Bora" Komorowskiego 4
Goclawek, Warsaw (south-east)

Sante

Ul. Przydrozna 1
Warsaw (north-east)
Tel: 811 50 37

Warszawa Vegetarian Society meets at ul. Elektoralna 12 on the first Thursday of the month.

KRAKÓW

by Zofia Torun

This year Kraków is the official European city of Culture and will be celebrating in style. It still remains the cultural and intellectual capital of Poland, home to Nobel prize winners for Literature Wisława Szymborska and Czesław Milosc, contemporary composer Krzysztof Penderecki and film directors Andrzej Wajda and Roman Polanski.

The Communists attempted to destroy and overshadow Kraków's rich past by building the huge steel works Nowa Huta on the outskirts in the seventies. Whilst not bringing about the industrial "dream", it has left instead a legacy of very serious pollution in the area.

Alongside the Wistula river, the Renaissance Wawel castle stands proud. Former home of the royal dynasties, its tiny cathedral is a royal resting-place. In more recent times, it was used as a barracks by invading Austrians and Nazis. Popular legend says that a dragon lives beneath the castle.

The old medieval city centre will enchant you, with its narrow cobbled street and lovely main square and Cloth Hall (Sukiennice). Kraków has a staggering number of beautiful churches, both baroque and gothic, such as Kosciol Mariacki (the restored Basilica) - listen out for the bugle. The Jagiellonian University is medieval in origin, where Mikolaj Kopernik (Copernicus) studied and where the present Pope lectured as a Bishop. Wadowice, just outside Krakow, is the birthplace of Pope John Paul II and therefore a place of interest and pilgrimage for many.

The incredible Wielicka salt mines lie 8 miles outside Krakow and are well worth a visit. The mines have been in operation for the last 700 years and are on UNESCO's World Heritage List. Venture down deep and behold the lakes, the ballroom complete with chandelier, the statues and the Chapel of Blessed Kinga, all made out of salt! Owing to its salubrious conditions, a sanatorium has been set up down in the mine.

Kazimierz, the Jewish Quarter since 1335, which Schindler's List made famous, is a must and just a short walk form the centre. Although it occupies such a small, dilapidated area, it is of great historic and cultural importance and is now enjoying an injection of new life and investment. Little remains, but there are seven synagogues to visit and the cultural centre puts on regular concerts and performances. Oswiecim, otherwise known as Auschwitz, the infamous Nazi concentration camp, is a haunting place where many wish to pay their respects. It is about one and three-quarter hours away.

After you've seen the delights of Kraków, head down into the Carpathian Mountains to Zakopane. You can ski in winter and in summer take a tranquil raft ride down the Dunajec river and Pieniny Gorge with a highlander guide. Look out for the eagles!

What goes on in Kraków? Opera, theatre, concerts, exhibitions, film festivals and more. Kraków boast an incredible diversity and an impressive programme for all tastes.

Kraków is quite good for vegetarians. There are a few Middle Eastern eateries in the centre so falafel snacks are easy to come by. Chinese, Mexican, Italian and Indian restaurants increase the veggie options. On the streets you can buy obwarzanki, which are similar to bagels and perfect if you're peckish.

Bar Vega

ul. Sw. Gertrudy 7
Tel: 422 3494
Open: 10-21.00 daily
Live pianist on Sundays. One of three Vega offering fantastic value. Soya kebabs, tofu, soups, cakes, pancakes, freshly made juices, the best pierogi! Extremely popular. Order food at the counter.

Bar Vega

ul. Krupnicza 22
Tel: 430 0846
Open: 9-23.00 daily
Another branch.

Vega

ul. Szeroka 3, Kazimierz
Open: 9-23.00 daily
And this one is an actual restaurant.

Salad Bar Rozowy Słon

Ul. Straszewskiego 24
Tel: 423 0757
Pay by weight of your food. Salads and a vast selection of pancakes. Fun wacky cartoon-strip décor. Very popular with students, bright and cheap.

Salad Bar Chimera

Ul. Sw. Anny 3, basement.
In a lovely 15th century cellar below its smarter (less veggie-friendly) restaurant. Great selection of fresh salads, fresh juices, big breakfasts. In the summer it spreads out into the pretty ground level courtyard.

Chimera II
Ul. Gołebia 2
Another salad bar with live music in the evenings. Excellent for brunch!

Health food shop
Ul. Zamenhofa 1
Tel/fax: 411 4868
Tel: 421 9353
Open: Mon-Fri 9-18.00, Sat 9-14.00.
Very good selection of organic food, toiletries and literature.

Another health food shop
Ul. Królewska 57
Tel: 637 1866 ext.663

Kraków Vegetarian Society
Tel: 422 2220
This has been running for eight years and meets twice a month for talks. On the first Sunday of the month they meet at 11am at Wojewódzki Osrodek Kultury, Rynek Główny 25. On the third Tuesday at 5pm at Klub Zaułek, ul.Poselska 9.

GDANSK, SOPOT & GDYNIA

by Anna Truszkowska

Gdansk, Gdynia and Sopot are all close together by the sea. There are great beaches nearby and you can get a boat to Scandinavia.

Green Way

Ul. Garncarska 4/6
Gdansk 80-894
Tel: 058-301 41 21
Bus or tram stop: Gdansk Głowny PKP or Hucisko
Open: Mon-Sun 10-22.00
All vegetarian cafe and takeaway with some vegan dishes. Calm and nice atmosphere inside. In season they may close much later than 22.00. Soup 3-3.5 zl always vegan. Different kinds of pitta 3.5-4.0 zl. Salads 1.5-2.0 zl. Main courses like soya or lentil cutlets, samosas, pakora served with rice, curry sauce and a few kinds of salads 6.5-8.5 zl. Desserts include pancakes with peaches, apples, strawberries or blueberries and cakes like granola, carrot cake, cheese cake with apple 2.0 zl. Non-alcoholic cocktails/smoothies 3.5zl, juices 2.5 zl, fruit tea 1.5 zl, coffee 2 zl.
Green Way also has branches in Sopot, Gdynia and Gdansk-Zabianka.

Green Way

PKP Station
Gdansk
Tel: 058-554 84 89
Open: Every day 11-23
See other entries for Green Way.

Green Way

Ul Abrahama 24
Gdynia 81 366
Tel: 058-620 15 23
Open: Every day 11-23.00
See other Green Way entries.

Restauracyjka Wegetarianska

Ul Bytomska 36
Gdynia-Orlowo 81 509
Tel: 058-664 60 84
Bus or trolley bus stop : Plac Gornoslaski
Open: Every day 12-21.00
Go to Gdynia -Orlowo, past Plac Gornaslaski, turn left and you'll get to the small but lovely cafe owned by two fashion design-ers. Friendly atmosphere and relaxed music. Tasty and healthy food with some vegan choices.

Starters like three sandwiches, two soya cutlets with slices of homemade bread and sauce or Greek salad 4.5-6.5 zl. Main dishes 10-12 zl for example soya or veg cutlets, grilled veg or veggie goulash with potatoes, rice or cereals, sauce and pick-led cucumber or salad. Mushroom or veg pizza 9 zl. Cakes 3zl. On Thursday "Porridge for Soul"- free of charge. Hot drinks 3 zl, cold drinks 2-5 zl. Homemade wholemeal bread 5-9.5 zl for a loaf. No smoking, no alcohol. They do take-away, organise ban-quets and special events.

Green Way

Ul Powstancow Warszawy 2/4/6
(w Rotondzie Panstowej Galerii Sztuki)
Sopot 81-718
Tel: 058-551 24 58
Open: Mon-Sun 11-to the last client
Located in rotunda with a terrace, near the pier and next door to the National Gallery of Art, beside the entry to the famous Mole in Sopot. A perfect place to rest after a nice walk on the

beach. Large windows,stylish and light interior. Same food as other Green Ways.
11am. It has a terrace. Near the pier.

Green Way

Ul.Bohaterów Monte Casino 67
Pavillion 14
Sopot 81 759
Tel: 0501-495 346
Open: Mon-Sun 11-23 sometimes later.
See other Green Way entries.

PORTUGAL

By Katrina Holland

Portugal is a wonderful country in so many ways. The scenery is beautiful, along the coast and inland. There are tiny villages scattered all over the country all with their own unique qualities. The people are very friendly and even though out of the main cities a great proportion don't speak English, communication always seems to be possible. They don't get frustrated with you if you can't speak Portuguese.

Lisbon is fantastic for vegetarians and vegans. Out of Lisbon, it is still possible to find vegetarian cafés and restaurants, but if you can't then most restaurants are happy to cater for you. Evora is a town you'll likely pass through on the way into Portugal from southern Spain.

EVORA

Pane & Vino

Páteo do Salema 22
Évora 7000
Tel: 266 746960
Open: 12.00-15.00 and 18.30-23.00
Omnivorous pizza and pasta restaurant. Has a large selecton of salads. A mixed salad costs 450$ and is quite tasty, consisting of a lot more than just lettuce and tomato. Vegetarian pizza is on the menu and they are happy to make it without cheese. The veggie pizza has a topping of tomato, capsicum, onion, mushrooms, artichoke hearts and broccoli and costs 1200$. They served complimentary freshly baked bread. If you are more in the mood for pasta, they have Napolitana sauce on the menu, which is vegetarian, but if you are vegan, check. Book a table if you are arriving much after 19.00, as although the

restaurant is large it fills up quickly. The menu is in English as well as Portuguese and our waiter spoke English.

LISBON

Celeiro Dieta

Rua Primeiro de Dezembro, 65
Lisbon 1200
Tel: 21-3422463
Metro: Restauradores
Open: 9.00-20.00

Large health food shop, which is part of a chain. Has everything from soy milk to ready made sandwiches and salads. If you are vegan and suffering withdrawal symptoms from chocolate and and icecream, this is where to get your fix. You can get soya icecream, yoghurts and Provamel desserts, as well as Plamil chocolate and mayonnaise. They also stock a large range of cruelty free toiletries. There is a vegetarian cafeteria downstairs which is open for lunch.

ESSENTIAL PORTUGUESE

I am a vegetarian
Eu sou vegetariano (m), Eu sou vegetariana (f)

I'm vegan
Eu sou vegan

I don't eat meat, chicken or fish
Eu não como carne, frango ou peixe

I don't eat eggs, milk, butter, cheese or honey
Eu não como ovos, leite, manteiga, queijo ou mel

Espiral

Praça da Ilha do Faial 14 A
Estefânia, Lisbon
Tel: (0) 21 357 3585
Metro: Saldanha
Open: 12.00-21.30 (until 23.00 on Sat)
Good macrobiotic food in a nice environment. Music on Saturdays. Vegan friendly.

Os Tibetanos

R. Salitre, 117
Av. da Liberdade
Lisbon
Tel: (0) 21 384 2028
Metro: Avenida
Open: 12.00-14.30 and 19.30-21.30. Closed Sun. Call to check on national holidays.
Vegetarian restaurant.   Good for food, yoga and Buddhism. Vegan friendly.

Restaurant O Sol

Calçada do Duque 23
Baixa, Lisbon
Tel: (0) 1 347 1944
Metro: Restauradores or Rossio
Open: Open for lunch and dinner.   Closes at 20.00.   Closed Sundays.
Vegetarian cafeteria style restaurant.   Mostly vegan.   Select your food from behind the counter and they will heat it up for you. Menu varies daily but the food available is generally salad, soup, tofu flan, rice, stir fry, croquettes and desserts. Reasonably priced. Licenced to sell beer. Fresh juice is available. Tables inside and outside.

Unimave

Rua Mouzinho da Silveira, 25
Marquês de Pombal, Lisbon
Tel: (0) 21 355 7362
Metro: Marquês
Open: 12.00-21.00 weekdays, 12.00-14.00 Sat, Closed Sun.
Restaurant with good vegetarian and macrobiotic food.   Vegan friendly.

Yin Yang

Rua dos Correeiros 14, piso 1
Baixa, Lisbon
Tel: (0) 21 342 6551
Metro: Rossio
Open: Lunchtime and dinnertime weekdays. Closed on week-ends.
Macrobiotic shop and restaurant. Vegan friendly.

VEGANS OF THE WORLD, UNITE!

I am vegetarian
Ya veghetarianyets (m), Ya veghetarianka (f)

I am vegan   Ya vegan (m), Ya veganka (f)

I do not eat meat, chicken
Ya nye yem nyee myasa, nyee kureetsoo, nyee reebee

I do not eat eggs, milk, butter, cheese or honey
Ya nye yem yaitsa, malako, maaslo, seer i myod

Please   Pozhalsta (zh like s in pleasure)
Thank you   Spaseeba
Yes   Da
No   Nyet

RUSSIA

MOSCOW

Being A Vegetarian in Moscow

by Tatyana Pavlova
President of the Russian Vegetarian Society

There is no statistic as to the number of vegetarians in Moscow, or even in Russia. There are quite a few of us because vegetarianism is becoming more and more popula and it does not sound funny any more to be a vegetarian, at least among the more civilised part of the public. Vegans are still scarce.

Having meals in towns has become a problem during the last few years. Before inflation and the economic difficulties, there were quite a lot of cafés and canteens around the city where one could have a meal at a reasonable price. Lately food has become rather expensive, the cafes and canteens supported by the state did not pay and were closed, so only private ones are functioning. They are too expensive for the Russian consumer and are patronised only by the rich.

The majority of Muscovites prefer to have meals at home which is cheaper, or to take a packed lunch from home. There still exist state supported canteens at colleges, publishing houses, ministries and so on which are less expensive than commercial establishments. They all serve meat. If a vegetarian visits such a canteen he or she can choose a milk soup (with noodles or rice for example), vegetables or cereals for the main course and sometimes pancakes. For a vegan the choice is narrower, it is mainly salads, vegetables or cereals (rice, buckwheat, pasta, mashed or fried potatoes). At most restaurants you are expected to order meat courses and will not find it easy to be served just grains or potatoes.

The Vegetarian Society in Moscow made attempts to co-operate with restaurants and persuade them to serve vegetarian food. None of them wished to take the risk, as most vegetarians are too poor or too busy to go across the city to have lunch or dinner in a restaurant.

Nevertheless, vegetarian cafes in Moscow have been opened. The first was a Hare Krishna café and lately two more appeared, one belonging to the society *The Way to Himself* oriented towards Eastern philosophy, and a kind of club of the group '*Pushkin*'. All of them are functioning not for the sake of profits but to promote the religous and ethical views of those societies. The Krishna Society is located near the Begovaya Metro station, 'The Way to Himself' is close to the Byelorussian Underground Station and the Pushkin club is in the centre of Tverskaya Street, in the First Greznikovsky Lane. The Krishna Society offers Indian food and so does the Pushkin Club.

The following supplementary information was provided by Toni Vernelli of PETA Europe.

There are western style restaurants in Moscow that are too expensive for Russians serving vegetarian and vegan food close to Red Square, particularly on and around Tverskaya Street. For example the Moscow Bombay Indian, a little Greek place that has separate vegetarian menus, and a Mexican place called La Cantina on Tverskaya Street. Paddy O'Pizza and Paddy O'Pasta are two new chains with vegan pizza or you can dive into their huge salad bars.

ST PETERSBURG

by Natalia Tsobkallo
St Petersburg Vegetarian Society

Troitsky Most

9/2 Kamennoostrovsky Prospekt
St Petersburg
Tel: 326 82 21
Metro station Gorovskaja
Open: Daily round the clock.
24 hour vegetarian café. Meals are delicious and not expensive.

Troitsky Most

35 Kronversky Pr
St Petersburg
Tel: 232 66 93
Metro station Gorovskaya
Open: All day
24 hour vegetarian café. Serves delicious and cheap food.

Idiot

Moyki 82
near Isaakievskaya Ploshad
St Petersburg
Tel: 812-315 16 75
Open: Every day 11.0024.00
Russian restaurant and bar with plenty for veggies and they told us they could do it without cheese (byez sira).

Kalifornia Grill

Nevsky Prospect 176
St Petersburg 193024
Tel: 2747470
Metro station Ploshad Aleksandra Nevskovo (Alexander Nevsky Sq.)
Open: 11.30-2 or 3 am (when last guest leaves)
Omnivorous American, Mexican and European food. Large TV showing sport and music channels. 13 vegetarian dishes 72-189 roubles including soups, veggie burgers, salads and tortillas with salsa, but sadly nothing appears to be vegan. House wine 120 R, beer 30-80 R, coffee 40 R. Takes Visa, Mastercard, Union Card, Eurocard, AmEx, JCB and Diners. English menu and English speaking staff.

Ochag

2 Zagorodny Prospekt
St Petersburg 191002
Tel: 812-1646642
Metro station Vladimirskaya, Dostoevskaya
Open: Every day 10-21.00
European, Oriental and Russian omnivorous restaurant / café in the very center of the city, not far from Nevsky Prospekt and near the beautiful Vladimirskaya church. Heaps of vegetarian dishes from 20 to 60 roubles (US$0.7-2.00). Starters include vegetable or mushroom or Russian country soup 30R, onion soup with toast 20R; Greek or vegetable salad 30R. Main courses tend to include cheese or sour cream so vegans make sure you have a copy of the Vegan Society's Vegan Passport: aubergines stuffed with vegetables 50R, potato pancakes with mushrooms 60R, fried potato with vegetable salad 50R. Desserts include fruit salad, pies, rolls, biscuits, cakes, ice-cream with nuts or fruit or chocolate 20R (probably not vegan, though we know that Swedish Glace is available in Moscow). Wine 90-300R (US$3-10) per bottle, beer 15-50R, coffee 15R. Outside seating in summer. No smoking. Menu in English, staff speak Russian.

Pizza Hut

96 Nevsky Prospekt
corner Moika embankment & Gorokhovaya St
St Petersburg
Tel: 812-315 77 05
Metro Mayakovskaya
Open: Every day 10.00-23.00
Not exactly a vegetarian restaurant but it's conveniently open all the time, they speak English, and of course vegans can ask for a pizza without cheese. Dine in, take out with slice bar open 24 hours.

Tandoor

2 Voznesensky Pr
near St. Isaac's Cathedral
St Petersburg 190000
Tel: 312 38 86
Open: Every day 12-23.00
Indian restaurant with good vegetarian selection. 14 Vegetarian and vegan dishes, average price 200 roubles, including vegetable samosas, pakoras, spinach and potato, vegetable korma. Can cater for special diets on request. They take Visa, Mastercard, Diners and AmEx cards. High chairs for children and children's portions. English menu and staff speak English.

SCOTLAND

EDINBURGH

by Jennifer Wharton

The Greenhouse

14 Hartington Gardens, Bruntsfield, Edinburgh EH10 4LD
Tel: 0131-622 7634
Website: www.greenhouse-edinburgh.com
Email: Greenhouse_Edin@hotmail.com
Open all year; Winter- ensuite £25 p/p, non-ensuite £20.
Summer ensuite £30/35.

This friendly vegetarian guesthouse is a twenty minute walk from the centre, and Hugh and Suzanne offer a warm welcome to all guests. Committed to both quality of service and lovers of vegetarian food, using organic and GM free ingredients where possible, they provide a veritable breakfast feast for veggies and vegans alike. On the standard menu you can choose from a full Scottish breakfast (vegan): rashers/organic tempeh, veggie sausage and mushrooms with baked beans, hashbrowns, tomatoes, and toast with scrambled tofu. Other breakfast choices include bagels with tofutti cream cheese (vegan); a selection of croissants or brioches; scrambled tofu with mushrooms on toast; pancakes with maple syrup. Always available soya milk, organic vegan margarine, fruit juices, various cereals, fruit salad and vegan yoghurt. All rooms include tea and coffee making facilities with vegan hot chocolate included. Even the soaps and the bedding are vegan and the rooms are decorated with environmentally friendly paint. Hugh and Suzanne also give guests a free map of Edinburgh with veggie places highlighted for easy reference. Families are welcome and children under three are free, 4-12 years £15. A number of parking spaces also available. All rooms are smoke free. Winter rates Oct-May and summer rates Jun-Sept.

Six Marys Place

6 Marys Place, Raeburn Place,
Stockbridge, Edinburgh EH4 1JH
*http://ourworld.compuserv.com/homepages/ECT_Socia_*
Tel: 0131-332 8965
3 single & 3 double £28-£30, 2 twin en suite £32-£35
Vegetarian guest house. Restored Georgian townhouse with dining conservatory and gardens, centrally located and a short walk from the Royal Botanical Gardens. With tea/coffee and tv in room if requested, also tv lounge. Usual veggie breakfasts and 3 course dinner for £9 which can be veganized. Also 5% discount for VSUK members.

Castle Rock Hostel

15 Johnston Street, near the castle,
Edinburgh EH1 2PW
0131-225 9666
Open all year
Flagship hostel and the largest of the three in Edinburgh run by Scotland's Top Hostels organization (others are High Street Hostel and Royal Mile Backpackers). Fantastic location next to the castle and 225 beds. Prices are the same as the High Street Hostel. They have a laundry service, and they feature a different movie every night. Again note price increase during festival.

High Street Hostel

8 Blackfriars Street,
Edinburgh EH11NE
101357.553@compuserv.com
0131-220 1869
Open all year
This is a 24 hour hostel with 140 beds costing £10.50 (add 30p if paying by credit card), increasing to around £12.00 during the festival. Facilities include a well-equipped kitchen, showers, pool table, juke box and dining area. There is no curfew and late bookings are usually accepted, although as with other hostels it is advisable to book first.

Royal Mile Backpackers

105 High Street, Edinburgh EH1 1SG
0131-557 6120

Open all year. Part of chain run by Scotland's Top Hostels organisation.

This centrally located hostel provides 38 beds at £10.50 per bed. Facilities include small basic kitchen with toaster and microwave (for residents use only), and reception area/diner. No curfew but last booking accepted at midnight. Dormitories sleep around eight people. Note that prices increase to £12.00 during the festival and booking in advance is always advisable. Residents can also do their cooking in their sister hostel the High Street Hostel.

The Engine Shed Cafe

19 St Leonards Lane, Edinburgh EH8 9SD
0131-662 0040
Mon-Thurs 10.30-15.30, Fri 10.30-14.30,
Sat 10.30-16.00, Sun 11.00-16.00.

Vegetarian café run by charitable organization Garvald Community Enterprises working with people with learning difficulties. Said to be the best value for money vegetarian food in town, weekdays the café is subsidised so low prices. Menu changes daily. Soup 85p, salads 65p a selection. Mains such as roast veg & cous cous, lasagne, baked spuds £1.95. Also organic bread supplied from nearby Engine Shed Bakery. Vegan desserts like apple crumble, fruit salad or passion pudding £1.25. Tea 60p, cafetiere of free-trade coffee 85p. A children -friendly café.

Ann Purna

45 St Patrick's Square, Edinburgh EH8 9ET
0131-662-1807
Mon-Fri 12.00-14.00 &17.30-23.00 Sun 17.00-22.00
Family run vegetarian Indian (Gujarati) restaurant, with staff happy to provide vegan versions of the few non-vegan menu items. The food is wonderful and they have special lunch prices Mon-Fri from £4.95. Sample vegan dishes include Milli-Jilli-Sabzi (mixed veg curry) £5.25, with brown rice £1.85; also Bahar-e-Nau-Korma (mixed veg curry in soya cream, coconut &almond) £5.90, with basmati rice £2.25.

Bann's Vegetarian Cafe

5 Hunter Square, (Royal Mile), Edinburgh EH1 1QW
Website: www.scoot.co.uk/banns/
0131-226 1112
Every day 10.00-23.00
Situated off the Royal Mile, combining modern décor with candlelight makes this eatery popular with tourists and locals alike. At least half the menu is vegan. Veggie breakfast £5, starters from £1.75 include bruschetta, patés, hummous, bhajis, etc. up to £5 for a tostada (tortillas with salsa and re-fried beans). Baked potatoes. Mains £5-£7.50 chilli, curry, veggie haggis, burgers, enchiladas, nut parcels etc. Selection of salads as mains or sides. Enticing desserts from £2.20. House wine £7.40. They do soyacinno. Students discount.

Black Bo's

57-61 Blackfriars Street, Edinburgh EH1 1NB
0131-557 6136
Mon-Sat 12.00-14.00 & Mon-Sun 18.00- 22.30
Has been acclaimed for its vegetarian cordon vert dishes with the chef dedicated to providing imaginative and fllavoursome meals. Four starters are vegan at £4.95 including chickpea chilli with coriander; avocado stuffed with passion fruit & lemon sorbet: 3 vegan main courses at £9.95 including mushrooms with back olive roulade; tomato and tarragon; haggis with shish-

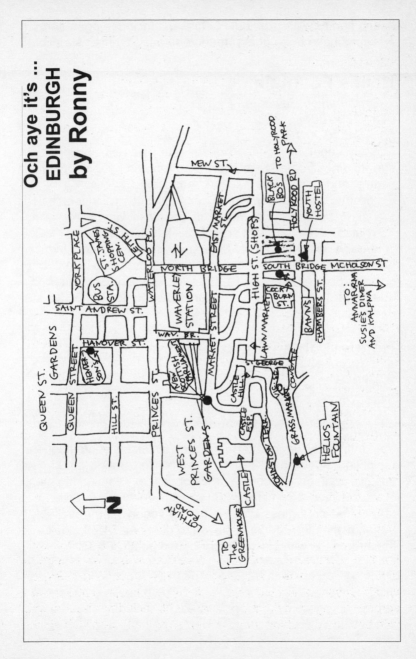

kebab flambé with drambuie. Desserts include vegan sorbert. All wines have been guaranteed vegetarian by their supplier.

Helios Fountain
7 Grassmarket, Edinburgh EH1 2HY
0131-229 7884
Mon-Sat 10.00-18.00, Sun 12.00-16.00
Friendly vegetarian coffee house, with pleasant and peaceful surroundings fronted by a charming craft and book shop. Many veggie and vegan dishes and reasonable prices. All of the soups and salads are vegan, examples being pasta salad, tabouleh, beetroot and melon in basalmic vinegar dressing. They also have a range of organic breads. Vegan mains include cottage pie with salad at £4.85 and savourary avocado tart with salad at £4.75. Vegan desserts include chocolate & coconut crunch 95p, orange cake £1.75, almond & cherry cookies 75p and sugar-free banana & yoghurt cake. Special offer for students soup + bread/rice cakes and 2 salads for £2.95.

Henderson's Bistro Bar
25B Thistle Street,
Edinburgh EH2 1DX
0131-225 2605
Mon-Sat 12.00-20.00, Sun 12.00-17.00. Extended hours during festival.
Vegan friendly vegetarian wine bar with cosy atmosphere. Lunchtime specials (12-3pm) available for around £6.95 gets you two courses and choice of tea or coffee. The evening menu starts between 4-7pm, for £8.50 you can enjoy two courses with tea, coffee or a glass of wine (some vegan wines available). Vegan dishes include lentil stew and potatoes £4.75; leek and mushroom pie with side salad or baked potato £4.75.

Henderson's Salad Table

94 Hanover Street, Edinburgh EH2 1DR
0131-225 2131
Mon-Sat 8.00-late, Sun 10.00-22.00.
Perhaps the most famous and oldest vegetarian restaurant in town. Porridge, muesli, croissants, toast etc. 95p-£1.95 for breakfast. All day menu includes soup, burgers, patties, pasties, quiches, pizza £1.20-£2.20. Selection of 16 salads with 3 salads for £2 or £1 each. Typical mains are nut loaf £3.20, veg haggis with neeps and taties £3.20; risotto, stuffed aubergine, lentil lasagne £3.50. Various desserts, some vegan (ask at counter), £2-3. Local real ales, organic wines. Live music ranging from jazz to Scottish folk every evening from 19.30.

Isabel's Café

Underneath Nature's Gate, 83 Clerk Street,
Edinburgh EH8 9JG
0131-662 4014
Mon-Sat 11.30-18.30, closed Sunday. (opens 10.30 during festival)
Relaxing basement wholefood vegan and vegetarian café. Starters £1.50-£2.25 like (vegan) soup, burger with roll £1.75, salads including carrot and coriander, and lentil dhal with potato. Mains £3.50 such as kebabs, pasta, stuffed marrow, crumble, haggis with neeps & tatties, baked potatoes with coleslaw or hummus. Desserts £1.45-1.75 include plum crumble, apple pie, baked bananas, and vegan cakes are always available. Herbal teas, mineral water and natural soda.

Kalpna

2/3 St. Patrick's Square,
Edinburgh EH8 9EZ
0131-667 9890
Mon-Fri 12.00-14.00, 17.30-23.00; Sat 5.30-23.00.
Open Sun in summer.
Multi-regional Indian wholefood vegetarian restaurant acclaimed for its fine foods. Not surprisingly Kalpna's is popular so booking is recommended for evening meals. Buffet lunch is available for the very reasonable price of £4.75 or regional gourmet buffet dinner for £8.95 on Wednesday evenings between 17.30-23.00. Kalpna's also offers discount to members of the Vegetarian Society.

Susie's Wholefoods Diner

51 -53 West Nicolson Street, opposite the pear tree,
Edinburgh EH8 9DB
susies@ednet.co.uk
0131-667 8729
Mon -Sat 9.00-22.00, Sun 12.30-21.00.
Extended hrs during festival.
Bountiful vegetarian/vegan café were you'll be spoilt for choice with at least 7 (3 or 4 vegan) hot dishes. Salads available every day, and limitless combinations of both. Relaxed menu rules allow you to combine several hot and cold dishes together, order a small plate is £3.95 or large £5.15 and make up your own veritable feast. Staff are happy to tell which dishes are vegan. Standard fare includes veggie-burgers, vegan soups, falafel and hummus combo plate. Also a range of hot and cold desserts including cakes and fruit crumbles with at least 2 vegan desserts with cashew nut cream. Susie's is licensed and offers many house wines and beers. Live music at the weekend and they play host to 'fabulous vege Belly Dancing Nights'

The Baked Potato Shop
Royal Mile, Edinburgh EH1 1PB
0131-225 7572
Mon-Sun 9.00-21.00 Extended hours during festival.
Not just your usual spud! For veggies on the go, vegetarian and vegan tattie shop with loads of hot and cold fillings from £2.35. Veg kebabs £1.60. Salads such as Greek salad, curried rice, Waldorf salad, soups, filled rolls and pastries. Also sell scrumptious looking vegetarian and vegan cakes from 55p. There is a small seating area for around 4 people.

Jordan Valley Wholefoods
8 Nicolson Street, Edinburgh EH8 9DJ
0131-556 6928
Mon-Sat 10.00-20.00, Sun 12.00-18.00
Jordan Valley make their own range of vegetarian and vegan pates, pies, dips and pastries.

Margiotta's
77 Warrender Park Road, Marchmont,
Edinburgh EH9 1ES
0131-229 2869
Mon-Sat 7.30-22.00, Sun 8.00-21.00
Margiotta's is recommended to be a reliable source for veggie and vegan snacks and they seem to be expanding with new branches across the city.

Real Foods
37 Broughton Street, Edinburgh EH1 3JU
0131-557 1911
Mon-Fri 9.00-18.00, Sat 9.00-17.30, Sun 11.00-17.00
Edinburgh's largest retailer of wholefood and health products. Many of their products are organic. As well as snack foods they sell organic breads, also vegan wines and foods that are clearly labeled. There is another branch at no. 8 Brougham Street EH3 9JH, which is open an hour later on Thurs. tel. 0131-228 1201.

I am vegetarian
Soy vegetariano (m), Soy vegetariana (f)

I'm a vegan
Soy vegano, Soy vegana

I do not eat meat, chicken, fish
Yo no como carne, pollo, pescado

I do not eat eggs, milk, butter, cheese or honey
No como los huevos, la leche, la mantequilla, el queso o la miel

Please   Por favor
Thank you   Gracias
Yes   Sí
No   No

SPAIN

by Katrina Holland

Spain is a fantastic getaway from the UK. Flights to Madrid, Malaga and Barcelona are getting more and more competitive. And once you are there it is a very easy country to travel around by bus and train. There is so much to do and see in Spain, but it is also a great place to just relax and unwind, especially out of the major cities.

Spain is not known as being a very accommodating country for vegetarians and vegans. However this is all changing. Vegetarian restaurants are popping up all over the country. Certainly in Madrid and Barcelona, there are plenty of restaurants and cafés to choose from. But even in the smaller cities like Seville and Granada, there are vegetarian restaurants around.

ALICANTE

by David Roman

Caña de Azucar
Calle Fora Mur, 3 bajos
03700 Denia, Alicante
Tel: 610-85 58 53
Open: every day 12-16.00, 19-23.00, winter open all day (breakfast included) as a teashop.
Tea shop and vegetarian restaurant with organically grown ingredients. Local cuisine, every day with a different menu ranging from 1100 to 1300 pesetas depending on the ingredients. Always inquire about the use of dairy and eggs. Quiet and very special atmosphere.

¿Habla Vegetariano?

FRUIT	FRUTAS	VEGETABLES	VERDURAS
apricots	albaricoques	aubergines	berenjenas
apples	manzanas	beetroot	remolacha
bananas	plátanos	broccoli	brécol
blackcurrants	casis /	carrots	zanahorias
	grosella negra	cabbage	col repollo
cherries	cerezas	cauliflower	coliflor
grapes	uva	courgettes	calabacines
kiwi fruit	kiwi	french beans	judías
lemons	limones	garlic	ajo
mangoes	mangos	kale	col rizada
melons	melones	leeks	puerros
oranges	naranjas	mushrooms	champiñones
pears	peras	onions	cebollas
peaches	melocotones	parsnips	chirivías
plums	ciruelas	potatoes	patatas
raspberries	frambuesas	spinach	espinaca
strawberries	fresas	swede	colinabo
		peppers	pimientos
DRIED FRUIT	**FRUTA SECA**	(yellow, green,	(amarillos, verdes,
apricots	albaricoques	red)	rojos)
	(orejones)	runner beans	habichuelas
dates	dátiles	sweet potatoes	boniatos
figs	higos		
prunes	ciruela pasa	**GRAINS**	**CEREALES**
raisins	pasas (uva pasa)	barley	cebada
sultanas	pasas sultanas	breakfast cereals	cereales para
			desayuno
SALAD	**ENSALADA**	millet	mijo
avocados	aguacates	noodles	tallarines
beansprouts	germinados (brotes)	rice noodles	tallarines de arroz
celery	apio	oats	avena
cucumber	pepino	oat cakes	tortas de avena
lettuce	lechuga	pasta	pasta
spinach	espinaca	pitta bread	pan de pita
spring onions	cebollas tiernas	popcorn	palomitas de maíz
tomatoes	tomates	rice	arroz
watercress	berros	long grain	grano largo
		short grain	grano corto
HERBS	**HIERBAS**	brown rice	arroz integral
basil	albahaca	basmati	arroz basmati
bay leaves	hojas de laurel	rice cakes	tortas de arroz
coriander	coriandro	wheatgerm	germen de trigo
oregano	orégano	wholemeal bread	pan integral
parsley	perejil		
rosemary	romero	**SEEDS**	**SEMILLAS**
sage	salvia	pumpkin seeds	pipas de calabaza
SPICES	**ESPECIAS**	sesame seeds	semillas de
chilli	chile (chilli)		sésamo
cumin	cominos	sunflower seeds	pipas de girasol
ginger	jengibre		
nutmeg	nuez moscada		

NUTS	**FRUTOS SECOS**	haricot beans	judías
almonds	almendras	mung beans	soja verde,
brazils	nueces del Brasil		judía mungo
cashew nuts	anacardos	pinto beans	judías pintas
hazelnuts	avellanas	red lentils	lentejas rojas
peanuts	cacahuetes		
peanut butter	mantequilla de	**CUPBOARD**	**DESPENSA**
	cacahuete	agar-agar	agar-agar
pine kernels	piñones	baking powder	levadura
walnuts	nueces	black pepper	pimienta negra
		blackstrap	melaza
TINNED FOOD	**ALIMENTOS**	molasses	
	ENLATADOS	burgamix	burgamix
baked beans	alubias cocidas	cider vinegar	vinagre de
coconut milk	leche de coco		manzana
chick peas	garbanzos		(o de sidra)
sweetcorn	maíz dulce	cocoa powder	cacao en polvo
kidney beans	alubias	cornflour	harina de maíz,
tinned tomatoes	tomates en		maicena
	conserva	custard powder	polvo para natillas
tomato purée	tomate triturado		o flan
		dried soya mince	soja picada seca
FROZEN	**CONGELADOS**	olive oil	aceite de oliva
peas	guisantes	extra virgin	extra virgen
soya ice-cream	helado de soja	olives	aceitunas, olivas
soya mince	soja picada	mustard	mostaza
veggie sausages	salchichas	jam	compota
	vegetales	marmalade	mermelada
veggie burgers	hamburguesas	salt	sal
	vegetales	sea salt	sal marina
		seaweed	algas marinas
CHILLED	**REFRIGERADOS**	nori	nori
hummous	humus	dulse	dulse
margarine	margarina	hiziki	hiziki
miso	miso	kelp	kelp
orange juice	zumo de naranja	wakame	wakame
soya cheese	queso de soja	soft brown sugar	azúcar moreno fino
soya mayonnaise	mayonesa de soja	sosmix	sosmix
soya yogurt	yogur de soja	soya cream	crema de soja
sundried tomato	puré de tomates	soya dessert	postre de soja
paste	secos	soya milk	leche de soja
tempeh	tempeh	sunflower oil	aceite de girasol
tofu	tofu	soya sauce	salsa de soja
tomato ketchup	salsa de tomate	tahini	tahín
	ketchup	vanilla essence	esencia de vanilla
vegan pesto	pesto vegano	yeast extract	extracto de levadura
		yeast flakes	copos de levadura
PULSES	**LEGUMBRES**	nutritional yeast	levadura nutricional
aduki beans	alubias aduki	vegetable stock	pastillas de caldo
blackeye beans	alubias negras	vegetal	
butterbeans	alubias de	cubes	
	manteca	vegetable bouillon	caldo vegetal
chick peas	garbanzos		
green lentils	lentejas verdes		

L'Indret

Calle García Morato 5
Alicante 03004
Tel: 96-521 66 14
Open: only for lunc 13.00-16.30h, closed Sunday and holidays and in August.
Vegetarian restaurant, they use no eggs, but some dishes may have yoghourt or cream in them. Local cuisine, along with some international dishes. Daily inexpensive menu 1200 pts includes salad, two courses and dessert. Homely atmosphere.

Restaurante Vegetariano

Calle Pedro Lorca 13
03180 Torrevieja, Alicante
Tel: 96-670 66 83
Open: every day in summer 12.30-15.45, 18.30-23.30, closed Mondays in winter.
Vegetarian restaurant with some eccentric decoration. A la carte only with the average price of a meal about 2000 ptas. A wide variety of dishes including salads, sandwiches, pizzas, homemade breads, natural juices, smoothies etc. Menu changes every two weeks. There are few vegan options on the menu, always inquire about the use of dairy and eggs as all items are cooked fresh to order.

Restaurante Mixto Vegetariano

Plaza Santa María 2
Alicante 03002
Tel: 96-520 08 42
Open: 09.00-16.30, 19.00-03.00
Omnivorous restaurant, with both daily vegetarian and non-vegetarian menus. Daily menu for 1250 ptas including two courses, drink, bread, dessert or coffee. Local cuisine, simple and cheap dishes. Our local resident researcher didn't find it the friendliest place, but you can eat outside in the quiet small square.

Spanish Onions

The guitar aroused my body
As the sun seduced my mind
And the excitement of flamenco
Helped my spirit to unwind

Like Picasso's Golden Goat
Life shone so brightly through the haze
No I will not forget the wonder
Of those heady Spanish days!

*Bespoke and 'Ready-to-Wear' Poetry & Cards
by Bernie Laprade at www.ThePoemShop.co.uk*

BARCELONA

by Katrina Holland

Juicy Jones

C/ Cardenal casañas 7
Barcelona
Tel: 93-3024 330
Open: Open every day continuously for lunch and dinner till about midnight.
Vegan café and juice bar with a vegan proprietor. It has a bar up the front where you can sit and have a quick juice, smoothy or coffee. Also has a restaurant down the back serving a set menu for 1000ptas. This consists of a soup, main dish and a dessert. The main dish is usually a serving of rice, two different mild curries and a salad. The dessert is a fruit compote. You can order just the main dish for 750 ptas. Organic beer and wine is served. Cappucinos and smoothies are available with soy milk or dairy milk. Waiters were very friendly and spoke good English.

Govinda Hindu Vegetariano

Plaza Villa de Madrid 4
Barcelona
Tel: 318 77 29
Metro: Cataluña
Open: Every day 13.00-16.00; Tue-Sat 20.30-23.30. Closed Sun and Mon evening.
Good and friendly Indian vegetarian restaurant, though in the evening it's more expensive than other European Hare Krishna restaurants. Weekday lunch 1275 pts, dinner a la carte 2000-2500 pts. Weekend three course set menu 1750 pts. There are some vegan dishes on the a la carte menu. Temple nearby.

L'ATELIER

*vegan and vegetarian guesthouse and cookery school
Southern Spain*

Award-winning chef Jean-Claude Juston welcomes you to his exclusively veggie guesthouse and restaurant in the unspoilt village of Mecina, high in the Alpujarras mountains between Granada and the sun-drenched shores of Southern Spain.

* ***gourmet vegetarian/vegan meals*** *with fresh organic local produce*

* single, double and family rooms, most with en suite facilities

* ***spectacular scenic walks*** *far from noise and pollution*

* bed and breakfast or full/half board

* ***picturesque villages and historic Granada*** *within easy reach*

* very reasonable rates

* ***English, French, Spanish and Portuguese spoken***

* facilities for groups (maximum 12 persons)

* *vegan/vegetarian* ***cookery courses*** *(minimum 3 persons)*

* discount for Vegetarian/Vegan Society members

* *a share of profits goes to help street children in Colombia*

Contact: Jean-Claude Juston, P.O. Box 126, 18400 Orgiva, Spain.
Tel/fax: +34-958 857 501 (Spain) or +44 (0)208 265 3277 (UK)

Email: mecinilla@yahoo.com   **Website:** www.ivu.org/atelier

Self Naturista

c. de Santa Anna 13
Barcelona
Tel: 93-318 2388, 3022130
Metro: Plaza de Cataluña
Open: Mon-Sat 11.30-22.00, closed Sun and public holidays.
Self service cafeteria style vegetarian restaurant. You take a tray, line up and select your food from behind a window. The food is not kept hot, but there are microwaves which you can use to heat it up. There are some vegan items available. Spanish speaking only, but that's hardly a problem.

Comme-Bio

Via Layetana 28
Barcelona 08003
Tel: 93-319 89 68
Open: Every day 08.00 right through till 01.00, restaurant closed 16-20.00.
Very nice health food store and restaurant near the cathedral which has been listed as vegetarian though they told us they do have some organic meat. Good place for a late night (by other countries' standards) feast before heading out to dance and drink till dawn. Choice of 5 or 6 set meals at the bar 1100-1500 pts before 8pm. Organic beer and wine.

"Cheap cafés, restaurants and Mediterranean take-aways proliferate in the tiny streets of the BARRIGOTTIC, the cheapest area to eat in Barcelona, where you can get hummus, felafel and Indian dishes." - Tony Weston

1	uno	6	seis
2	dos	7	siete
3	tres	8	ocho
4	cuatro	9	nueve
5	cinco	10	diez

GRANADA

by Katrina Holland

Naturii Albayzin

Calle de la Caldereria Nueva 10
Granada
Vegetarian restaurant with some vegan options. Quite nice yet we had problems finding out what was vegan as neither the waiter nor the cook spoke English. Wear a coat if you are going during the winter as there is no heating in the restaurant. Not licenced.

Raices

avenida Pablo Picasso 30
(Aluminares)
Granada 18006
Tel: 958-12 01 03
Open: 13.30-16.00, 21.00-24.00
Vegetarian restaurant with varied international menu. Also a shop. Sometimes closed Sunday or Monday.

11	once	30	treinta
12	doce	35	treinta y cinco
13	trece	40	cuarenta
14	catorce	50	cincuenta
15	quince	60	sesenta
16	dieciséis	70	setenta
17	diecisiete	80	ochenta
18	dieciocho	90	noventa
19	diecinueve	100	cien
20	veinte	101	ciento uno
21	veintiuno	102	ciento dos
22	veintidós		

MADRID

by Katrina Holland

El Estragón Vegetariano
C/ Costanilla de San Andrés, 10 (Plaza de la Paja)
Los Austrias area.
Madrid
Tel: 91-365 89 82
Metro: La Latina
Open: every day 13.00-17.00 and 20.00-00.30 a.m. (01:30 on
weekends)
Creative ovo-lacto-vegetarian cuisine with some vegan items
available a la carte. Daily lunch menu 1200 pesetas, dinner
and weekends 2750 pesetas.

El Granero de Lavapiés
C/ Agumosa, 10
Madrid
Tel: 91-467 76 11
Metro: Lavapiés
Open: Mon-Sat 13.00-16.00, also Fri-Sat 20.30-23.00
Vegetarian restaurant serving a wide variety of dishes made
with seasonal organic fruits and vegetables. Daily lunch menu
except Sundays and holidays for 1200 pesetas, including 2
courses, dessert, coffee or tea or herb tea and bread. They
also have a health food shop at Calle Fé 9.

Restaurant La Biotika

Calle del Amor de Dios, 3
Madrid
Tel: 91-429 07 80
Metro: Antón Martin
Open: every day 13.00-16.30 and 20.00-23.30
(approx, this is España)

Vegetarian restaurant which is almost all vegan, macrobiotic oriented but with varied cuisine. It has a daily set menu for 1200 pesetas, 1300 on weekends and holidays. This consists of soup, a main course, a dessert of cake or baked apple and a cup of tea. The set menu is always vegan, but some dishes a la carte have eggs or dairy (sometimes soya milk). There is also a small health food shop at the front where you can stock up on soy milk. Licenced for alcohol.

Restaurant Integral Artemisa

C/ Ventura de la Vega, 4
(Frente a las Cortes)
Madrid
Tel: 91-429 50 92
email: artemisa@la_red.com
Metro: Antón Martin or Sevilla
Open: Lunch 14.00 onwards. Dinner 20.00 onwards.

Advertised as a vegetarian restaurant, yet unfortunately they have a few chicken dishes on the menu listed under 'non vegetarian items'. Despite this it is a very nice restaurant, with a relaxed atmosphere and delicious food.   They have a good selection of salads, entrées, mains and desserts, all reasonably priced. Some items are suitable for vegans, but if they aren't they are happy to adapt most of them. The service was very friendly and the waiters spoke English. Menus were available in English or Spanish. A great place to relax at the end of a long day's sightseeing. Open for lunch and dinner. Licenced. Fresh juice available.

Restaurant Integral Artemisa

C/ Tres Cruces, 4
(Plaza del Carmen)
Madrid
Tel: 91-521 87 21
artemisa@la_red.com
Metro: Gran Via or Sol
Open: Lunch 13.30-16/00, dinner 21.00-24.00
The second branch of Artemisa. Has the same menu and opening times. The waiters here are not as friendly and do not speak English as well. The atmosphere here is not as relaxing as the other branch and is probably more suitable for a quick meal.

Falafel Ali-ba-ba

Calle Velarde 6
Madrid
Tel: 91-448 55 20
Metro: Tribunal
Open: 12.30-16.00 and 20.00-24.00 every day
Israeli style falafel served in pitta bread, with a choice of salads and tahini sauce, 350 ptas. With hommous 50 ptas extra. Eat in or take away.

100	cien	700	setecientos
200	doscientos	800	ochocientos
300	trescientos	900	novecientos
400	cuatrocientos	1,000	mil
500	quinientos	2,000	dos mil
600	seiscientos	5,000	cinco mil

MALAGA

by Francisco Martin & Vanessa Clarke

El Legado Celestial

Calle Pelegrino no. 2
Malaga 29002
Tel: 95-235 15 21
Metro: near Alameda station and the post office
Open: Daily 13.00-16.00; 20.00-23.00 not Monday.
Chinese vegan restaurant, cheap and friendly, which unusually for Chinese places has plenty of salads. All you can eat for 850 pesetas, an incredible deal.

Comedor Naturo Vegetariana or Sonavema

Calle Carretaria 82, 1st floor
Malaga 29008
Tel: 952-47 85 72
Open: Mon-Sat 13.30-16.00, closed Sun.
Vegetarian restaurant and shop where Malaga Vegetarian Society meet. No smoking.

El Vegetariano de la Alcazabilia

Pozo del Rey 5
(opposite Albeniz cinema)
Malaga
Tel: 95-221 48 58
Open: Mon-Sat 13.30-16.00 and 21.00-23.00, closed Sun.
Average vegetarian restaurant. Mon-Fri daily set menu 1000 pesetas with soup, salad with side dishes, main course (vegetable pie or similar), dessert (kefir - a kind of sour yoghourt - or wholefood cakes). No vegan options on the menu, but they can fix up something for you.

Salomón

Calle Salomón 8
Malaga 29013
Tel: 95-226 21 46
Open: Daily 13.30-16.30, closed evenings.
Vegetarian restaurant. Daily menu for only 850 pesetas, including 3 courses and dessert.   Non smoking.

hello	hola
do you have...?	¿Tiene...?
I'd like ..., please	por favor, quisiera ...
how much?	¿Cuanto es?
OK	vale
thank you	gracias
goodbye	adiós

SEVILLE

by Katrina Holland

Bar Vegetariano Jalea Real

Sor Angela de la Cruz 37, Seville
Tel: 95-42 16 103
Open: Mon-Sat 13.30-17.00, 20.30-23.30.
Closed Sunday night.
Vegetarian restaurant that was closed when we visited and they just don't answer their phone. Let us know if you liked it.

Ha Ba Ni Ta (Previously Zucchero)

C/ Golfo 3 (Plaza Alfalfa), Seville
Tel: 606-71 64 56
Open: 12.30-16.30, 20.00-00.30, closed Sunday night.
Omnivorous restaurant with a good vegetarian selection, of which some are vegan. Cuban and Mediterranean specialties. Choice of salads. Dishes available in snack, medium or large sizes. Two dishes we tried were rice with black bean sauce and rice with 7 mushrooms. Homemade desserts including chocolate cakes. Both were simple but very nice. Licenced for alcohol. Tables inside and outside.

La Mandràgora

Calle Albuera 11, Seville
Tel: 95-422 01 84
Open: Tue-Sat 14.00-16.00, Thu-Sat 21.30-23.30.
Sun-Mon closed.
100% vegetarian, several dishes available for vegans. Daily lunch menu 1575 pesetas with several options to choose from for your two courses, drinks not included. Dinner a la carte only. Homely atmosphere. Special diets no problem, for example their traditional "gazpacho" is made with no vinegar, lemon or bread in order to avoid any incompatibilities, but still tastes excellent.

VALENCIA

by David Roman

Restaurante Casa Salud

Calle Conde de Altea 44
Valencia 46005
Tel: 96-374 43 61
Open: 13.30-16.00, 20.30-24.00
Chinese restaurant which is exclusively vegan. Eastern cuisine as well as local, with a huge variety of dishes. Very inexpensive menu at 995 pts, self-service. Also take-away food.

La Lluna

Calle San Ramón 23
(Barrio del Carmen)
Valencia 46003
Tel: 96-392 21 46
Vegetarian restaurant, with inexpensive menus. Tiny stylish place.

Les Maduixes

Calle Daoiz y Velarde 4
Valencia 46021
Tel: 96-369 45 96
Open: Mon-Sat 13.30-16.00, also Thu-Sat 21.00-23.30, closed Sunday.
Vegetarian restaurant with an inexpensive daily menu for 1300 pesetas, including salad, soup, main course (rice, quiche, pies) and herb tea, although additional dishes are somewhat more expensive. Usually made with organic produce. Always inquire about the use of dairy and eggs. Very friendly, nice and quiet atmosphere.

Restaurante Ana Eva

Calle Turia 49
Valencia 46008
Tel: 96-331 53 69
Open: 13.30-16.00, 20.30-23.00. Closed Sunday night and Mondays.
Vegetarian restaurant, located near the Quart Towers with a very nice indoor covered patio. Menu 1600 pesetas only for lunch from Tuesday to Friday, otherwise a la carte.

SWEDEN

STOCKHOLM

By **Monica Engström, Henrik Sheutz and Ulla Troëng**

Stockholm is a beautiful city built on seven islands, modern and cool with plenty of history. Everyone speaks English and there is plenty of vegetarian and vegan food. Get yourself a map and check out the islands in turn:
Gamla Stan is the central island with the Old Town.
To the north, **Norrmalm** contains the Central Station.
Kungsholmen to the west contains the City Hall.
Södermalm to the south is full of cafes.
Långholmen is a nature park.
Djurgården is unspoilt.
Skeppsholmen has the Moderna Museet in the middle.

Manna
Åsögatan 102
(Sodermalam, underground to Medborgarplatsen)
Tel: 08-640 59 69
Open: Mon-Sat 11-21.00
Brand new vegetarian restaurant which has about five vegan gourmet dishes on the menu with organic ingredients for SEK 65-85. There are also vegan cakes, coffee and a lot of teas. There is also a little store where you can buy organic vegetables, fruits, drinks, vitamins and minerals. Right now many people consider this to be the best vegetarian restaurant in town. It is also a nice place to meet other vegans, vegetarians and animal activists.

Lao Wai

Luntmakaregatan 74
close to Sveavägen
Stockholm
Tel: 08 673 78 00
Open: Tue-Sun, closed Mon, closed in Summer
Virtually vegan restaurant (except for one dessert) with very tasty, spicy food. One of the few fancy vegan places, expensive, meals cost around 100kr.

Govinda's

Fridhemsgaten 22
Stockholm
Tel: 08 654 90 02
T-station Fridhemsplan
Open: Mon-Fri 11-21.00. Sat 12-21.00
Vegetarian Hare Krisna restaurant. Little for vegans as milk is used extensively, so make sure your vegan dish really is vegan.

Malaysia

Luntmakaregatan
close to Sveavägen
Stockholm
Tel: 08 673 56 69
Open: Mon-Fri 11-14.30 and 17-22.00, Sat 15-23.00
Popular Asian restaurant. Expensive, but tasty food such as soya 'mock duck'.

Manna

Soderhallarna
Stockholm
Tel: 08 643 18 05
T- Station Medborgarplatsen
Open: Mon-Fri 11-18.00
Environmentally-friendly restaurant very popular with vegans. Two hot dishes available, along with cakes and cappuccinos.

Organic Green
Rehnsgatan 24
Stockholm
Tel: 08 612 74 84
Open: Mon-Fri 11-16.30, Sat 10-15.00
Vegetarian organic restaurant with a buffet.

Chutney
Katarina Bangata 17
Stockholm
Tel: 08 640 30 10
Open: Mon-Fri 11-22.00, Sat-Sun 11-21.00
Very nice restaurant serving 2-3 vegan meals for around 50 kr, including bread, salad, coffee and juice.

Hermans Höjdare
Fjällgatan 23 A
at Halsans Hus
Stockholm
Tel: 08 64 39 80
Open: Mon-Sat 11-21.00, also 21-23.00 in Summer
Restaurant serving vegetarian food with a fine view of the city.

Stockholm Information Service
P.O. Box 7542
S-103 93 Stockholm
Tel +46-8-789 24 00, fax +46-8-789 24 50
Email: Info@stoinfo.se, Web: www.stoinfo.se
Stockholm Information Service are pleased to inform you about the beautiful capital of Sweden. The official Stockholm website is constantly updated with information on events, activities and conferences and also lists the addresses, opening hours and admission charges for all the city's museums and attractions. The site also includes a gudie to all the city's hotels and hostels.

MALMÖ

by **Kirsten Jungsberg**

La Empanada

Sjaelbodgatan 10
opp Saint Petri church
Malmö
Tel: 040 120 262
Open: Mon-Sat 11-21.00
Large omnivorous Latin American/Mexican restaurant. Very popular and cheap place with many dishes for vegetarians and vegans. Very large portions. For example chili sin carne with a bottle of pure juice kr 39. No smoking or alcohol. Coffee, tea and herb tea kr 5.

SWEDISH

I am vegetarian
Jag är vegetarian

I am vegan
Jag är vegan

I do not eat meat, chicken or fish
Jag äter inte kött, höna, kyckling, fisk

I do not eat eggs, milk, butter, cheese or honey
Jag äter inte ägg, mjölk, fil, smör, ost, honung

Please	Tack
Thank you	Tack
Ja	Yes
Nej	No

Animalen

Gasverksvaegen 13
Malmö
Tel: 040 6110261
Open: Mon-Fri 15-17.30
The oldest and biggest animal protection society in Sweden called Animals Rights. They have a little shop where they sell vegan food and books and give away information. You can also get a nice cup of herb tea there.

Two paths met in a forest.
I chose the road less travelled
And that has made all the difference.

SWITZERLAND

ZURICH

by Alex Bourke

Bahnhof Buffet

Corner of the Central Station, (Im Hauptbahnhof)
Zurich 8001
Tel: 01-217 15 15
Open: Every day 11.30-14.00, 17.30-21.30 last orders,
doors close 23.00.
What a fine idea, a completely vegetarian buffet restaurant at
the main station, on a corner of the building. 18 SF for a small
plate, 25 SF for a large plate, or all you can eat 35 SF gets you
starter, main course, soup and dessert. They have 10 dishes
such as salads, vegetables, lentils, aloo gobi, dhal, and vegans
can eat well as they use things like coconut milk, apart from
being stuck with fruit salad for dessert. But they did say "we'll
have to do something about that." Still, it'll leave more room for
vegan Swiss chocolate. Drinks extra. They have theme food
months like Arab, Thai or Chinese. British Rail could learn a lot
from this place.

Hiltl

Sihlstrasse 28, Zurich 8001
close to Jelmoli department store, off Bahnhoffstrasse
Tel: 01-227 70 00
Open: Mon-Sat 07.00-23.00, Sun 11-23.00
Now this, this is history. The oldest vegetarian restaurant in
Europe according to the Guinness Book of Records, in the trail-
blazing Hiltl family since 1898, and deserving of an extensive
review for setting a fine example to the world. Who dared to say
the Swiss never invented anything? There are many Indian,
continental and Far Eastern specialities and some vegan dishes but no vegan desserts apart from fruit salad, and they don't

have soya milk, though owner Ralph Hiltl told us he'd look into stocking soya ice-cream. Breakfast 7-10am Mon-Sat is a buffet, 2.80 SF per 100g, with muesli, fruit, bread etc. From 10.30 am the all-day lunch or dinner buffet 16-25 SF allows you to eat as much as you want from the salad bar and pay 3.90 SF per 100gm. There are 50 kinds of salad, hot snacks like potato wedges, onion rings and falafel. From 5pm they move the salads to the back of the table and add a 30 dish Indian buffet too then it's all-you-can-scoff including dessert for 38 SF. The buffet means you can have lunch whenever you're hungry regardless of whether it's 10.30am or 4pm. You can go as many times as you like right up until closing time or you explode, whichever comes first. A la carte offers 30 dishes for 16-27SF, e.g. mushroom stroganoff, vegetable paella, lots of Indian dishes. Desserts 4-8 SF. Oodles of wines, some organic, bottle from 25 SF up to 100 SF, glass from 4.80 SF to 8 SF. 15 freshly squeezed juices 1dl 3.20 SF, 2.5 dl 5.8 SF, 22.50 for a litre to share in a carafe. All juices and in fact the whole menu are available as take-away for about 30% less. The menus are in English and 70% of the staff speak English. Website www.hiltl.ch.

Limmathof "Pot au Vert"

Limmatquai 142
Zurich, 8001
Tel: 01-261 42 20
Open: Mon-Fri 11.30-14.00, 18.00-21.30 kitchen,
closed weekend.

Vegetarian restaurant in the centre, 5 minutes from the station. A la carte 17.50-24.50 SF for one dish or economise with the 2 course lunch enu with soup or salad and main course 14.50 SF, evening 4 course fixed menu 38 SF. Vegans can have a vegetable dish, or salads with tofu. Usual desserts 7.50-9.50 SF but they don't acknowledge vegans at all in this department. Local and organic wines from 4-5 SF glass, 25 SF for a bottle, beers with or without alcohol. Menu in English and staff speak English. Small terrace in the summer where you can sit outside overlooking the central square.

Govinda Kulturtreff

Preyergasse 16
Zurich, 8001
Tel: 01-251 88 59
Open: Mon-Sat 11-14.00, closed Sunday.
Vegetarian Indian restaurant in Niederdorf, with food cooked in the Hare Krishna temple twenty minutes walk away on the hill. 14 SF for a plate of lunch with rice, dhal, two kinds of vegetables and chutney with a drink. Their sweets are made with milk or cheese - sorry vegans. There is a possibility that, after 15 years, they may have to move to another less expensive location after June 2000.

Gleich

Seefeldstr. 9
Zurich, 8009
Tel: 01-251 32 03
Open: Mon-Fri 06.00-21.00, Sat till 16.00, closed Sun
Breakfast from 06.00 till 11.00, 11-21.00 lunch. We believe this to be a fine vegetarian restaurant, but unlike 298 or the other 299 places in this book they were always "too busy" to speak with us no matter how many times we called. In our experience anywhere that's this busy must be really really good. The only other place in Europe this popular is Buxs in Munich.

MERRY CHRISTMAS
HAPPY BIRTHDAY
DIWALI GREETINGS
HAPPY ANNIVERSARY

say it with a vegetarian guide
the year long gift in the
best possible taste
see end pages

BON VOYAGE

Vegetarian Organizations

CONTACT FELLOW VEGGIES IN EUROPE

If you're in a European country for a long time, particularly if you speak the language, here are some organisations to join and make new friends, or get active in. Send a stamp or international reply coupon for details in their language. *Please remember these are hard-pressed, cash strapped, time starved charities struggling to make Europe safe for animals and they cannot answer letters in English and certainly don't provide school project or tourist info. If you think it's tough being a campaigner in Britain or America, you ain't seen nothing'!* But they do welcome your leftover foreign money!

Now for the rant, but we're only trying to keep the movement in Europe on target. Just in case anyone missed the last paragraph, please don't write to these organisations for information on restaurants and places to stay. (You can always write to Veggie Guides - we *love* to hear from and help our customers!) Only write to them if you're moving to their country, want to get involved in animal rights, preferably in their language, and then a donation would be nice, at the very least an international reply coupon from your post office.
Also they don't welcome unannounced personal callers, they are not drop in centres, the address might even be someone's home. If you're staying in the country long term, speak the language and would like to volunteer, then of course they'd love to hear from you.   If you want to meet veggie friends, go on a demo where you'll meet like minded folk and some of them may wish to practise their English.

Got a couple of hours? Here are two website that have lists of member societies with links to their websites. Some parts are in English, otherwise you can have fun improving your language skills working out the rest with a dictionary.

International Vegetarian Union: www.ivu.org (all in English)
European Vegetarian Union http://www.ivu.org/evu/
(quite a lot of it in English)

AUSTRIA

Internationale Vegetarische Initiative
Johannesstrasse 38
2344 Maria Enzersdorf
Tel: +43-2236-86933
email: ivi@ivu.org

Österreichische Vegetarier-Union
Postfach 1
8017 Graz
Tel: +43-316-463717 or +43-676-347 6346
http://www.vegetarier.at/   email: erwin.lauppert@styria.com

Vegane Gesellschaft Österreich
Postfach 27
1238 Wien
www.vegan.at/   Email: info@vegan.at

BELGIUM

Association Végétarienne
1346 bte Chausée de Wavre
B-1160 Bruxelles
Tel: +32-2-660 2124

GAIA (Global Action in the Interest of Animals)
Paleizenstraat 90, B-1030 Brussels
Tel: +32-2-245 2950. Fax: +32-2-215 0943.
www.gaia.be, email: gaia:advalvas.be

Vegetariërsvereniging vzw
(Flemish Vegetarian Society)
Kerseveldmeers 53, 1745 Opwijk
Tel/fax: 052-35 83 00
E-mail: vegetariersvereniging@altavista.net
http://dine.at/vegetariersvereniging

DENMARK

Dansk Vegetarforening
Gillesager 252 2.tv
DK-2650 Hvidovre
Tel: +45-7022 4001
email: nb@dmu.dk

FINLAND

Finnish Association of Living Food
Museokatu 9 C 25
FIN-00100 Helsinki
Tel/fax: +358-9-491 267
www.kolumbus.fi/ery   Email: ery@kolumbus.fi

Vegaaniliitto
(Finnish Vegan Society)
Martti Bergestadt
P.O. Box 320
FIN-00151 Helsinki
Tel: +358-9-296 3025
Fax: +358-9-221 5696
www.vegaaniliitto.fi/ email: mbstad@clinet.fi

FRANCE

Alliance Végétarienne
Lionel et Marie Reisler
Beauregard
85240 St Hilaire des Loges
Tel: +33-5-49 06 03 87
Fax: +33-5-49 25 10 41
email: avf@ivu.org, www.ivu.org/avf

One Voice (formerly Talis)
8 rue des Morillons, 75015 Paris
Tel: +33-1-56 56 62 70
www.onevoice-ear.org (or try www.talis-ear.org)
Inspired by PETA with a high media profile, campaigning for vegetarianism and animal welfare. No group has had a bigger impact here, with spectacular TV successes exposing, for example, BSE and making vegetarianism cool for the first time in France. 100F annual subscription, plus 60F to receive their quarterly magazine.

GERMANY

'Die Ratten' Alternativer Tierschutz
Werner Joergensen
Hansastr. 10
D-45478 Mülheim/Ruhr
Tel: +49-208-593400
Fax: +49-208-593401
E-Mail: Werner_Joergensen@du.maus.de

MUT (Mensch Tier Umwelt)
Tierschutzpartei
Dr. Gisela Bulla
Curtiusstr. 5
D-86165 Augsburg
Tel/Fax: +49-821-791982

Vegetarier Bund Deutschlands
Blumenstraße 3
D-30159 Hannover
Tel: +49-511-363 2050
Fax: +49-511-363 2007
www.vegetarierbund.de/   email: info@vegetarierbund.de

Vegetarische Initiative
Postfach 1136
D-21383 Amelinghausen
Tel/Fax: +49-4131-83199

HUNGARY

Vegetarianus Barati Kor
Vass Gyorgy Bodizsar
1 Regzofu u
H-1165 Budapest

IRELAND

Vegetarian Society of Ireland
Box 3010
Dublin 4
Tel: +353-1-8730451
www.ivu.org/evu/english/news/news981/ireland.html

ITALY

Associazione Vegetariana Italiana
Viale Brianza 20
20127 Milano
Tel: +39-2-26113546
Fax: +39-2-28340631
www.vegetariani.it/   Email: avi@ivu.org

Società Vegetariana
Via Chiari 5
I-20155 Milano
Tel/Fax: +39-3300 1176
www.ivu.org/svi   Email: svi@ivu.org

Improve your Italian veggie and campaigning vocabulary.
Campaign Against Cruelty - an animal activist's handbook
by Alex and Ronny, Italian translation by Marina Berati
is online at
www.freeweb.org/animali/bacheca_animalista/manuale/

LUXEMBOURG

De Vegabond
Dr. Claude Pasquini (President)
c/o B.P. 44
3107 Rumelange
www.ivu.org/devegabond/   email: devegabond@ivu.org

MALTA

International Animal Rescue Malta
Max Farrugia, Chairman
 www.ivu.org/iarm   Email: iarm@ivu.org

The Vegetarian Society of Malta
Katherine Azzopardi, Secretary
c/o 48 Church Avenue
Paola PLA 05 Malta
Tel. 07-356-695 812
email: mnajdra@mail.waldonet.net.mt
www.ivu.org/malta

NETHERLANDS (HOLLAND)

Nederlandse Vegetariërsbond
Larenseweg 26
NL-1221 CM Hilversum
Tel: +31-35-6834796. Fax: +31-35-6836152.
www.vegetariers.nl/   Email: info@vegetariers.nl

Nederlandse Vereniging voor Veganisme
Postbus 1087, 6801BB Arnhem
www.vegansime.non-profit.nl
Email: info@veganisme.non-profit.nl

NORWAY

NOAH Oslo (head office)
Osterhausgate 12
N-0183 Oslo
Tel/Fax: +47-2-211 4163
www.noahonline.no

NOAH Bergen
Postboks 680
N-5002 Bergen
Tel: +47-55-324 114

Norsk Vegetarforening
Postboks 101
Blinderen
N-03114 Oslo

POLAND

Get the monthly magazine *Wegetarianski Swiat* (Vegetarian World) from kiosks with extensive listings of what's going on around the country.

BEEK
PO Box 67
PL-81-806 Sopot 6

Ruch Promocji Wegetarianizmu
Krzysztof Zolkiewski
Tysiaclecia 80/141, PL-40-871 Katowice

Towarzysto Zwollenikow Wegetarianizmu
Krystyna Chomicz-Jung
ul. Gdanska 2 m. 97, PL-01-633 Warszawa
Tel: +48-22-331045

Verdaj Brigadoj
Andrzej Zwawa
Slawkowska 12/24
PL-31014 Krakow
Tel/Fax: +48-12-4222147
www.gemini.most.org.pl/zb

PORTUGAL

Sociedade Portuguesa de Naturlogia
Rua do Alecrim 38-3
P-1200 Lisboa
Tel: +351-1-346 3335

RUSSIA

St Petersburg Vegetarian Society
Box 37
191011 St. Petersburg
email: lag@infopro.spb.su

Vegetarian Society of Russia
Tatyana Pavlova
Volzhsky bulvar d39 k3 kv23
RUS-109462 Moscow
eMail: vegsoc@glasnet.ru

SPAIN

Asociación Vegetariana Canaria
Dr. Luis Vallejo Rodriguez
Apartado 3557
E-35080 Las Palmas
Canary Islands
Tel: +34-28-242834
email: bulchand@arrakis.es

Asociación Vegana Española
Francisco Martìn
Apartado 478
Torre del Mar
29740 Malaga
Tel/Fax: +34-95-251 3981
www.ivu.org/ave/   email: ave@ivu.org

Federacion Naturista Vegetariana Española
Manuel Tinoco Pérez, Presidente
'Sonavema', C/ Carreteria, 82, 1°
29008 Malaga, Spain
Email: c/o vegania@ivu.org

Fundación Sakahari Vegetariana
Plaza Picasso, 4, 4° I
29640 Fuengirola, Malaga

Societat Vegetariana de Barcelona (SVB)
(Barcelona Veggies)
Sofia de Paz & Enric Llacay
Aribav 320, 1-4
08006 Barcelona
Tel/Fax: +34-3-2022980
email: grw@pangea.org

SWEDEN

Animal Rights Sweden
Box 2005
S-125 02 Älvsjö
(visitor address: Gamla Huddingevägen 437)
Tel: +46-8-555 914 00
Fax: +46-8-555 914 50
email: info@djurensratt.org
Website: www.djurensratt.org
Magazine: Djurens Rätt (Animal Rights) five times a year
Sweden's biggest animal rights organisation with 50,000 members, founded in 1882, previously called the Swedish Society Against Painful Experiments on Animals. They run campaigns throughout the year including International Animal Day and Fur Free Friday. Main areas of concern are alternatives to animal testing, cosmetics not tested on animals, improving the situation of farm animals, banning of battery cages, stopping keeping animals for fur production, veganism and vegetarianism. The main reason for changing its name was to show that the society deals with all kinds of animal rights issues, cooperating internationaly with WSPA, IAAPEA, The European Coalition to End Animal Experiments and Eurogroup for Animal Welfare.

Swedish Vegan Society
Klövervägen 6
647 30 Mariefred
Tel/Fax: +46-159-344 04
email: u.troeng@strangnas.mail.telia.com
Magazine: Vegan four times a year.
Founded in 1976 and has always focused on education and providing information, particularly to municipalities, organisations and authorities. Interest in veganism in Sweden has increased greatly, especially among young people during the last five years. The Society sells national and international literature on veganism.

Svenska Vegetariska Föreningen
(Vegetarian Society Sweden)
Sågargatan 4
S-116 36 Stockholm
Tel: +46-8-702 11 16, Fax: +46-8-702 11 17
email: svf@vegetarian.se, Website: www.vegetarian.se
Magazine: Vegetar four times a year.
The Vegetarian Society (Sweden) was founded in 1903 and will celebrate its 100th anniversary in 2003 by hosting the European Vegetarian Union (EVU) Congress. Every 1st October, World Vegetarian Day, the society, together with the Swedish Vegan Sociey and Animal Rights Sweden, organises seminars, vegetarian cooking competitions and exhibitions. The Vegetarian Society aims to iinform and inspire people to adopt a healthy vegetarian lifestyle, mainly through giving advice by telephone, its quarterly magazine and lectures.

Föreningen Justa Bananer
Lunda Vägen 62
23252 Åkard
Tel: +46-40-461682
www.algonet.se/~tyling/   email: jbanana@ivu.org

SWITZERLAND

Action pour le Respect des Animaux
Christina Maier
Case Postale 2071
CH-1002 Lausanne
Tel: +41-21-616 8182. Fax +41-21-616 0959.
email: asv@vegetarismus.ch

Schweiz. Vereinig für Vegetarismus (SVV)
Renato Pichler
Postfach
CH-9466 Sennwald
Tel: +41-81-757 1586. Fax: +41 81-757 2819.
www.vegetarismus.ch/   Email: renato@vegetarismus.ch

UNITED KINGDOM

London Vegans
7 Deansbrook Road
Edgware, Middlesex HA8 9BE
Tel: +44-20-7603 4325
www.veganlondon.freeserve.co.uk
Check out the website for our next restaurant visit, last Wednesday monthly
meeting, weekend walks, demos and other events then come and hang out with
this friendly social and campaigning group.

Oxford Vegetarian Society
Paul & Galina Appleby
57 Sharland Close
Grove, Oxon OX12 OAF
Tel: +44-1235-769425
www.ivu.org/oxveg/   Email: oxveg@ivu.org
Regular social activities.

The Vegetarian Society (UK)
Parkdale, Dunham Road
Altrincham WA14 4QG, Cheshire
Tel: +44-161-928 0793
Fax: +44-161-926 9182
www.vegsoc.org
email: info@vegsoc.demon.co.uk
Has a network of campaigning and social groups for members.

The Vegan Society
7 Battle Road
St Leonards-on-Sea TN37 7AA
Tel: +44-1424-427 393
Fax: +44-1424-717064
www.vegansociety.com
email: info@vegansociety.com
Local contacts around the country will help new vegans.

Viva! (Vegetarians International Voice for Animals)
12 Queen Square
Brighton, E.Sussex BN1 3FD
Tel: +44-1273-777688
Fax: +44-1273-776755
www.viva.org.uk
email: info@viva.org.uk
Lots of campaigning groups around the country, specialising in youth and school talks.

For a comprehensive listing of thousands of animal rights and vegan business-es in the UK and abroad, check out the **Animal Contacts Directory** produced by Veggies of Nottingham on the web at www.veggies.org.uk. Or buy a 200 page printed copy for £4.95 + postage from Veggie Guides, see end of this book or our website www.vegetarianguides.co.uk.

They who travel far
can tell many stories.

Why we don't promote egg and cheese dishes

by listing them in restaurant descriptions

The authors of this book are all ethical vegans. We were vegetarians for a long time before, but we changed when we realised that **all** the moral and health benefits of being vegetarian come **exclusively** from the vegan part of the diet. Most of the ingredients that make meals so tasty are vegan anyway. Animal products like cheese and eggs are actually quite bland and are certainly unnecessary for a balanced diet.

Animal farming causes all kinds of ethical problems with regards to human and animal rights and environmental degradation. There isn't room in this book to go into the issue in depth, but please consider the following points.

The **egg** and **chicken** industries both involve similar amounts of suffering and killing. After 18 months the hens are killed even though they could naturally live for seven years. The fluffy newly hatched male chicks are a waste product of the industry. They are gassed or crushed alive and used for fertiliser or, would you believe it, chicken feed. How many males have you seen even on a "free range" farm? Eggs are the richest natural source of cholesterol. These days doctors recommend that you should not eat more than one or two a week. We don't know of any such restriction on scrambled tofu!

Cows only produce milk when they have calves. In order for the dairy industry to be profitable, the cows are impregnated every year, which is stressful and exhausting for them, so they are killed when worn out at a relatively young age. The calves are taken away from their mothers at less than a week old. Most are killed immediately or reared in stalls for cheap meat, veal or pet food, but some females are returned to the dairy herd.

While meat has typically 40% of calories from fat, **cheese** has 70% of calories from fat, most of it saturated. It doesn't contain fibre or carbohydrate. It doesn't even contain significant iron. Grains, nuts and beans on the other hand do contain protein, carbohydrate, fibre, iron and many other good things.

The idea that you need milk products for calcium is a myth. There is not a single case in the medical literature of calcium deficiency in a calorie sufficient diet. **Osteoporosis** is not a disease of calcium deficiency but a disease of calcium loss. The main cause of the loss is consuming more protein than you need, normally by eating protein-crammed animal foods. Getting rid of that excess protein requires mineral salts, and the easiest way to get them is to take calcium from the bones.

Far from being calcium-deficient, people who don't use cow's milk, like vegans, Chinese in China or Africans, don't get osteoporosis. Whereas the countries with high dairy consumption such as Holland, Scandinavia, Britain, USA and Canada have an epidemic of osteoporosis.

Soya milk, oat milk, rice milk, cashew milk and almond milk are cruelty free and don't contain the animal proteins that cause osteoporosis.   Instead of a veggie meal topped with cheese, why not try something different? If the vegan dishes in your restaurant are limited or boring, refer them to *Ronny's Top Tips for Restaurateurs* elsewhere in this guide.

Ronny Worsey and **Alex Bourke** are trustees of The Vegan Society. They can be contacted at info@vegetarianguides.co.uk.

If you have internet access, check out the following sites:
The Vegan Society: www.vegansociety.com
Physcians Committee for Responsible Medicine: www.pcrm.org
People for the Ethical Treatment of Animals:
 www.peta-online.org and www.milksucks.com
Milk - The Deadly Poison: www.notmilk.com
Vegetarian Resource Group: www.vrg.org
Or write with a stamped addressed envelope in UK or two international reply coupons to The Vegan Society, Donald Watson House, 7 Battle Road, St Leonards-on-Sea, East Sussex TN37 7AA, England. Tel (+44) 01424-427 393, fax 01424-717 064.

Ronny's Top Tips for Restaurateurs

The vegan population is growing rapidly, much faster than vegetarianism, and awareness about food allergies and cholesterol is also increasing. Therefore a very significant number of your customers will be actively avoiding eggs and dairy products as well as meat. If you make sure that many of your meals are completely animal free, you will tap into a significant market. Here are some suggestions:

1. There are numerous brands of vegetarian **sausages, burgers and bacon substitutes**. All are quite similar, but some brands contain egg. If you always buy egg-free ones, you will be able to cater for both vegetarians and vegans at the same time. For a total vegan breakfast feast, offer **scrambled** (mashed and lightly fried) **tofu** as an alternative to scrambled eggs.

2. Always have **soya milk**. It keeps for over a year unopened and up to 5 days when opened. **Soya dessert** and **soya cream** also keep for a long time. Soya milk makes excellent cappuccinos and is perfect for making custard and rice puddings.

3. Try serving **Tofutti** or **Swedish Glace** or **Provamel** ice cream, either on its own or to accompany hot pies and puddings. Just try it and you won't need any further convincing!

4. **Soya cheese** can be used to create some amazing vegan dishes, yet is rarely used in catering. It is easily available prepacked at wholefood stores, or in bulk blocks from manufacturers and wholesalers. Redwood Foods make a very popular brand called 'Cheezley'. It has a longer shelf life than dairy cheese, even after you open it. Or make your own using **The Uncheese Cookbook** by Joanne Stepaniak, from www.vrg.org or amazon.com, or ask at your bookshop.

5. Vegan salads are easy to prepare. **Egg-free mayonnaise** is available in small jars from wholefood stores or buy the excellent Plamil brand in bulk tubs from wholesalers. Alternatively make your own mayonnaise-style dressing by blending vegetable oil with roughly equal quantities of vinegar and soya milk. You could also offer a **vinaigrette** made with olive oil, herbs, mustard and lemon juice or vinegar. If you make up a big batch of this, it will keep for weeks, just shake before serving.

6. **Vegan dips** are no problem. You can easily buy or make hummous, and guacamole can be made just as well without yogurt. Try roasting aubergines and liquidising with olive oil and black pepper for a very rich and creamy baba ganoush dip.

7. For an uncooked **vegan breakfast**, serve a muesli that doesn't have honey or whey in it, or offer toast, crumpets or muffins with vegan margarine. Most brands of vegetable margarine are not vegan as they contain whey powder, but virtually all supermarkets stock at last one vegan brand. Catering size tubs can be bought from wholesalers.

8. Avoid glazing **pastries** with egg, and make sure that the pastry itself as well as the contents are vegan. Bulk packs of frozen puff, filo and shortcrust pastry are widely available from wholesalers.

9. Aim to **make at least half your starters and main courses vegan**. If only one out of four or six options is vegan we don't have any choice. Cheese, cheese or cheese isn't much of a choice for veggies either.

10. It is very frustrating that so many restaurants offer a choice of vegan starters and main courses, but no **dessert**. When there is a dessert, it is often completely unimaginative. Vegans are as fed up with fruit salad and sorbet as vegetarians are with omelettes and cheese salad! Why not offer vegan ice cream (see above) with fruit salad, or better still, experiment with egg-free recipes for cakes and puddings. It is possible to make deli-

cious trifles, flans and cheesecakes which are completely vegan.

If you have any questions, or would like some free vegan cake recipes, write to me c/o Vegetarian Guides. You could also contact the Vegan Society for their catering pack (which includes a list of wholesalers of vegan food and alcohol) and their merchandise catalogue full of cookbooks. Alternatively, see what's on offer in any of the restaurants listed that are particularly good for vegans. The IVU and VRG websites are also a great source of inspiration.

Ronny has been a vegan campaigner and caterer for many years, has written *The Complete Scoffer* cookbook and co-authored *Campaign Against Cruelty - an activist's handbook*. She currently works at a central London veggie cafe and has just published a new cake cookbook *The Cake Scoffer*. (see next page). Check out some of Ronny's recipes at CampaignAgainstCruelty.co.uk

Top websites for recipes & cookbooks

International Vegetarian Union: www.ivu.org

The Vegetarian Society (UK): www.vegsoc.org
Parkdale, Dunham Rd, Altrincham, Cheshire WA14 4QG, UK
Tel (+44) 0161-928 0793, Fax 0161-926 9182. Email: info@vegsoc.org

Vegetarian Resource Group: www.vrg.org
PO Box 1463, Baltimore, MD 21203, USA.
Tel 410-366 8343. Fax 410-366 8804. Email: vrg@vrg.org

The Vegan Society: www.vegansociety.com
Donald Watson House, 7 Battle Rd, St Leonards-on-Sea, East Sussex TN37 7AA, UK. Tel (+44) 01424-427 393. Fax 01424-717064.
Email: info@vegansociety.com

American Vegan Society, PO Box 369, Malaga, NJ 08328.
Tel 856-694. Fax 856-694 2288. Fabulous catalog of vegan cookbooks.

VEGETARIAN EUROPE
READER RESPONSE FORM

We are relying on **YOU** to help make the next edition of *Vegetarian Europe* even better. The best letters will receive a free copy of your choice of one of our guides. Please feel free to continue on another sheet. Thank you.

Are there any improvements you'd like to see in the guide?

Any places you would like to see featured in the next edition?

Any places you would like to see removed, and why?

Any descriptions you would like to see changed?

Where did you buy your guide? _____

Are you: veggie __   vegan __   other _____

Your name: . . . .

Address: . . . .

. . . .

. . . . Email . . . .

Vegetarian Guides Ltd, PO Box 2284, London W1A 5UH, UK
UK Fax: (+44) 0870-121 4721 USA Fax: (+1) 509-272 1463
info@vegetarianguides.co.uk

VEGETARIAN EUROPE

NEW RESTAURANT
& ACCOMMODATION FORM

Are you the proprietor of a vegetarian guest house or restaurant not listed in this guide? Then please please tell us about yourselves to ensure your **FREE** listing in the next edition of *Vegetarian Europe*.   Please feel free to enclose your menu or brochures - the more you send, the more we'll write! Thanks.

Name of establishment: . . . .

Proprietor / Manager: . . . .

Address: . . . .

. . . .

. . . . Postcode . . . .

Phone: . . . .   Fax: . . . .

Website: . . . .

Email: . . . .

Veggie   . . .   Vegan . . . Other . . . .

Restaurant . . . .   Café . . .   Tea room . . .   Pub . . . Other . . . .

Hotel . . .   B&B . . .   Guest house . . .   Hostel . . .   Other . . . .

Additional info:

Vegetarian Guides Ltd, PO Box 2284, London W1A 5UH, UK
UK Fax: (+44) 0870-121 4721 USA Fax: (+1) 509-272 1463
info@vegetarianguides.co.uk

VEGETARIAN
BRITAIN

by Alex Bourke and Alan Todd
Foreword by Paul and Linda McCartney

Hankering for a day trip or weekend
away and wondering if you should pack a hamper first? Now
you can dump the veggie emergency kit, safe in the knowl-
edge that wherever you go, you'll be able to refuel at totally
vegetarian and vegan eateries and sleeperies.

This 256 page guide features hundreds of vegetarian restaurants, cafés, hotels and guest houses all over Britain with
opening times, prices and full descriptions including what's on
the menu for vegans. The most comprehensive and detailed
veggie guide ever.

Available from UK bookshops, price £7.99

SPECIAL OFFER - MAIL ORDER ONLY
Vegetarian Britain + London + France £15
(regular price £7.99 + 5.99 + 6.99 = £20.97, save £5.97)

That's **500** places to eat and sleep in Britain
400 restaurants and shops in London
150 places to eat and sleep in France
plus a free bonus pocket fold out **map of Paris**
a total of **600 pages, 1,000 veggie oases**

Add UK postage £1.50 for all three books total £16.50. Europe airmail or
worldwide surface £2.25, total £17.25. Worldwide airmail £3, total £18.
Order online at www.vegetarianguides.co.uk
or send UK cheque or Visa/Mastercard details to
Vegetarian Guides Ltd, PO Box 2284, London W1A 5UH, UK

VEGETARIAN
FRANCE

*By Alex Bourke and Alan Todd, with
an introduction by Roselyne Masselin
of La Cuisine Imaginaire and
foreword by Paul and Linda McCartney.*

France is a veggie-lover's paradise, but only if you know where to find it! This **128 page** guide features:

150 places to eat out and crash out, over **20** veggie restaurants in Paris alone, vegetarian hotels and guest houses all over France, all-you-can-eat vegan buffet in Marseille, veggie vocabulary, maps, the hitch-hiker's guide to the south of France on 50 francs a day, connect with fellow veggies in France!

"A lot of people think it's impossible to find vegetarian food in France, but this little cracker of a book proves them wrong. Vegetarian France is an invaluable guide to finding really good vegetarian food in the most unexpected places. Bon appetit!"

Paul and Linda McCartney, from the Introduction.

Available from UK bookshops, price £6.99.

Order direct from Vegetarian Guides and get a free fold out pocket map of Paris to help plan your trip.

Add UK postage first book £1.50, then £1 per book.
Europe airmail or worldwide surface £2.25 first book then £1.50 per book.
Worldwide airmail £3 first book then £2 per book.
Order online at www.vegetarianguides.co.uk
or send UK cheque or Visa / Mastercard details to Vegetarian Guides Ltd, PO Box 2284, London W1A 5UH, UK.

new super improved
VEGETARIAN
LONDON

By Alex Bourke and Paul Gaynor

120 vegetarian and vegan restaurants, plus a further 80 ethnic restaurants with huge veggie menus, and a complete listing of all wholefood and health food stores telling you which ones offer take-away food. Plus juice bars, alcohol, accommodation, local veggie groups, a map of where to find central restaurants, postcode maps, and comprehensive indexes. New for this 3rd edition is an index of 17 bargain all-you-can-eat buffets. 224 pages.

"A thorough run-down of health and food shops, restaurants serving vegetarian food, green shops and places to buy cruelty-free cosmetics and clothes." **Time Out**

"For people living in or visiting the capital, this book is more important than the A-Z." **The Vegetarian Society (UK)**

"From Wood Green to Wimbledon, the book is a comprehensive catalogue of the best restaurants, shops and tourist attractions in the capital." **The Big Issue**

"By the time I've tried every food in every place in this book I'll be 196 years old. You'll have no trouble finding nosh with this remarkably thorough guide to everything vegetarian in London. So join me, get out there and get scoffing!"
Tony Banks, MP

Available from UK bookshops £5.99
or mail order from Vegetarian Guides

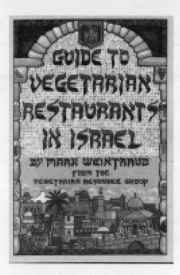

VEGETARIAN
ISRAEL

by Mark Weintraub

Jerusalem, Tel Aviv, Jaffa, Haifa, Tiberias, Galilee resorts, Moshav Amirim, Eilat.   Indispensable for the vegetarian, health-concerned, or kosher traveller. Restaurants range from Italian to Indian; from cafe and nightlife to upscale hotel and resort. Find a restaurant which is a favourite hangout for Israeli journalists, has a stone mill on the premises for grinding flours, or displays unique artwork. Includes health food stores in Jerusalem, Tel Aviv and Haifa. 88 pages.

£6.99 + postage mail order from Vegetarian Guides

Available in USA $9.95 postage included from Vegetarian Resource Group, PO Box 1463, Baltimore, MD 21203. Tel 410-366 8343. http://www.vrg.org
(Maryland residents add 5% sales tax)

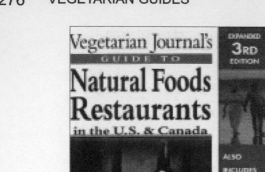

VEGETARIAN
USA & CANADA

by the Vegetarian Resource Group
foreword by Lindsay Wagner

Over 2,000 brilliant places to eat and sleep all over North America. Plus vacation spots, camps, tours and local groups. Fantastic value with a massive 370 pages.

£9.99 + postage mail order from Vegetarian Guides

Available in USA $12.95 postage included from Vegetarian Resource Group, PO Box 1463, Baltimore, MD 21203. Tel 410-366 8343. http://www.vrg.org
(Maryland residents add 5% sales tax)

VEGETARIAN
IRELAND

by Steph Daly

Ireland is great for touring. This guide features veggie guest houses and restaurants all over Ireland with a map showing their locations. Plus a complete listing of all the wholefood shops, environmental and earth-friendly organisations.

£3.00 + postage from Vegetarian Guides

Add UK postage first book £1.50, then £1 per book.
Europe airmail or worldwide surface £2.25 first book then £1.50 per book.
Worldwide airmail £3 first book then £2 per book.
Order online at www.vegetarianguides.co.uk
or send UK cheque or Visa / Mastercard details to Vegetarian Guides Ltd, PO Box 2284, London W1A 5UH, UK.

VEGAN GUIDE TO
NEW YORK

by Rynn Berry & Max Friedman with Dan Mills. 7th edition revised and updated for 2000-01. From Harlem to Wall Street, Manhattan is vegan and veggie nirvana with over 100 restaurants plus health food stores, ethnic cuisine, famer's markets, bookstores, even where to buy vegan shoes. Handy map of the favorite 22 NYC eating places. Also includes Queen's and Brooklyn.

£3.99 + postage from Vegetarian Guides

Also available in USA from the publisher $5 + 75c postage to
Rynn Berry, 159 Eastern Parkway, Suite 2H, Brooklyn, NY 11238.

VEGETARIAN OXFORD

by Paul Appleby
of Oxford Vegetarians

Have a great day out or weekend in the centre of England sightseeing and cafe hopping in this ancient university town. This excellent guide covers the whole of the surrounding county too with guest houses, youth hostels, restaurants and cafes, pubs, health food and wholefood shops, tourist information centres throughout Oxfordshire, and other businesses catering for vegetarians. 24 pages.

£0.95 + postage from Veggie Guides

VEGETARIAN NOTTINGHAM

by Veggies of Nottingham

Enjoy a historic day sightseeing and scoffing in the heart of England. Robin Hood's home town is great for vegheads, with heaps of places to eat out, shop and meet new friends. Pubs, bars, cafes, restaurants, accommodation, shops, maps, places of interest, museums, caves, lace centre, local contacts. 96 pages.

£2.50 + postage from Veggie Guides

THE VEGAN SHOPPER

by The Vegan Society (UK)
5th edition July 2000, 270 pages

Britain is vegan heaven with this pocket size guide to products which are free of animal ingredients and involve no animal testing. Sections include food, drink, footwear, toiletries, cosmetics, remedies, baby & child care, animal care, garden and leisure, home and office, and now chocolate. Lists additives, mail order addresses, vegan contacts, glossary of animal substances. GM-free products highlighted.

£5.95 + postage from Vegetarian Guides

Or order direct from the Vegan Society (+44) 01424-427 393

VEGAN PASSPORT

edited by George Rodger of the Vegan Society

We've all been in a foreign restaurant and explained to the waiter in basic English what we want, only for the cook to serve up soup with a bone at the bottom or salad with tuna. Not any more! This passport sized book contains a page for each of the 38 most common languages covering 90% of the world's population, saying what vegans do and don't eat in great detail.

Let the waiter show it to the cook and you'll be sure of a totally animal free feast even if no one speaks a word of your language. Includes all of the European Community, Arabic, Bengali, Chinese, Croatian, Czech, Gujarati, Hebrew, Hindi, Hungarian, Indonesian, Japanese, Korean, Malay, Marathi, Persian, Polish, Romanian, Russian, Sinhalese, Slovak, Swahili, Tagalog, Thai, Turkish, Urdu, Vietnamese and Esperanto. Plus a page of pictures of what we do and don't eat if all else fails.

The essential companion to *Vegetarian Europe*.

£2.99 + postage from Vegetarian Guides

ANIMAL
CONTACTS
DIRECTORY

by Veggies of Nottingham, 204 pages

The vegan campaigner or business person's bible. Locate allies, suppliers, sales or import-export partners.

Comprehensive directory of 7,000 businesses and animal rights groups all over Britain and overseas, including websites and emails.

Vegan Business Connection trading directory with every animal friendly business in the UK. (no animal testing and no animal ingredients)

600 national UK animal groups from Animal Aid to Zoocheck plus 600 local contacts. 270 local animal rights groups, the backbone of the animals' movement, coordinating campaigns in towns and cities throughout the British Isles. 1,000 rescue, rehabilitation, rehoming centres and sanctuaries.

1,000 international animal contacts in 94 countries from Albania to Zimbabwe. Environmental, conservation and key human rights organisations.

Health care and natural healing organisations. Cross reference indexes.

£4.95 + postage from Vegetarian Guides

VEGETARIAN GUIDES

mapping the world for vegetarians and vegans

Our own guides, available from bookshops: **EUROPE £9.99**
BRITAIN £7.99, FRANCE £6.99, LONDON £5.99

SAVE £5.97: BRITAIN + FRANCE + LONDON for £15
(mail order only) and only pay postage on the first book

The following guides we buy in and are available *mail order only*.
AUSTRALIA/NZ £4.99, IRELAND £3.00, ISRAEL £6.99
USA/CANADA £9.99, WORLDWIDE £9.99, NEW YORK £3.99
CAKE SCOFFER £1, NOTTINGHAM £2.50, OXFORD 95p
VEGAN PASSPORT £2.99, VEGAN SHOPPER £5.95, ACD £4.95

- -

Please send me:
[ ] *Vegetarian Europe £9.99*
[ ] *Vegetarian Britain + France London £15*
      (counts as one book for postage)
[ ] *Vegetarian Britain £7.99*
[ ] *Vegetarian France £6.99*
[ ] *Vegetarian London £5.99*
[ ] *Vegetarian Ireland £3.00*
[ ] *Vegetarian Israel £6.99*
[ ] *Vegan Guide to New York City £3.99*
[ ] *Vegetarian Oz/NZ £4.99*
[ ] *Vegetarian USA/Canada £9.99*
[ ] *Worldwide Vegetarian Guide £9.99*
[ ] *Vegetarian Nottingham £2.50*
[ ] *Vegetarian Oxford £0.95*
[ ] *Vegan Passport £2.99*
[ ] *The Cake Scoffer £1.00*

[ ] *Vegan Shopper (UK) £5.95*
[ ] *Animal Contacts Directory £4.95*
[ ] *Rainbows & Wellies cookbook £14.95*

Postage & packing rates:
UK one book £1.50, then £1 per book.
[ ] Airmail to Europe, surface other
countries, £2.25 then £1.50 per book.
[ ] Airmail to rest of world one book £3
then £2 per book.

Money back guarantee: if for any reason you are not entirely satisfied, return within 28 days for a full, no quibble refund. This guarantee is in addition to your statutory rights.

Sub total £ . . . . . . plus p&p £ . . . . . .   TOTAL £ . . . . . .
[ ] I enclose a UK sterling cheque/PO/money order payable to 'Vegetarian Guides Ltd'
[ ] Please debit my Visa/Mastercard/Access/Eurocard/Visa Delta/Connect/Switch/Solo

Card number . . . . Start date . . . . . Expiry . . . . .

Switch Issue No . . . Name on card . . . . Signature . . . .

Name: . . . . Telephone: . . . .

Address: . . . .

. . . . Postcode . . . .

Email: . . . . Today's date: . . . .
Mail to: Vegetarian Guides Ltd, PO Box 2284, London W1A 5UH, England.
Or fax to (outside UK +44) 0870-121 4721. USA fax: +1-509-272 1463.
Order online at www.vegetarianguides.co.uk, enquiries info@vegetarianguides.co.uk

About Veggie Guides

Alex Bourke gave up a career as a software engineer to set up Vegetarian Guides to map the world for vegetarians and vegans. His aim was to make it easy to eat cruelty free anywhere in the world. Since 1991 he's travelled widely on four continents, working with the world's leading veggie and vegan activists and creating an unrivalled research network. As well as publishing our own guides, Vegetarian Guides buys in great veggie travel guides from other publishers to sell mail order and can provide info on eating pretty much anywhere in the world. We just haven't gotten around to writing it all down yet. That's where we hope you'll come in.

If you want to work with Vegetarian Guides you should be vegan, office skilled, perfectly bilingual, have a track record of activism (i.e. contacts in your country), and be committed to our vision of creating a cruelty free vegan world.

We don't do the usual naff reviews by a person who's tasted one dish at 1,000 restaurants in 3 months. Instead we list all the nice looking vegan dishes with prices, and get as much info as we can from local veggies who eat there all the time. We don't judge. If a place isn't up to standard we leave it out. We figure if it's still open someone likes it, so we give enough info for the students to pick the cheapie places, the couples to spot the ones with candles, and the business types to know where to go to impress. Of course if a place delights everyone we might rave about it.

Vegetarianism is growing explosively. Veganism is growing even faster within vegetarianism. The veggie market is bigger than the gay market, yet hardly addressed at all by the media and travel guides beyond a few token listings. We are building the first truly comprehensive series of guides, in partnership with the people best placed to write them, the coordinators of local and national vegetarian organisations in each country. We are doing for veggies what Lonely Planet, Rough Guides, Let's Go and Moon have done for independent travellers, making full use of the opportunities provided by the internet, cheap international phone calls and travel.

When there's a veggie guide to every city and country, it will be easy for everyone in the world to eat vegan, and we will retire. We are looking forward to the day when we will sit in the park and the children will say "Why are you always talking about the time when people ate meat? No one's done that for 20 years."

If you'd like to help us to map the rest of the world and fill in the the gaps in Europe, write (or publish - we'll tell you how) a guide for your town or a section of one of our guides, or you have some suggestions or recommendations, we'd love to hear from you.

Happy travels!

www.vegetarianguides.co.uk
info@vegetarianguides.co.uk
Vegetarian Guides Ltd
PO Box 2284, London W1A 5UH, UK.

CITY INDEX

ADVERTISERS INDEX

DIALING CODES

Flying out for the weekend? Restaurants can be very busy
Friday or Saturday night, but now you can reserve ahead.

AUSTRIA	**+43**		ROME	06
SALZBURG	662		VENICE	041
VIENNA	1		**LUXEMBOURG**	**+352**
BELGIUM	**+32**		**NETHERLANDS**	**+31**
BRUSSELS	2		AMSTERDAM	20
CROATIA	**+385**		**NORWAY**	**+47**
CZECH REPUBLIC	**+420**		OSLO	-
PRAGUE	2		BERGEN	-
DENMARK	**+45**		**POLAND**	**+48**
COPENHAGEN	-		GDANSK, SOPOT & GDYNIA	58
ENGLAND	**+44**		KRAKÓW	12
LIVERPOOL	151		WARSAW	22
LONDON	20		**PORTUGAL**	**+351**
OXFORD	1865		EVORA	266
FINLAND	**+358**		LISBON	21
HELSINKI	9		**RUSSIA**	**+7**
FRANCE	**+33**		MOSCOW	095
PARIS	1		ST PETERSBURG	812
GERMANY	**+49**		**SCOTLAND**	**+44**
BERLIN	30		EDINBURGH	131
BREMEN	421		**SPAIN**	**+34**
FRANKFURT	69		ALICANTE	96
HAMBURG	40		BARCELONA	93
MUNICH	89		GRANADA	958
OLDENBURG	441		MADRID	91
GREECE	**+30**		MALAGA	95
ATHENS	1		SEVILLE	95
HUNGARY	**+36**		VALENCIA	96
BUDAPEST	1		**SWEDEN**	**+46**
IRELAND	**+353**		MALMÖ	40
CORK	21		STOCKHOLM	8
DUBLIN	1		**SWITZERLAND**	**+41**
ITALY	**+39**		ZURICH	1
FLORENCE	055			
MILAN	02			

BON APPETIT! BUON APPETITO! SMACZNEGO!